Early One Spring 早春二月

An Intermediate Chinese Reader

Early One Spring 早春二月

An Intermediate Chinese Reader
to Accompany the film Video
February

王施璧倫   王若韶

Pilwun Shih Wang & Sarah Wang

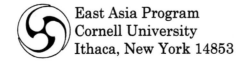
East Asia Program
Cornell University
Ithaca, New York 14853

The Cornell East Asia Series is published by the Cornell University East Asia Program (distinct from Cornell University Press). We publish affordably priced books on a variety of scholarly topics relating to East Asia as a service to the academic community and the general public. Standing orders, which provide for automatic billing and shipping of each title in the series upon publication, are accepted.

If after review by internal and external readers a manuscript is accepted for publication, it is published on the basis of camera-ready copy provided by the volume author. Each author is thus responsible for any necessary copy-editing and for manuscript formatting. Address submission inquiries to CEAS Editorial Board, East Asia Program, Cornell University, Ithaca, New York 14853-7601.

Number 112 in the Cornell East Asia Series
Copyright © 2003 by Pilwun Shih Wang and Sarah Wang. All rights reserved
ISSN 1050-2955
ISBN 1-885445-12-1 pb
Library of Congress Control Number: 2003107102
Printed in the United States of America
18 17 16 15 14 13 12 11 10 09 08 07 06 03   9 8 7 6 5 4 3 2 1

Cover illustration: Chen Hongshou (Chinese, 1768-1822), *Plum Blossoms* (detail). Hanging scroll: ink on paper. Courtesy of Herbert F. Johnson Museum of Art, Cornell University, Museum Associates Purchase Fund, 74.74.1. Cover design by Karen K. Smith.

♾ The paper in this book meets the requirements for permanence of ISO 9706:1994.

早春二月寒未盡

迎來溫馨暖人间

二○二二年春　謝鐵驪

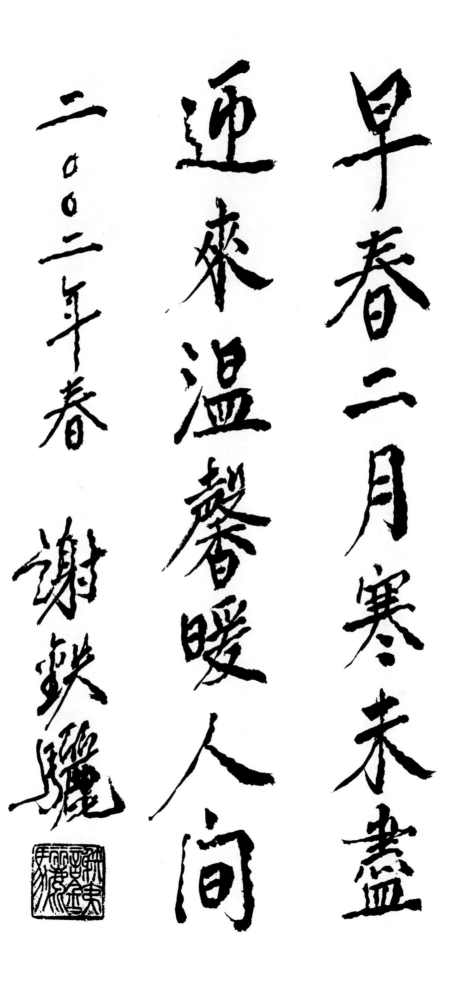

目錄　　　Contents　　　目录

Guide to the Reader

電影劇本   **Screenplay**   电影剧本

A transcript of the film in narrative form; divided into sixty-two scenes, with the lines numbered for easy reference; formatted with the text in traditional and simplified characters on facing pages.

生詞   **Vocabulary**   生词

Entries listed in order of first occurrence, keyed to scene and line number. For example, the entry 般, listed under 7.44, appears first in scene 7, line 44. Each entry includes both traditional and simplified characters, *pinyin* romanization, and gloss. Alternative pronunciations are listed in alphabetical order of *pinyin*. Each gloss lists first a grammatical designation of the entry as used in the text, followed by some common alternative usages. However, please note that these listings are by no means intended to be comprehensive. Characters with multiple meanings, usages, and/or pronunciations have separate entries for each alternative, but are cross-referenced for the reader's convenience.

練習   **Exercises**   练习

The sixty-two scenes of the screenplay are divided into nine sets of exercises, identified by arabic numeral in italics. Each exercise set is made up of five sections: reading comprehension, grammar, vocabulary usage (fill-in-the-blank), speaking and writing. The grammar section consists of seven grammar points, each of which is identified by roman numeral. Thus for example, the entry 般, listed as *1.III*, can be found in the third grammar point of the first set (scenes 1-5). Formatted with the text in traditional and simplified characters on facing pages. A fill-in-the-blank answer key is appended at the end of this section.

索引   **Index**

Lists every occurrence of all characters in both traditional and simplified forms appearing in the vocabulary and grammar sections of the exercises. Arranged alphabetically according to *pinyin* romanization, with homophones listed in order of their appearance in the text. Entries of single character words (字) with their own individual glosses are underlined; characters with multiple pronunciations are cross-referenced.

Grammatical Terms

A	Adverb: includes only those expressions that function primarily as adverbs, and not verbs with the adverbial ending 地 (see (A) below); 地 thus appears in the entries only where necessary, and is enclosed in parentheses where optional
(A)	Verbal form that appears in the screenplay text as an adverb, usually marked by the adverbial ending 地
APP	Appellation: term of address
AT	Attributive: special set of noun modifiers like stative verbs, but they cannot be used verbally
AV	Auxiliary Verb: precedes the main verb; may take adverbial modifiers
C	Conjunction
Cf.	Compare: cross-references different pronunciations, meanings and/or usages
CV	Coverb: subordinated verb that takes objects; it precedes and modifies the main verb; often corresponds roughly to prepositions in English
CVO	Coverb-Object compound: typically consisting of two characters; often corresponds roughly to prepositional phrases in English modifying the main verb
CV Ph	Coverb Phrase: often appears at the beginning of sentences before the topic; often corresponds roughly to prepositional phrases in English modifying the sentence
L	Locative: words that indicate spatial position
L Ph	Locative Phrase: consists of locative indicating the spatial position in relation to a particular noun, e.g. 懷裏/怀里: "in one's arms"
M	Measure Word: counting unit for nouns; e.g. "flock" (of sheep)
MA	Movable Adverb: adverb that may occur either directly before the verb or at the beginning of a sentence without affecting meaning
N	Noun
Nu	Number
ON	Onomatopoeia

P   Particle: grammatical function word(s); includes interjections and exclamations, as well as prepositions

PAT   Grammatical Pattern

PN   Proper Noun

Pn   Pronoun

Pre-pivotal Verb that takes an object which functions also as the subject of a following verb

Q   Question Word

RV   Resultative Verb: compound verb consisting of a verb and a complement that describes a result of the verb

S   Subject or topic *(for use only in grammatical patterns)*

SE   Set Expression

See   References the main listing for the character

SV   Stative Verb: intransitive verb that describes a quality or condition; may modify nouns; often corresponds to the English construction, "to be/ to become + adjective"

T   Time Word(s): noun expression that indicates time; may also function as a movable adverb

V   Verbal Formation: includes simple verbs, compound verbs, verbal set phrases modified by adverbs

VE   Verbal Expression: general term for all types of verb formations, including stative verbs and verb-object compounds *(for use only in grammatical patterns)*

VO   Verb-Object formation: typically allows for separation between the verb and object components, for example, by the aspect marker 了, by measure words and/or by other modifiers; construction may include adverbial modifiers or more than one object

( )   Parentheses indicate that the character(s) enclosed within are optional

[ ]   A grammatical term, such as CVO, CV Ph, or VO, enclosed in square brackets appearing at the end of the gloss, indicates the actual grammatical structure of the vocabulary entry; often contrasts with the idiomatic usage listed at the beginning of the gloss, which treats the entry more as a unified expression that typically does not allow for separation between the individual components of the expression

/   "Or": marks alternative grammatical usages at the beginning of each gloss; the first one listed describes the vocabulary term as it appears in the text

o o o   "Blank": may be filled with a range of grammatical possibilities, from simple nouns and verbs all the way through full clauses with subject-verb constructions *(for use only in grammatical patterns)*

Preface

Steadily increasing numbers of students learning Chinese in recent years have led to an ever-greater demand for course materials. Students at more advanced levels face the particular challenge of making the transition from the level of the textbook to that of general literacy and fluency. In reading for example, while students may have advanced beyond the simplified, fully explicated language of the textbook, their training often still leaves them unprepared for the world of unabridged, unglossed materials intended for the general Chinese language audience. Similarly, in writing and speaking, students may have progressed beyond the communication of simple, concrete thoughts common in everyday life, only to find that they have yet to develop their ability to express fluently more abstract concepts such as ideas and feelings, give extensive descriptions, or relate a narrative.

Story Content

Zǎochūn èryuè 早春二月, (*Early One Spring*) is a new intermediate Chinese reader designed to help prepare students with this transition. It uses as the basis for its text, our transcript of the dialog from the 1963 film of the same name (but rendered into English as "February"),[1] embedded in an adaptation of a narrative version of the screenplay written by the director of the film, Xiè Tiělí 謝鐵驪/谢铁骊 .[2] This film and screenplay in turn is adapted from the short story "Èryuè 二月 (The Second Lunar Month)" by Róu Shí 柔石 (1901-1931),[3] a young follower of the great fiction writer, Lǔ Xùn 魯迅 (1881-1936). Written during the 1920's at a time of intense cultural self-examination, the story dramatizes issues of family, marriage, and the status of women that result from the clash between the recent influx of western thought and traditional social values. This ambivalent relationship with the west, often conflated with issues of modernization, has played a significant role in Chinese culture to this day, particularly with respect to the ways that China sees herself and her place in the world.

We choose this material because, first and foremost, it tells a good, engaging story. Second, it presents intellectually challenging issues that introduce well some basic themes of modern Chinese literature. In this way, we hope that students may not only gain proficiency in language skills, but also gain an appreciation for Chinese literature. Third, the story's emphasis on such issues such as marriage, family, and the status of women work well pedagogically in that it provides continuity to the various intermediate textbooks that have also covered these themes, if in a more contemporary context.[4] Such textbooks' introduction of these issues of cultural difference between China and the west provides a good

---

[1] The 120 minute film is available on videotape through the Nan Hai Arts Center, 510 Broadway, Suite 300, Millbrae, CA 94030.

[2] *Zǎochūn Èryuè* 早春二月 (Beijing: Zhongguo dianying chubanshe, 1979).

[3] There is also an English translation of the story, called "Threshold of Spring," by Sidney Shapiro, collected in *Threshold of Spring* (Beijing: Foreign Languages Press, 1980), 1-133.

[4] See for example, Chou Chih-p'ing, *Intermediate Reader of Modern Chinese* (Princeton: Chinese Linguistics Project, 1992); Irene Liu, with Li Xiaoqi, *A Chinese Text for a Changing China* (Boston: Cheng & Tsui, 1995), and Foreign Service Institute, *Module 7: Society in the Standard Chinese: A Modular Approach series*, (1980).

foundation for this text, which explores the history of these issues in the context of the May Fourth Movement.

Pedagogical Goals

Our main goal in developing 早春二月 has been to provide for students an experience of a typical Chinese text written for the general Chinese language audience, and thus increase proficiency and confidence in reading at an advanced level. Like many film guides, this textbook provides a transcript of the dialog from the film. However, our presentation is structured as a narrative form, so that it may also include sustained descriptions of the film's settings and characters. The language of the text is fairly literary, in that it is representative of much of modern Chinese writing that lies beyond the scope of language textbooks. As the screenplay may be read as a narrative piece in its own right, our text has the flexibility to work both as a film guide and as an introductory reader.

早春二月 thus introduces students to the language of modern Chinese print culture, but it does so at a level appropriate for advanced intermediate students. As discussed above, the screenplay itself is a simplified version of the original short story that nevertheless retains its authenticity as a general audience Chinese language text. Our narrative version of the film transcript, together with the vocabulary gloss and reading comprehension questions (the first section of each of the nine sets of exercises), may function by itself as a reader for more advanced students studying on their own. At the same time, it is also designed to work in the classroom in conjunction with the film. Obviously, the film itself can play an important pedagogical role in providing visual cues that greatly enhance comprehension, in terms of both the literal language and the cultural issues raised in the story.

In this way, we have designed a flexible format in order to reach the greatest numbers of students possible. Further, we have formatted the entire text in both traditional and simplified characters, and also added a vocabulary gloss comprehensive enough to accommodate students with a roughly second year reading vocabulary even though our reader focuses on a level more suited for third year students. We have done this in order to address as well the needs of an ever-growing variety of Chinese language students, in particular those heritage speakers with their very individual language backgrounds. Although many of these students have not pursued formal study of Chinese in the classroom before, and thus lack the more "standard" beginning levels of written vocabulary, they nevertheless already possess strong grammar and usage skills that need to be exercised at more advanced levels. Our text offers a way for such students to balance the acquisition of basic vocabulary with the practice of more advanced usage.

While 早春二月 seeks to develop students' reading skills and confidence in approaching texts for the general Chinese language audience, it also seeks to develop strategies of both oral and written expression, particularly the articulation of more complex and abstract ideas and the construction of sustained narratives. The narrative form of the screenplay, with its descriptions of the film's settings and characters, plays a significant role in this text's pedagogy, for it provides real examples of how scenes visualized in the film may be translated into the written language.

Further, our reader centers on vocabulary that 1) portrays characters' thoughts, feelings, and motivations, as seen in their speech and actions; and 2) describes the physical environment, or setting. Oral discussion and written essay exercises accordingly emphasize such narrative descriptions, as based on the screenplay models. Rather than requiring just a simple phrase or sentence as part of a set drill response, these exercises must be completed in paragraph form, consisting of several sentences that are clearly marked by a beginning and end. In this way, the Exercises promote the incorporation of individual vocabulary items into the larger construction of paragraphs necessary for exposition and narration.

At a more fundamental level, we have included in the Vocabulary several features that help students with the acquisition of vocabulary in terms of active usage. We have provided as part of each gloss grammatical information on usage. However, we do not give only the usage of each entry as it appears in the text, but have also included common alternate usages. Further, we have cross-referenced variations in meaning for various characters where semantic relationships as translated into English are not obvious. We have done this in order to emphasize to students the flexible nature of written Chinese, especially as it begins to approach the classical language. A single character may act as a noun, verb, or modifier with equal ease. The exact designation of grammatical usage may also depend on regional variation, age of the speaker, and conventions in apparent disregard of grammatical rules. Similarly, a single character may also convey a number of disparate meanings. In listing the different usages and cross-listing alternative meanings, we hope to help students to begin to think of vocabulary not as concrete terms with a one-to-one correspondence to objects in the world, or direct word-for-word translations in English, but as semantic fields that can cover a number of different grammatical functions and meanings. Moreover, we believe that acquainting students with the various uses of characters helps to hone a sense of context for the vocabulary they learn. Rather than depending solely on the often limited, and therefore misleading, denotations of glosses, students may concentrate more on learning the arenas of convention in which a particular vocabulary item might appear. In this way they develop their ability and confidence to use the vocabulary they learn in the appropriate contexts.

Our emphasis on mastering the active usage of vocabulary continues in the Exercises. In the vocabulary section, we have designed fill-in-the-blank vocabulary exercises that demand a familiarity with the usage of the vocabulary beyond mere passive comprehension. Students must have developed some understanding of the vocabulary before they can complete the exercises. There is an answer key to this section in order to allow students more independence outside of class in this aspect of their study, as well as to free up precious class time. The grammar section also focuses on vocabulary acquisition in terms of usage: it mainly treats 1) function words, 2) grammar previously introduced in earlier texts but that have proven difficult to master, and 3) the more advanced four-character set phrases. Building on this work, the remaining exercise sections, consisting of oral discussions and written essays, offer students a more open-ended form of practice of vocabulary usage as they work on developing their narrative and descriptive skills. We hope that students can thereby develop a sense of the subtleties of the vocabulary and its usage, while building on their strategies of articulation.

Teaching Suggestions

We suggest that the book be used second semester, third year for a period of about thirty contact hours. We have provided more than enough exercise materials for this amount of teaching, and suggest teachers tailor the materials to the needs of their particular classes. However, we do recommend that teachers spend extra time on the first ten scenes (and first two sets of exercises) in order to build a strong foundation that will help the class through the rest of the text. We have found that this is a critical period in which students need extra time to familiarize themselves with the characters, the setting, along with the style of the text. Once this initial foundation has been laid, then students have a much easier time getting involved in the story, and reading becomes progressively faster and easier, as the story gains momentum. For the rest of the story, the teacher may select as appropriate, particular scenes for focused examination.

The book is divided into nine sections, each with a set of exercises. A typical section should take about three class periods. After the students have read the text and watched the corresponding piece of film, we suggest that the class go over the reading comprehension questions (the first section of each exercise set) together, and discuss particular parts students do not understand. This activity segues easily into the next, which is to practice speaking. Freezing the video on particular scenes, students may describe the scenes and their characters, or provide narration of the events depicted. This type of activity may also be used in conjunction with the speaking exercises (the fourth section). Next, the class may choose to go over the vocabulary and grammar exercises. While the vocabulary may be done at home, we recommend that the grammar be done in class. Teachers may supplement or skip drills as necessary. Finally, the class uses what they have learned above in terms of vocabulary and grammar to have a discussion about the events, themes, along with the issues that they raise. The students may then use this class discussion as the basis of their last exercise, the written essay. We hope that through this learning process, students will gain confidence in handling general audience Chinese language texts, enrich their articulation strategies, and most of all, enjoy this introduction to the wonderful world of Chinese literature.

Acknowledgments

In conclusion, we would like to express our thanks to the many people who participated in the preparation of this book. The teachers and students in the Chinese program at Cornell University who field-tested the material, particularly Paul Festa, Jr., provided invaluable feedback. Special thanks go to Julian Wheatley for his generous encouragement and advice throughout the project, and to Jerry and Stella Norman for their willingness to help in linguistic matters large and small. We would also like to include a special note of thanks to Peter Feng, Professor of Law at East China Normal University, Shanghai, who so generously advised us on the intricacies of Chinese copyright law. Funding was provided in part by the Consortium for Language Teaching and Learning. Finally, we are indebted to our friends and family; we could never have completed this project without their enormous support and forbearance.

Pilwun Wang 王璧倫 and Sarah Wang 王若韶

人物表
Cast of Characters

| 蕭澗秋 | 萧涧秋 | Xiāo Jiànqiū | 外地來的青年
A young person from outside the area | 外地来的青年 |

| 文嫂 | | Wén Săo | 青年寡婦
A young widow | 青年寡妇 |

| 采蓮 | 采莲 | Căilián | 文嫂的女兒
Wén Săo's daughter | 文嫂的女儿 |

| 阿寶 | 阿宝 | Ābăo | 文嫂的兒子
Wén Săo's son | 文嫂的儿子 |

| 陳奶奶 | 陈奶奶 | Chén Năinai | 文嫂的鄰居
Wén Săo's neighbor | 文嫂的邻居 |

| 陶慕侃 | | Táo Mùkăn | 芙蓉中學的校長
The principal at Hibiscus Town Middle School | 芙蓉中学的校长 |

| 陶嵐 | 陶岚 | Táo Lán | 陶慕侃的妹妹
Táo Mùkăn's little sister | |

| 陶媽媽 | 陶妈妈 | Táo Māma | 陶羨慕的母親
Táo Mùkăn's mother | 陶羨慕的母亲 |

| 錢正興 | 钱正兴 | Qián Zhèngxīng | 芙蓉中學的教師
A teacher at Hibiscus Town Middle School | 芙蓉中学的教师 |

| 方謀 | 方谋 | Fāng Móu | 芙蓉中學的教師
A teacher at Hibiscus Town Middle School | 芙蓉中学的教师 |

| 王福生 | | Wáng Fúshēng | 芙蓉中學的學生 | 芙蓉中学的学生 |
| A student at Hibiscus Town Middle School |

| 阿榮 | 阿荣 | Āróng | 芙蓉中學的校役 | 芙蓉中学的校役 |
| A custodian at Hibiscus Town Middle School |

| 吳媽 | 吴妈 | Wú Mā | 陶慕侃家的佣人 | 陶慕侃家的用人 |
| Táo Mùkǎn's family servant |

電影劇本

diànyǐng jùběn

Screenplay

电影剧本

第一景

　　陰曆的二月。梅花還在落瓣，柳樹已經吐出了嫩芽，天氣異常地和暖。

　　女佛山至芙蓉鎮的班輪在平靜的內河裏行駛着。統艙裏擠滿了人，大多是做小生意的客商，還有一些是從女佛山朝香回來的穿着長裙的老太婆。他們在談論着買賣的行情，談論着天氣與菩薩。一個賣瓜子的也擠在其中叫賣。

　　在人羣中顯得不調和的是一位青年。看起來他的年齡已近三十，身穿一套嗶嘰的學生裝，足下是一雙黑色深統皮鞋全身帶着長遠路途的風塵。在他腿旁的舊皮箱上幾乎貼滿了北京、上海等地的托運標籤。艙內的煙霧和嗡嗡的談話聲使他氣悶，頭昏。他擠在那裏無法轉身，只好盡力將頭扭向窗外。他身旁緊挨着一個商人模樣的胖子，正在打盹。那肥碩的腦袋不時地磕碰着他的肩頭。這位青年實在忍受不了，抽身擠出艙去。

第二景

　　當那青年一踏上了船頭就覺得輕鬆許多。他貪婪地吸着清新的空氣，望着兩岸的自然景色。忽然一個橘子滾到了他的腳邊。他俯身將橘子拾起，一個眼秀頰紅的女孩正向他跑來。他將紅橘交給女孩，同時注意到靠近船舷的欄杆處坐着一個青年婦人，身穿破舊的夾襖，滿面愁容地凝視着水面。從她的兩眼內，可以瞧出極度的悲哀。婦人懷裏抱着一個兩歲的男孩，已經睡熟了。

第一景

　　阴历的二月。梅花还在落瓣，柳树已经吐出了嫩芽，天气异常地和暖。

　　女佛山至芙蓉镇的班轮在平静的内河里行驶着。统舱里挤满了人，大多是做小生意的客商，还有一些是从女佛山朝香回来的穿着长裙的老太婆。他们在谈论着买卖的行情，谈论着天气与菩萨。一个卖瓜子的也挤在其
5　中叫卖。

　　在人群中显得不调和的是一位青年。看起来他的年龄已近三十，身穿一套哔叽的学生装，足下是一双黑色深统皮鞋，全身带着长远路途的风尘。在他腿旁的旧皮箱上几乎贴满了北京、上海等地的托运标签。舱内的烟雾和嗡嗡的谈话声使他气闷，头昏。他挤在那里无法转身，只好尽力将头扭向
10　窗外。他身旁紧挨着一个商人模样的胖子，正在打盹。那肥硕的脑袋不时地磕碰着他的肩头。这位青年实在忍受不了，抽身挤出舱去。

第二景

　　当那青年一踏上了船头就觉得轻松许多。他贪婪地吸着清新的空气，望着两岸的自然景色。忽然一个橘子滚到了他的脚边。他俯身将橘子拾起，一个眼秀颊红的女孩正向他跑来。他将红橘交给女孩，同时注意到靠近船舷的栏杆处坐着一个青年妇人，身穿破旧的夹袄，满面愁容地凝视着水面。
5　从她的两眼内，可以瞧出极度的悲哀。妇人怀里抱着一个两岁的男孩，已经睡熟了。

女孩回到婦人膝前，珍惜地玩弄着那隻橘子，熱切地問她媽媽：「媽媽，到家就能吃橘子了吧？」

離婦人不遠處，有位五十多歲的老奶奶，對孩子說：「采蓮，你要吃就吃吧。別問你媽媽了，啊。」

一個乘客問道：「你孫女兒幾歲了？」

「不是。我們是鄰居。」

「哦。」

「他爸爸是革命軍，在廣州那邊兒打仗打死了。嗐，丟下這孤兒寡婦的，往後這日子可怎麼過呢？」

為強烈的同情心所驅駛，那位青年的目光已經落到這位婦人身上了。他想探索出婦人悲哀的根由。這時候婦人正呆呆地看着懷裏的孩子的臉，似乎孩子白嫩熟睡的臉可以安慰一些她內心的酸痛和絕望。女孩仍是癡癡地微笑，玩弄着手裏的紅橘。

第三景

1   渡頭，小船。

第四景

芙蓉中學的兩位青年教師跨進陶家的大門。這是一座老式的大家庭的房子，廊簷的朱柱已為久遠的日光曬得變黑了。他們穿過庭院，走向廳堂。

廳堂裏陳設着舊式的紅木家具，壁上掛着大幅的淡墨山水，顯得寬敞而幽靜。

陶校長的妹妹陶嵐，約二十三、四歲，是個非常美貌的人。她坐在廳堂中看書，兩手隨便編織着毛線，像無聊似地消磨着自己的時光。

兩位青年教師走了進來。衣着漂亮的錢正興顯得特別親切，帶着幾分扭捏地向陶嵐問：「嵐，客人還沒到吧？」

女孩回到妇人膝前，珍惜地玩弄着那只橘子，热切地问她妈妈：「妈妈，到家就能吃橘子了吧？」

离妇人不远处，有位五十多岁的老奶奶，对孩子说：「采莲，你要吃就吃吧。别问你妈妈了，啊。」

一个乘客问道：「你孙女儿几岁了？」

「不是。我们是邻居。」

「哦。」

「他爸爸是革命军，在广州那边儿打仗打死了。嗐，丢下这孤儿寡妇的，往后这日子可怎么过呢？」

为强烈的同情心所驱驶，那位青年的目光已经落到这位妇人身上了。他想探索出妇人悲哀的根由。这时候妇人正呆呆地看着怀里的孩子的脸，似乎孩子白嫩熟睡的脸可以安慰一些她内心的酸痛和绝望。女孩仍是痴痴地微笑，玩弄着手里的红橘。

第三景

渡头，小船。

第四景

芙蓉中学的两位青年教师跨进陶家的大门。这是一座老式的大家庭的房子，廊檐的朱柱已为久远的日光晒得变黑了。他们穿过庭院，走向厅堂。

厅堂里陈设着旧式的红木家具，壁上挂着大幅的淡墨山水，显得宽敞而幽静。

陶校长的妹妹陶岚，约二十三、四岁，是个非常美貌的人。她坐在厅堂中看书，两手随便编织着毛线，像无聊似地消磨着自己的时光。

两位青年教师走了进来。衣着漂亮的钱正兴显得特别亲切，带着几分扭捏地向陶岚问：「岚，客人还没到吧？」

　　　　陶嵐一見這位紈絝子弟就有一種厭惡的感覺。她隨即拿起毛線和書
10　本，不作回答就走向內房。

　　　　老臉皮的方謀故意叫道：「欸！欸，密斯陶！」

　　　　陶嵐不得不停步轉頭，睜着一雙大眼看着他。

　　　　方謀緊接着問：「陶校長呢？」

　　　　陶嵐微微一搖頭，翩然進入內房。

15　　　方謀無可奈何地看了錢正興一眼。他正很不快意地走向一把椅子坐
　　下。方謀也隨着坐下去，偷眼看着錢正興，暗自好笑，卻又安慰似地說：
　　「她是因為見了你啊，有點兒不好意思！」

　　　　錢正興心不在焉地勉強笑了一聲。

　　　　從房內出來了陶嵐的母親。她是一位六十歲左右，面貌慈祥的老婦人，
20　對兩位教師非常客氣。「你們來啦！」

　　　　錢正興馬上站了起來，彬彬有禮地回答：「伯母您好。伯母，慕侃去接
　　客人了嗎？」

　　　　「是啊，也該回來了。」陶媽媽讓他們坐下。

第五景

　　　　芙蓉鎮的市街。各色的店鋪也帶有城市風味，不過規模都顯得狹小些。
　　一兩個伙友坐在店櫃裏，特別清閑。唯有一家當鋪門前生意興隆，一些窮人
　　夾着棉衣進去，拿着當票出來。

　　　　街道上行人稀少。校役阿榮擔着行李、網籃走過，陶校長陪着蕭澗秋──
5　──船上的那位青年──走來。

　　　　陶校長三十四、五歲，身材微胖，面貌給人以渾厚的印象。他邊走邊
　　說：「我們足足有六年沒有見面了。澗秋，這些年，你跑了不少地方吧。」

　　　　蕭澗秋苦笑了一下。「是啊！我幾乎跑遍了大半個中國。城市的生活使
　　我感到厭倦了。」

10　　　「所以，我就不願意出去。這個小小的芙蓉鎮倒真是個世外桃源呢！」
　　陶校長露出幾分得意的神色。

陶岚一见这位纨袴子弟就有一种厌恶的感觉。她随即拿起毛线和书本，不作回答就走向内房。

老脸皮的方谋故意叫道：「欸！欸，密斯陶！」

陶岚不得不停步转头，睁着一双大眼看着他。

方谋紧接着问：「陶校长呢？」

陶岚微微一摇头，翩然进入内房。

方谋无可奈何地看了钱正兴一眼。他正很不快意地走向一把椅子坐下。方谋也随着坐下去，偷眼看着钱正兴，暗自好笑，却又安慰似地说：「她是因为见了你啊，有点儿不好意思！」

钱正兴心不在焉地勉强笑了一声。

从房内出来了陶岚的母亲。她是一位六十岁左右，面貌慈祥的老妇人，对两位教师非常客气。「你们来啦！」

钱正兴马上站了起来，彬彬有礼地回答：「伯母您好。伯母，慕侃去接客人了吗？」

「是啊，也该回来了。」陶妈妈让他们坐下。

第五景

芙蓉镇的市街。各色的店铺也带有城市风味，不过规模都显得狭小些。一两个伙友坐在店柜里，特别清闲。唯有一家当铺门前生意兴隆，一些穷人夹着棉衣进去，拿着当票出来。

街道上行人稀少。校役阿荣担着行李、网篮走过，陶校长陪着萧涧秋——船上的那位青年——走来。

陶校长三十四、五岁，身材微胖，面貌给人以浑厚的印象。他边走边说：「我们足足有六年没有见面了。涧秋，这些年，你跑了不少地方吧。」

萧涧秋苦笑了一下。「是啊！我几乎跑遍了大半个中国。城市的生活使我感到厌倦了。」

「所以，我就不愿意出去。这个小小的芙蓉镇倒真是个世外桃源呢！」陶校长露出几分得意的神色。

兩人沿着河邊走着，穿過一座小橋，看着市街。

陶校長又問：「澗秋，這個芙蓉鎮，你印象如何？」

蕭澗秋也隨着高興起來。「它很幽靜。要是可能的話，我倒願意在這兒多住幾年。」

「那太好了，我要為孩子們高興呢！」陶校長似乎快樂得全身發抖起來。

市上來了個面生的人，大家不由得用好奇的目光注視他一會兒。有的人看了看也就算了。有的人卻指點着他，與別人議論：「欸，這是誰呀？」

「沒見過。也許是上面兒派下來查學的吧。」

蕭澗秋覺得自己引起了別人的注意，雖然沒有甚麼羞慚，總覺得有點不自在，只垂眼看着腳前的路。

陶校長似解釋地說：「走啊。鎮上人口很少，幾乎大家都面熟。只要來一個外鄉人就會引起大家的注意。這也許是一種尊敬的表示吧！」

末了一句顯然是一種玩笑的口吻，蕭澗秋回以淡淡的一笑。

第六景

陶校長領着蕭澗秋一跨進陶家庭院的大門，就見方謀和錢正興正迎出門來。於是連忙向錢、方兩位介紹道：「來，來，來，來，我給你們介紹一下。這位就是我常跟你們提起的蕭澗秋，蕭先生。」

錢、方兩位連聲說着：「哦，久仰，久仰。」

陶校長繼續給他們介紹：「這位是錢正興，錢先生。這位是。。。」

方謀忙接過來說：「敝姓方，草字謀。」

他們相互點頭微笑。

「好，大家屋裏坐。」陶校長將他們讓進廳堂。

於是三人互讓着進了屋。

陶校長自己卻返回向阿榮吩咐：「阿榮，你先把行李提到下房去。吃完晚飯，跟蕭先生一塊兒回學校去。」

阿榮答應着。陶校長又忙碌地奔向廚房。

两人沿着河边走着，穿过一座小桥，看着市街。

陶校长又问：「涧秋，这个芙蓉镇，你印象如何？」

萧涧秋也随着高兴起来。「它很幽静。要是可能的话，我倒愿意在这儿多住几年。」

「那太好了，我要为孩子们高兴呢！」陶校长似乎快乐得全身发抖起来。

市上来了个面生的人，大家不由得用好奇的目光注视他一会儿。有的人看了看也就算了。有的人却指点着他，与别人议论：「欸，这是谁呀？」

「没见过。也许是上面儿派下来查学的吧。」

萧涧秋觉得自己引起了别人的注意，虽然没有什么羞惭，总觉得有点不自在，只垂眼看着脚前的路。

陶校长似解释地说：「走啊。镇上人口很少，几乎大家都面熟。只要来一个外乡人就会引起大家的注意。这也许是一种尊敬的表示吧！」

末了一句显然是一种玩笑的口吻，萧涧秋回以淡淡的一笑。

第六景

陶校长领着萧涧秋一跨进陶家庭院的大门，就见方谋和钱正兴正迎出门来。于是连忙向钱、方两位介绍道：「来，来，来，来，我给你们介绍一下。这位就是我常跟你们提起的萧涧秋，萧先生。」

钱、方两位连声说着：「哦，久仰，久仰。」

陶校长继续给他们介绍：「这位是钱正兴，钱先生。这位是。。。」

方谋忙接过来说：「敝姓方，草字谋。」

他们相互点头微笑。

「好，大家屋里坐。」陶校长将他们让进厅堂。

于是三人互让着进了屋。

陶校长自己却返回向阿荣吩咐：「阿荣，你先把行李提到下房去。吃完晚饭，跟萧先生一块儿回学校去。」

阿荣答应着。陶校长又忙碌地奔向厨房。

第七景

廳堂裏，三位青年在閑談着。

方謀說：「蕭先生的光臨帶來了春天哪！今天天氣是特別地和暖。」

蕭澗秋僅以微笑作答。

錢正興卻說：「我倒覺得暖得早了一點兒。」

方謀不同意。「按時令也該是暖和的時候了。」

「哪裏。我今天換了兩次衣服。上午換了一件紫羔，下午又換了這件灰鼠的。」錢正興翻起長袍角，一面接下去：「還是熱！哼！難道非叫我穿單的不成啊？啊？」

方謀同意着，「是，是。」

錢正興又繼續道：「蕭先生，這是不祥之兆，我看今年又要有災難。」

蕭澗秋也笑着表示了他的意見。「我看天氣的變化是自然的現象。至於人間的災難嘛，。。。」

方謀看了蕭澗秋一眼，就順水推舟地接下去道：「唉，災難是年年不免的。近幾年來災難可太多了，啊？你看啊，直奉戰爭、甘肅地震、河南土匪、山東又鬧水災。唉，現在革命軍在廣東打得很厲害。。。」

這時候陶校長走進房內。「澗秋，我妹妹想見見你。這就是我們家的皇后。」

陶嵐在門口出現了，她大方又活潑。「哥哥，你別說了。」

大家都大笑起來。

於是陶校長說：「好吧，那麼你自己介紹吧。」

陶嵐微笑着，「我有甚麼好介紹的？還不是都知道了，以後我們認識就是了。」

陶校長拿出一包香煙請客人抽，同時抱歉地說道：「不抽煙，忘記了招待客人。」又轉向蕭澗秋問道：「你，還是不抽？」

陶嵐卻在凝思，似乎在回憶中尋找着甚麼。一會兒，她微笑着說：「蕭先生，我好像。。。在哪兒見過你。」

「是嗎？」蕭澗秋竭力地追憶着。

「不會吧！」陶校長看着蕭澗秋說。「唔，也許是。。。」

第七景

厅堂里，三位青年在闲谈着。

方谋说：「萧先生的光临带来了春天哪！今天天气是特别地和暖。」

萧涧秋仅以微笑作答。

钱正兴却说：「我倒觉得暖得早了一点儿。」

5　　方谋不同意。「按时令也该是暖和的时候了。」

「哪里。我今天换了两次衣服。上午换了一件紫羔，下午又换了这件灰鼠的。」钱正兴翻起长袍角，一面接下去：「还是热！哼！难道非叫我穿单的不成啊？啊？」

方谋同意着，「是，是。」

10　　钱正兴又继续道：「萧先生，这是不祥之兆，我看今年又要有灾难。」

萧涧秋也笑着表示了他的意见。「我看天气的变化是自然的现象。至于人间的灾难嘛，。。。」

方谋看了萧涧秋一眼，就顺水推舟地接下去道：「唉，灾难是年年不免的。近几年来灾难可太多了，啊？你看啊，直奉战争、甘肃地震、河南土

15 匪、山东又闹水灾。唉，现在革命军在广东打得很厉害。。。」

这时候陶校长走进房内。「涧秋，我妹妹想见见你。这就是我们家的皇后。」

陶岚在门口出现了，她大方又活泼。「哥哥，你别说了。」

大家都大笑起来。

20　　于是陶校长说：「好吧，那么你自己介绍吧。」

陶岚微笑着，「我有什么好介绍的？还不是都知道了，以后我们认识就是了。」

陶校长拿出一包香烟请客人抽，同时抱歉地说道：「不抽烟，忘记了招待客人。」又转向萧涧秋问道：「你，还是不抽？」

25　　陶岚却在凝思，似乎在回忆中寻找着什么。一会儿，她微笑着说：「萧先生，我好像。。。在哪儿见过你。」

「是吗？」萧涧秋竭力地追忆着。

「不会吧！」陶校长看着萧涧秋说。「唔，也许是。。。」

　　　陶嵐臉紅了一下，不好意思地笑了。「那也許是我認錯人了。蕭先生，
30　我說話是很隨便的。以後你還多原諒我呀。我哥哥常說起你，他說你學問
好，又走過很多地方。以後我甚麼都要向你來請教，你能不客氣地指教我
嗎？」

　　　她這樣滔滔地說着，簡直房內好像是她一人佔領着似的。她的神態非
常自然和柔媚，又帶着幾分嬌養的習氣。蕭澗秋注意地瞧着她，她是個非常
35　美麗的人。

　　　他向陶慕侃說道：「我簡直不知道應該怎麼回答才好了。」

　　　陶嵐隨即笑了一笑。「就這麼回答吧。我還要你怎樣回答呢？」

　　　陶校長嬉笑起來。「怎麼樣，澗秋，你跑遍了中國南北，怕沒有看見過
像我妹妹這樣脾氣的。高興起來，說個沒完。不高興的時候，誰都不理！」

40　　　錢正興面色凝重，似乎有些異樣的感觸。

　　　陶嵐繼續旁若無人地說：「他們都說我脾氣古怪。其實我不過是不懂得
人情世故罷了。蕭先生，你對哲學一定很有研究，希望你教我一點真正做人
的知識。」

　　　蕭澗秋似受到諷刺一般。「做人的知識，我還不知道到哪兒去學呢！按
45　閱歷來說，慕侃該是我們的先生了。」

　　　陶校長得意地快樂起來，卻又謙遜地說：「哪裏，哪裏。妹妹對我就不
信任。欸，錢先生，你說是嗎？」

　　　陶嵐不等錢正興回答，就接下去問道：「蕭先生，聽說你鋼琴彈得很
好。能教教我嗎？」

50　　　「多年不彈了。手指已經很生疏了。」

　　　錢正興不知是因為受到了冷落，還是為忌妒心所驅駛，他站了起來，慢
慢走出房去。他的行動引起在座的人的注意。蕭澗秋不知所以地看着。

　　　房間內呈現出一片沈寂。

陶岚脸红了一下，不好意思地笑了。「那也许是我认错人了。萧先生，我说话是很随便的。以后你还多原谅我呀。我哥哥常说起你，他说你学问好，又走过很多地方。以后我什么都要向你来请教，你能不客气地指教我吗？」

她这样滔滔地说着，简直房内好像是她一人占领着似的。她的神态非常自然和柔媚，又带着几分娇养的习气。萧涧秋注意地瞧着她，她是个非常美丽的人。

他向陶慕侃说道：「我简直不知道应该怎么回答才好了。」

陶岚随即笑了一笑。「就这么回答吧。我还要你怎样回答呢？」

陶校长嬉笑起来。「怎么样，涧秋，你跑遍了中国南北，怕没有看见过像我妹妹这样脾气的。高兴起来，说个没完。不高兴的时候，谁都不理！」

钱正兴面色凝重，似乎有些异样的感触。

陶岚继续旁若无人地说：「他们都说我脾气古怪。其实我不过是不懂得人情世故罢了。萧先生，你对哲学一定很有研究，希望你教我一点真正做人的知识。」

萧涧秋似受到讽刺一般。「做人的知识，我还不知道到哪儿去学呢！按阅历来说，慕侃该是我们的先生了。」

陶校长得意地快乐起来，却又谦逊地说：「哪里，哪里。妹妹对我就不信任。欸，钱先生，你说是吗？」

陶岚不等钱正兴回答，就接下去问道：「萧先生，听说你钢琴弹得很好。能教教我吗？」

「多年不弹了。手指已经很生疏了。」

钱正兴不知是因为受到了冷落，还是为忌妒心所驱驶，他站了起来，慢慢走出房去。他的行动引起在座的人的注意。萧涧秋不知所以地看着。

房间内呈现出一片沉寂。

第八景

　　廚房裏，陶媽媽站立在案板前切菜。案板上放着各色各樣正待烹調的菜餚。吳媽坐在灶台口燒火，阿榮幫着打雜。

　　錢正興走進來，叫了一聲「伯母。」

　　陶媽媽説：「錢先生，你們都餓了吧？」

　　錢正興連忙説：「哦，不，不。我是來看伯母做菜呢！」

　　「都是些粗魚笨肉的。」陶媽媽説着將菜端向灶台。又接下去道：「人家蕭先生是走過大地方的，恐怕吃不來。」

　　「不會，不會。看他那樣兒，也不會吃過甚麼山珍海味。」

　　陶媽媽將碟中切好了的菜投入熱油鍋內，發出嘎的一聲。錢正興連忙往後退，怕油濺上他那件青緞袍子。

第九景

　　廳堂的吊燈已經燃上。室內的紅木家具耀着燈光，交映出淡紅的顏色。八仙桌上設了四份杯箸，四個碟子，兩碗菜，還有一大壺酒。陶校長陪着客人圍坐在桌子四邊。

　　方謀正在高談闊論。「如果一個青年人沒有信仰的話，那就失掉了青年的意義。所以現在，凡是想救國的青年，都應該信仰三民主義。我就是這樣的。」

　　這時陶嵐走了進來，倚在一個高桌邊。

　　錢正興説：「密斯陶，一起來喝一杯酒吧。」

　　「不，我不喝，」陶嵐笑嘻嘻地説。「我是來聽你們談話的，長長見識。」

　　錢正興興致勃勃地，一邊做着手勢説：「三民主義我不反對。可是幹嗎要節制資本呢？我看，要和外國競爭，要救中國，那就得先大大地發展資本主義。」

　　「欸，三民主義也並不排斥資本主義呀。」方謀一面説一面轉向蕭澗秋。「欸，蕭先生，你信仰甚麼主義呢？」

第八景

厨房里，陶妈妈站立在案板前切菜。案板上放着各色各样正待烹调的菜肴。吴妈坐在灶台口烧火，阿荣帮着打杂。

钱正兴走进来，叫了一声「伯母。」

陶妈妈说：「钱先生，你们都饿了吧？」

钱正兴连忙说：「哦，不，不。我是来看伯母做菜呢！」

「都是些粗鱼笨肉的。」陶妈妈说着将菜端向灶台。又接下去道：「人家萧先生是走过大地方的，恐怕吃不来。」

「不会，不会。看他那样儿，也不会吃过什么山珍海味。」

陶妈妈将碟中切好了的菜投入热油锅内，发出嘎的一声。钱正兴连忙往后退，怕油溅上他那件青缎袍子。

第九景

厅堂的吊灯已经燃上。室内的红木家具耀着灯光，交映出淡红的颜色。八仙桌上设了四份杯箸，四个碟子，两碗菜，还有一大壶酒。陶校长陪着客人围坐在桌子四边。

方谋正在高谈阔论。「如果一个青年人没有信仰的话，那就失掉了青年的意义。所以现在，凡是想救国的青年，都应该信仰三民主义。我就是这样的。」

这时陶岚走了进来，倚在一个高桌边。

钱正兴说：「密斯陶，一起来喝一杯酒吧。」

「不，我不喝，」陶岚笑嘻嘻地说。「我是来听你们谈话的，长长见识。」

钱正兴兴致勃勃地，一边做着手势说：「三民主义我不反对。可是干吗要节制资本呢？我看，要和外国竞争，要救中国，那就得先大大地发展资本主义。」

「欸，三民主义也并不排斥资本主义呀。」方谋一面说一面转向萧涧秋。「欸，萧先生，你信仰什么主义呢？」

「我沒有。」蕭澗秋微微地搖一搖頭。

方謀不肯罷休地發出了一聲「欸！」

錢正興也跟着說：「太客氣了。像蕭先生這樣的人，一定會有個高妙的主義的。」

蕭澗秋微笑地答：「主義到了高妙的程度，還有甚麼用處呢？所以我沒有。」

「好！妙，妙極了！」方謀笑着轉過頭來，好似帶着酒興。「欸，欸，密斯陶，你呢？」

陶嵐看了蕭澗秋一眼，然後冷冷地帶刺地說：「我不會像你們那樣會說漂亮話。我是只顧自己的個人主義。」

方謀還想開口，陶校長攔阻道：「我看，不要談甚麼主義了。目前喝酒最實際。來吧，乾了這杯。」

方謀、錢正興隨着陶校長一飲而盡，蕭澗秋僅舉杯呷了一口示意而已。

這時，吳媽端着一個熱氣騰騰的火鍋放在桌子上。

方謀看着窗外說：「欸，下雪了。」

錢正興也搭腔道：「你看，我說氣候不正常嘛。」

陶校長只顧招待着大家，「請，請。。。」

方謀說：「哦，好。」

「欸，方先生，你怎麼也客氣起來了？」陶校長繼續讓着客人，「欸，澗秋，來，來，來，吃菜，吃菜。。。。」

大家靜寂了一下。

陶嵐走近桌邊憂愁地說：「哥哥，聽說文嫂回來了。白跑了一趟，撫恤金一個也沒領到。」

「是呀！上海那麼大地方，又是孫傳芳的天下，哪兒能找到革命黨的機關？」

陶嵐沒有等她哥哥說完就轉向蕭澗秋問：「欸，蕭先生，你今天在船上，有沒有看到一位年青的婦人，領着兩個孩子的？」

蕭澗秋非常不願提起似地答：「有的。」

「我没有。」萧涧秋微微地摇一摇头。

方谋不肯罢休地发出了一声「欸！」

钱正兴也跟着说：「太客气了。像萧先生这样的人，一定会有个高妙的主义的。」

萧涧秋微笑地答：「主义到了高妙的程度，还有什么用处呢？所以我没有。」

「好！妙，妙极了！」方谋笑着转过头来，好似带着酒兴。「欸，欸，密斯陶，你呢？」

陶岚看了萧涧秋一眼，然后冷冷地带刺地说：「我不会像你们那样会说漂亮话。我是只顾自己的个人主义。」

方谋还想开口，陶校长拦阻道：「我看，不要谈什么主义了。目前喝酒最实际。来吧，干了这杯。」

方谋、钱正兴随着陶校长一饮而尽，萧涧秋仅举杯呷了一口示意而已。

这时，吴妈端着一个热气腾腾的火锅放在桌子上。

方谋看着窗外说：「欸，下雪了。」

钱正兴也搭腔道：「你看，我说气候不正常嘛。」

陶校长只顾招待着大家，「请，请。。。」

方谋说：「哦，好。」

「欸，方先生，你怎么也客气起来了？」陶校长继续让着客人，「欸，涧秋，来，来，来，吃菜，吃菜。。。。」

大家静寂了一下。

陶岚走近桌边忧愁地说：「哥哥，听说文嫂回来了。白跑了一趟，抚恤金一个也没领到。」

「是呀！上海那么大地方，又是孙传芳的天下，哪儿能找到革命党的机关？」

陶岚没有等她哥哥说完就转向萧涧秋问：「欸，萧先生，你今天在船上，有没有看到一位年青的妇人，领着两个孩子的？」

萧涧秋非常不愿提起似地答：「有的。」

陶校長皺一皺眉，表示一下悲哀，然後說：「欸，對了，澗秋，你還記
45　得我們在師範學院的時候，有一個會演講的姓李的同學？」

「哦，你說的是李志豪嗎？」

「對。你看到的就是他的家小。」

「怎麼了？他。。。」

陶校長接着感嘆地說：「志豪是一個有志氣的人，可是一直總不得志。
50　東奔西跑了幾年，後來考取了黃埔軍校。誰知前途剛有希望，竟在去年十
月，攻打惠州的時候，陣亡了！」

方謀驚訝地問道：「甚麼，蕭先生和李志豪是同學呀？」

蕭澗秋想了一想，說：「唔，他比我高一班。五四運動那年。。。」

陶校長也想起來了。「對了。我記得那個時候，他帶了一批同學去搜查
55　日貨、上街遊行。你不是也在一起嗎？」

「對。」蕭澗秋點頭嘆氣。「這幾年來，一直沒有通信。沒想到他
。。。」

錢正興打斷話題：「好了，好了。我們不談這些了。來，我們乾了這一
杯。」

60　錢正興與方謀舉杯對飲。蕭澗秋也無心地舉杯，像又增加一層負擔似
的。陶嵐在一旁注視着他。

第十景

1　陶嵐在蕭澗秋的房間裏。

第十一景

蕭澗秋進了西村，走到一間低矮的小屋前。

他直立在門外躊躇了一下，才輕輕地敲了幾下門。門開處出現了船上
遇見的那位婦人——文嫂。她一見這位陌生的青年，隨即想將門關上。

陶校长皱一皱眉，表示一下悲哀，然后说：「欵，对了，涧秋，你还记
45 得我们在师范学院的时候，有一个会演讲的姓李的同学？」

「哦，你说的是李志豪吗？」

「对。你看到的就是他的家小。」

「怎么了？他。。。」

陶校长接着感叹地说：「志豪是一个有志气的人，可是一直总不得志。
50 东奔西跑了几年，后来考取了黄埔军校。谁知前途刚有希望，竟在去年十
月，攻打惠州的时候，阵亡了！」

方谋惊讶地问道：「什么，萧先生和李志豪是同学呀？」

萧涧秋想了一想，说：「唔，他比我高一班。五四运动那年。。。」

陶校长也想起来了。「对了。我记得那个时候，他带了一批同学去搜查
55 日货、上街游行。你不是也在一起吗？」

「对。」萧涧秋点头叹气。「这几年来，一直没有通信。没想到他
。。。」

钱正兴打断话题：「好了，好了。我们不谈这些了。来，我们干了这一
杯。」

60 钱正兴与方谋举杯对饮。萧涧秋也无心地举杯，像又增加一层负担似
的。陶岚在一旁注视着他。

第十景

1 陶岚在萧涧秋的房间里。

第十一景

萧涧秋进了西村，走到一间低矮的小屋前。

他直立在门外踌躇了一下，才轻轻地敲了几下门。门开处出现了船上
遇见的那位妇人——文嫂。她一见这位陌生的青年，随即想将门关上。

　　　　蕭澗秋卻順手將門推住，溫和地説：「請原諒，這裏是不是李先生的家？」

　　　　文嫂一下子答不出話來，緩了一緩才問道：「先生，你是。。。？」

　　　　蕭澗秋慢慢地説：「我姓蕭，我是芙蓉鎮中學的教師，過去和李先生是同學。」

　　　　文嫂哽咽着，「他。。。」

　　　　「李先生的不幸，陶校長已經告訴我了。我今天是特地來看看孩子的。」

　　　　文嫂一時手足無措，兩眼含着淚向他看了一看，才説：「那，請進來坐吧。」

　　　　她衣單，全身為寒冷而顫抖。蕭澗秋低頭跟她進去。

　　　　她掩好了門，説：「屋裏可不像樣子。」

　　　　屋内是灰暗的，四壁滿是灰塵。兩個孩子在一張破舊的大床上坐着，圍着七穿八孔的棉被，冷得不能起來。

　　　　文嫂客氣地説：「請坐。」

　　　　「好。」

　　　　她對女孩子説：「采蓮，這位伯伯來看你了！」

　　　　采蓮睜大眼睛望着來客。

　　　　蕭澗秋走到床前，湊近采蓮問：「小妹妹，你還認識我嗎？」

　　　　采蓮搖搖頭。

　　　　「昨天在船上，你還記得嗎？你掉了一個橘子，是不是？」

　　　　采蓮就笑了起來。

　　　　他繼續説：「可惜我今天忘記帶橘子了。過兩天我一定給你帶幾個來，啊。」

　　　　文嫂説：「先生，你。。。你坐呀。」

　　　　「好。」蕭澗秋回到桌邊坐下。他看了一看文嫂，才説：「我想問一問，以後的生活，有甚麼打算嗎？」

　　　　文嫂奇怪地看他一眼，嘆了一口氣答：「還説不上呢。我。。。我連想都不敢想。」

萧涧秋却顺手将门推住，温和地说：「请原谅，这里是不是李先生的家？」

文嫂一下子答不出话来，缓了一缓才问道：「先生，你是。。。？」

萧涧秋慢慢地说：「我姓萧，我是芙蓉镇中学的教师，过去和李先生是同学。」

文嫂哽咽着，「他。。。」

「李先生的不幸，陶校长已经告诉我了。我今天是特地来看看孩子的。」

文嫂一时手足无措，两眼含着泪向他看了一看，才说：「那，请进来坐吧。」

她衣单，全身为寒冷而颤抖。萧涧秋低头跟她进去。

她掩好了门，说：「屋里可不像样子。」

屋内是灰暗的，四壁满是灰尘。两个孩子在一张破旧的大床上坐着，围着七穿八孔的棉被，冷得不能起来。

文嫂客气地说：「请坐。」

「好。」

她对女孩子说：「采莲，这位伯伯来看你了！」

采莲睁大眼睛望着来客。

萧涧秋走到床前，凑近采莲问：「小妹妹，你还认识我吗？」

采莲摇摇头。

「昨天在船上，你还记得吗？你掉了一个橘子，是不是？」

采莲就笑了起来。

他继续说：「可惜我今天忘记带橘子了。过两天我一定给你带几个来，啊。」

文嫂说：「先生，你。。。你坐呀。」

「好。」萧涧秋回到桌边坐下。他看了一看文嫂，才说：「我想问一问，以后的生活，有什么打算吗？」

文嫂奇怪地看他一眼，叹了一口气答：「还说不上呢。我。。。我连想都不敢想。」

「是不是有些田地啊?」

「連屋後的那小塊兒菜園,都被他賣光了!」

「有親戚嗎?」

文嫂搖了搖頭。

蕭澗秋一時沈默,想不出適當的話來說。他站起來,在桌邊踱了幾步。

文嫂卻說道:「蕭先生,就是。。。有了這個孩子,他們得活下去。」

「是啊,得活下去啊。俗話說,『天無絕人之路』啊。」

「天!先生,我已經不相信有甚麼天了!天的眼睛在哪兒?」文嫂不禁哭出聲來。

蕭澗秋一時慌亂了起來,好不容易才找出一句安慰她的話來。「我相信,好人終究不會受委曲的。」

文嫂很快收住了眼淚,緩了一下,說:「蕭先生,你請坐。我去給你燒點兒水去。」

蕭澗秋聽到此處,就立刻阻止道:「哦,不,不用了。不要客氣了。」又強裝着平靜,好像怕使人受驚地說:「我想跟你說一件事情。我今天到這兒來,就是為了。。。」他的話在孩子的哭聲中繼續下去:「。。。我以後打算頁擔一點兒這兩個孩子的責任。我自己沒甚麼頁擔,可以盡一點兒小小的力量。」

文嫂簡直呆了似地睜眼看着他。「先生,你是。。。」

「請你不要見外吧。我對志豪素來是很敬佩的。哦。。。」他從口袋內掏出一張五元的鈔票放在鍋蓋上,說:「現在你可以去買米了。」

「不!不!蕭先生,我不。。。」文嫂用顫抖的手拿起鈔票要還給他。

蕭澗秋輕輕推開她的手說:「你不用介意了,為了孩子你得收下。好,我該走了。」他連忙抽身跑了出去。

文嫂拿着錢立在那裏,她又是惶恐又是感激地看着他走去的背影。

「是不是有些田地啊？」

「连屋后的那小块儿菜园，都被他卖光了！」

「有亲戚吗？」

文嫂摇了摇头。

萧涧秋一时沉默，想不出适当的话来说。他站起来，在桌边踱了几步。

文嫂却说道：「萧先生，就是。。。有了这个孩子，他们得活下去。」

「是啊，得活下去啊。俗话说，『天无绝人之路』啊。」

「天！先生，我已经不相信有什么天了！天的眼睛在哪儿？」文嫂不禁哭出声来。

萧涧秋一时慌乱了起来，好不容易才找出一句安慰她的话来。「我相信，好人终究不会受委曲的。」

文嫂很快收住了眼泪，缓了一下，说：「萧先生，你请坐。我去给你烧点儿水去。」

萧涧秋听到此处，就立刻阻止道：「哦，不，不用了。不要客气了。」又强装着平静，好像怕使人受惊地说：「我想跟你说一件事情。我今天到这儿来，就是为了。。。」他的话在孩子的哭声中继续下去：「。。。我以后打算负担一点儿这两个孩子的责任。我自己没什么负担，可以尽一点儿小小的力量。」

文嫂简直呆了似地睁眼看着他。「先生，你是。。。」

「请你不要见外吧。我对志豪素来是很敬佩的。哦。。。」他从口袋内掏出一张五元的钞票放在锅盖上，说：「现在你可以去买米了。」

「不！不！萧先生，我不。。。」文嫂用颤抖的手拿起钞票要还给他。

萧涧秋轻轻推开她的手说：「你不用介意了，为了孩子你得收下。好，我该走了。」他连忙抽身跑了出去。

文嫂拿着钱立在那里，她又是惶恐又是感激地看着他走去的背影。

第十二景

　　蕭澗秋在雪上走，有如一隻鶴在雲中飛翔一樣。他這時才貪戀田野中的雪景。他顧盼着，他跳躍着，他的內心竟有一種說不出的微妙的愉悅。他很快就回到了校內。

　　他向自己的房門一手推進去，不料陶嵐卻站在他的書架面前翻書。她聽到聲音立即將書合攏，放回原處。蕭澗秋一時似乎不敢走進去。

　　陶嵐卻微笑地迎上來說：「蕭先生，我在你的房間裏，已經待了很久了。你不會覺得我冒昧吧！」

　　「不，不，沒有甚麼。」蕭澗秋關上門，一邊拿下圍巾一邊說。

　　「你的書我幾乎都翻遍了。」

　　「哦，實在亂得很。還沒來得及整理呢。」蕭澗秋拿起兩本書放好，又拉出椅子來。「請坐吧。」

　　「你這麼客氣幹甚麼？」陶嵐覺得她已經是蕭澗秋的老朋友了。

　　蕭澗秋笑了起來。「坐吧。」

　　「好。」

　　「這些書恐怕你並不喜歡吧。」蕭澗秋邊說邊倒茶請陶嵐喝。

　　「為甚麼？」

　　「聽說你是學理科的。這兒並沒有這方面的書啊。」

　　「謝謝。」陶嵐接過茶來答道：「不。我現在已經不學它了。我本來是喜歡藝術的。就因為別人說，女的不能作數學家，我才偏要去學理科，可是實在是不感興趣。」

　　蕭澗秋又笑了。

　　陶嵐卻又主人似地說：「欸，你坐呀。」

　　兩人就一起在桌邊坐下。

　　陶嵐繼續說：「後來我想，窮人打官司總是輸。將來我還是作個律師替窮人寫狀紙，為被壓迫的人出庭辯護。可是現在知道，不可能了。蕭先生，我想看點哲學的書籍，能介紹我一本嗎？」

　　「好啊，我替你找一找。」蕭澗秋走到書架前抽下一本書遞給她。「你看這本可以嗎？」

第十二景

萧涧秋在雪上走，有如一只鹤在云中飞翔一样。他这时才贪恋田野中的雪景。他顾盼着，他跳跃着，他的内心竟有一种说不出的微妙的愉悦。他很快就回到了校内。

他向自己的房门一手推进去，不料陶岚却站在他的书架面前翻书。她听到声音立即将书合拢，放回原处。萧涧秋一时似乎不敢走进去。

陶岚却微笑地迎上来说：「萧先生，我在你的房间里，已经待了很久了。你不会觉得我冒昧吧！」

「不，不，没有什么。」萧涧秋关上门，一边拿下围巾一边说。

「你的书我几乎都翻遍了。」

「哦，实在乱得很。还没来得及整理呢。」萧涧秋拿起两本书放好，又拉出椅子来。「请坐吧。」

「你这么客气干什么？」陶岚觉得她已经是萧涧秋的老朋友了。

萧涧秋笑了起来。「坐吧。」

「好。」

「这些书恐怕你并不喜欢吧。」萧涧秋边说边倒茶请陶岚喝。

「为什么？」

「听说你是学理科的。这儿并没有这方面的书啊。」

「谢谢。」陶岚接过茶来答道：「不。我现在已经不学它了。我本来是喜欢艺术的。就因为别人说，女的不能作数学家，我才偏要去学理科，可是实在是不感兴趣。」

萧涧秋又笑了。

陶岚却又主人似地说：「欸，你坐呀。」

两人就一起在桌边坐下。

陶岚继续说：「后来我想，穷人打官司总是输。将来我还是作个律师替穷人写状纸，为被压迫的人出庭辩护。可是现在知道，不可能了。萧先生，我想看点哲学的书籍，能介绍我一本吗？」

「好啊，我替你找一找。」萧涧秋走到书架前抽下一本书递给她。「你看这本可以吗？」

「可以。」陶嵐珍惜地翻了一下。然後又問，「下午你還出去嗎？」

「不了。」蕭澗秋自供一般地說：「剛才我去西村走了一下，去看了看志豪他兩個孩子。」

「我知道。」陶嵐回答得非常奇怪，一會兒又補充着，「哦，是阿榮告訴我的。他們現在怎麼樣了？」

蕭澗秋低着頭，搓着手，慢慢地說：「可憐得很。所以我想替他們想點兒辦法。」

陶嵐簡短地回答了「我知道，」三個字。

蕭澗秋覺得有些奇怪，笑着問：「事情還沒有做呢，你怎麼就知道了？」

她又天真地笑起來。「我當然知道的。要不然，你為甚麼到他們那兒去？我們又為甚麼不去呢？下着這麼大的雪，哥哥他們都在爐邊喝酒，為甚麼你一個人去呢？」

這時蕭澗秋驚奇地睜大眼睛看着她。她不僅是美麗，而又是那麼聰慧。

陶嵐慢慢低下頭。「我不知道自己會怎麼樣。我很奇怪，沒有甚麼人管我，可我總把自己關在房間裏。外面的世界甚麼樣子，我一點兒不知道。我恐怕是飛不出去了。」

「你為甚麼要說這樣的話呢？」

「這麼想就這麼說了。」

沈默。蕭澗秋在房中踱了兩步。

陶嵐又說：「蕭先生，我還沒有把我的來意告訴你呢。你不是答應過教我鋼琴的嗎？我今天一大早把鋼琴位置擺好，就來找你。可惜你不在家。下午你願意到我家去嗎？」

「好！我一定去。」

陶嵐又高興起來。「那太好了！我的要求都滿足了，沒有理由再坐了。」她走到門邊又回頭說：「別忘了帶琴譜。」

「好。」

她快樂地返身走出門去。

「可以。」陶岚珍惜地翻了一下。然后又问，「下午你还出去吗？」

「不了。」萧涧秋自供一般地说：「刚才我去西村走了一下，去看了看志豪他两个孩子。」

「我知道。」陶岚回答得非常奇怪，一会儿又补充着，「哦，是阿荣告诉我的。他们现在怎么样了？」

萧涧秋低着头，搓着手，慢慢地说：「可怜得很。所以我想替他们想点儿办法。」

陶岚简短地回答了「我知道，」三个字。

萧涧秋觉得有些奇怪，笑着问：「事情还没有做呢，你怎么就知道了？」

她又天真地笑起来。「我当然知道的。要不然，你为什么到他们那儿去？我们又为什么不去呢？下着这么大的雪，哥哥他们都在炉边喝酒，为什么你一个人去呢？」

这时萧涧秋惊奇地睁大眼睛看着她。她不仅是美丽，而又是那么聪慧。

陶岚慢慢低下头。「我不知道自己会怎么样。我很奇怪，没有什么人管我，可我总把自己关在房间里。外面的世界什么样子，我一点儿不知道。我恐怕是飞不出去了。」

「你为什么要说这样的话呢？」

「这么想就这么说了。」

沉默。萧涧秋在房中踱了两步。

陶岚又说：「萧先生，我还没有把我的来意告诉你呢。你不是答应过教我钢琴的吗？我今天一大早把钢琴位置摆好，就来找你。可惜你不在家。下午你愿意到我家去吗？」

「好！我一定去。」

陶岚又高兴起来。「那太好了！我的要求都满足了，没有理由再坐了。」她走到门边又回头说：「别忘了带琴谱。」

「好。」

她快乐地返身走出门去。

蕭澗秋目送着她，心中有一種不平靜的感覺。他很快地從床下拖出一
58 隻箱子，從箱子裏找出幾本琴譜。

第十三景

　　在陶家的一間廂房裏。陶嵐全神貫注地翻閱着琴譜。蕭澗秋搓搓手坐
在琴前，隨便地彈了幾個音階。他等着陶嵐給他琴譜。

　　陶嵐翻到一本手抄的樂譜。她輕聲念出「徘徊曲」三字，抬頭問道：「這
是哪個作曲家的作品？」

5　　蕭澗秋笑了笑答：「不是甚麼作曲家。那是我在三年以前，一時感情衝
動，胡亂寫的。不成其為甚麼曲調。」就隨手要收起來。

　　陶嵐卻又把《徘徊曲》譜紙放在上面。「就請你彈它吧！」

　　蕭澗秋考慮了一下，然後微笑地说：「那，你可不要見笑。」

　　陶嵐高興地答應了一聲「唔。」

10　　於是蕭澗秋開始彈奏起來。

　　陶嵐起初是一面聽，一面注意他的指法。後來，她完全為音樂的旋律所
感染，慢慢地走到門邊凝神地聽着。她彷彿感到在哪裏聽過這首樂曲，太奇
怪了。

　　她凝視着蕭澗秋的臉，喚起了一段回憶。

第十四景

　　夏天夜晚的西湖。月色曚曨，微風吹蕩着垂柳。一位留着長髮的青年在
湖邊徘徊，有時癡癡地凝視着水面。遊人已經稀少，陶嵐和一位女同學方苹
挽着膀子向回家的路上走去。當她倆在那位徘徊的青年身旁走過的時候，
陶嵐不時地回頭看他。最後，她終於站定了。

5　　方苹奇怪地問：「你認識他？」

　　「不。」陶嵐凝神地说。「我們再坐一會兒吧！」

　　她拉着方苹坐到路旁的一把長椅上。

萧涧秋目送着她，心中有一种不平静的感觉。他很快地从床下拖出一只箱子，从箱子里找出几本琴谱。

58

第十三景

在陶家的一间厢房里。陶岚全神贯注地翻阅着琴谱。萧涧秋搓搓手坐在琴前，随便地弹了几个音阶。他等着陶岚给他琴谱。

陶岚翻到一本手抄的乐谱。她轻声念出「徘徊曲」三字，抬头问道：「这是哪个作曲家的作品？」

萧涧秋笑了笑答：「不是什么作曲家。那是我在三年以前，一时感情冲动，胡乱写的。不成其为什么曲调。」就随手要收起来。

5

陶岚却又把《徘徊曲》谱纸放在上面。「就请你弹它吧！」

萧涧秋考虑了一下，然后微笑地说：「那，你可不要见笑。」

陶岚高兴地答应了一声「唔。」

于是萧涧秋开始弹奏起来。

10

陶岚起初是一面听，一面注意他的指法。后来，她完全为音乐的旋律所感染，慢慢地走到门边凝神地听着。她仿佛感到在哪里听过这首乐曲，太奇怪了。

她凝视着萧涧秋的脸，唤起了一段回忆。

第十四景

夏天夜晚的西湖。月色曚昽，微风吹荡着垂柳。一位留着长发的青年在湖边徘徊，有时痴痴地凝视着水面。游人已经稀少，陶岚和一位女同学方苹挽着膀子向回家的路上走去。当她俩在那位徘徊的青年身旁走过的时候，陶岚不时地回头看他。最后，她终于站定了。

方苹奇怪地问：「你认识他？」

5

「不。」陶岚凝神地说。「我们再坐一会儿吧！」

她拉着方苹坐到路旁的一把长椅上。

方苹勉強坐下來。「怎麼，你怕他自殺？」

「也許我是多餘了。」陶嵐像監視犯人似地看着他。

那位青年發現有人在注意他，就停住腳步，也不時地回頭看着她們。最後，倒是那位青年感到僵窘了，他對她們笑了一笑就大步走開了。

方苹責怪地說：「你看你，叫人家笑話我們了！」

第十五景

想到此處，陶嵐不禁笑出聲來。琴聲突然中斷了，蕭澗秋奇怪地抬起頭來。

陶嵐沒等他開口就連忙解釋道：「蕭先生，請你不要誤會！我是想起了過去的一件事情。三年前的那個夏天，你在杭州的葛嶺住過嗎？」

她還沒有說完，蕭澗秋也笑了起來。「住過。哦！那天晚上，有兩個女同學在監視着我，其中有一個就是你吧！」

陶嵐似乎有些不好意思。「是的，我真傻，我還以為你要。。。？」

「那倒不會。」

「那你為了甚麼呢？」

「那個時候，五四運動像一場風暴一樣過去了。有不少同學被學校開除了。也有的人作了官，得發了。我徬徨得很，不知道怎麼辦才對。」蕭澗秋說着，又用力彈起來。

陶嵐呆呆地看着他，兩人一時沈默着。

「你怎麼不說話呢？」蕭澗秋問。

陶嵐低下頭，慢慢地說：「你使我想到了自己。」

「我們不談這些個吧！我卻無意中在你的面前暴露了我自己的弱點。不過，我後來還是克服了這種徬徨。我現在開始同意你哥哥的看法。教育也許是有意義的。」

陶嵐對他的每一句話、每一個字都在認真地思索着。

方苹勉强坐下来。「怎么，你怕他自杀？」

「也许我是多余了。」陶岚像监视犯人似地看着他。

那位青年发现有人在注意他，就停住脚步，也不时地回头看着她们。最后，倒是那位青年感到僵窘了，他对她们笑了一笑就大步走开了。

方苹责怪地说：「你看你，叫人家笑话我们了！」

第十五景

想到此处，陶岚不禁笑出声来。琴声突然中断了，萧涧秋奇怪地抬起头来。

陶岚没等他开口就连忙解释道：「萧先生，请你不要误会！我是想起了过去的一件事情。三年前的那个夏天，你在杭州的葛岭住过吗？」

她还没有说完，萧涧秋也笑了起来。「住过。哦！那天晚上，有两个女同学在监视着我，其中有一个就是你吧！」

陶岚似乎有些不好意思。「是的，我真傻，我还以为你要。。。？」

「那倒不会。」

「那你为了什么呢？」

「那个时候，五四运动像一场风暴一样过去了。有不少同学被学校开除了。也有的人作了官，得发了。我彷徨得很，不知道怎么办才对。」萧涧秋说着，又用力弹起来。

陶岚呆呆地看着他，两人一时沉默着。

「你怎么不说话呢？」萧涧秋问。

陶岚低下头，慢慢地说：「你使我想到了自己。」

「我们不谈这些个吧！我却无意中在你的面前暴露了我自己的弱点。不过，我后来还是克服了这种彷徨。我现在开始同意你哥哥的看法。教育也许是有意义的。」

陶岚对他的每一句话、每一个字都在认真地思索着。

第十六景

1   學校大門前的攤子。

第十七景

學校裏。上課鈴「噹!噹!噹!」地響着,男女同學跑向自己的課堂。陶校長陪着蕭澗秋從教務室裏出來,走向初中一年級的教室。

教室裏,學生們都好奇地向窗外張望。忽然聽到一聲「來了,來了!」就都坐上了位子,小聲地議論着。

5   陶校長與蕭澗秋一跨進門,學生們立刻肅靜了。在級長「一!二!三!」的號令下起立、鞠躬、坐下,他們的目光都盯在這位新來的教師身上。

陶校長跨上講台,演講似地說:「同學們,我來介紹一下。這位就是你們的級任老師,蕭澗秋先生。蕭先生能夠接受敝校的聘請從遠地來任教,真是我校的光榮,也是同學們的幸福。蕭先生到過很多的地方,見識廣闊,學10   問淵博。。。。」

蕭澗秋截住了他的話:「你不要在同學們面前窘我了。」

「哪裏,哪裏。」陶校長笑了一笑,又轉向同學們說:「蕭先生還有謙遜之美德,可以稱得起是品學並茂。他的一切都值得你們仿效,你們要用心求教才是。現在就請蕭先生來給你們上課。拍手!」

15   學生們在校長的提示下鼓起掌來。

蕭澗秋有些窘迫地走上講台,看着桌子上的點名簿說:「現在我開始點名,藉此和你們大家認識一下。」

他開始叫學生的姓名。陶校長滿意地笑了笑,輕輕地退出教室。

「余志雄。」

20   「到。」

「黃文平。」

「到。」

「你坐下吧。」

第十六景

1　　　学校大门前的摊子。

第十七景

学校里。上课铃「当！当！当！」地响着，男女同学跑向自己的课堂。陶校长陪着萧涧秋从教务室里出来，走向初中一年级的教室。

教室里，学生们都好奇地向窗外张望。忽然听到一声「来了，来了！」就都坐上了位子，小声地议论着。

5　　　陶校长与萧涧秋一跨进门，学生们立刻肃静了。在级长「一！二！三！」的号令下起立、鞠躬、坐下，他们的目光都盯在这位新来的教师身上。

陶校长跨上讲台，演讲似地说：「同学们，我来介绍一下。这位就是你们的级任老师，萧涧秋先生。萧先生能够接受敝校的聘请从远地来任教，真是我校的光荣，也是同学们的幸福。萧先生到过很多的地方，见识广阔，学10　问渊博。。。。」

萧涧秋截住了他的话：「你不要在同学们面前窘我了。」

「哪里，哪里。」陶校长笑了一笑，又转向同学们说：「萧先生还有谦逊之美德，可以称得起是品学并茂。他的一切都值得你们仿效，你们要用心求教才是。现在就请萧先生来给你们上课。拍手！」

15　　　学生们在校长的提示下鼓起掌来。

萧涧秋有些窘迫地走上讲台，看着桌子上的点名簿说：「现在我开始点名，借此和你们大家认识一下。」

他开始叫学生的姓名。陶校长满意地笑了笑，轻轻地退出教室。

「余志雄。」

20　　　「到。」

「黄文平。」

「到。」

「你坐下吧。」

蕭澗秋點到的同學都站起來應聲，他也總要抬頭看一看。當他點到林月仙，林月仙要站起來的時候卻站不起來，她的辮子被後座的同學綁在椅背上了。同學們都笑了起來。

蕭澗秋說：「後面那位同學，請你站起來。你叫甚麼名字？」

「我叫段王海。」

蕭澗秋看了看他，才說：「你坐下吧！」

當他點名叫到王福生時，卻沒有回聲。同學們的目光都投在一張空桌位上。

他又復叫了一次，轉向級長問：「他請假了嗎？」

任級長的學生站起來答：「他經常遲到。」

蕭澗秋用手示意讓他坐下，繼續點名。

校門口，賣早點的擔子正在收拾，準備離去。一個十三歲帶着鄉村氣息的孩子從遠處跑來。他滿頭大汗，神色有些緊張。他跑進校門後，腳步卻放慢了下來。

他好像怕別人發現他似的，悄悄走向初一的教室。當他看見新老師已在講課，害怕地站住了。

坐在窗邊的級長發現了他，隨即向老師報告：「他就是王福生。」

正在黑板上寫着課文的蕭澗秋，轉身望着門外，向他招一招手說：「你進來吧！」

王福生羞愧地低着頭，慢慢地走了進去。

「你怎麼遲到了？」蕭澗秋特別溫和地問。

王福生直立在那裏，沒有回答。

「你家離這兒遠嗎？」

「有三里多路。」

「那你每天甚麼時候起床呢？」

「天沒亮就起來了。」因為老師態度溫和，王福生緊張的程度減低了一些。

蕭澗秋奇怪地問：「那你為甚麼遲到呢？是到哪兒去玩兒了嗎？」

萧涧秋点到的同学都站起来应声，他也总要抬头看一看。当他点到林月仙，林月仙要站起来的时候却站不起来，她的辫子被后座的同学绑在椅背上了。同学们都笑了起来。

萧涧秋说：「后面那位同学，请你站起来。你叫什么名字？」

「我叫段王海。」

萧涧秋看了看他，才说：「你坐下吧！」

当他点名叫到王福生时，却没有回声。同学们的目光都投在一张空桌位上。

他又复叫了一次，转向级长问：「他请假了吗？」

任级长的学生站起来答：「他经常迟到。」

萧涧秋用手示意让他坐下，继续点名。

校门口，卖早点的担子正在收拾，准备离去。一个十三岁带着乡村气息的孩子从远处跑来。他满头大汗，神色有些紧张。他跑进校门后，脚步却放慢了下来。

他好像怕别人发现他似的，悄悄走向初一的教室。当他看见新老师已在讲课，害怕地站住了。

坐在窗边的级长发现了他，随即向老师报告：「他就是王福生。」

正在黑板上写着课文的萧涧秋，转身望着门外，向他招一招手说：「你进来吧！」

王福生羞愧地低着头，慢慢地走了进去。

「你怎么迟到了？」萧涧秋特别温和地问。

王福生直立在那里，没有回答。

「你家离这儿远吗？」

「有三里多路。」

「那你每天什么时候起床呢？」

「天没亮就起来了。」因为老师态度温和，王福生紧张的程度减低了一些。

萧涧秋奇怪地问：「那你为什么迟到呢？是到哪儿去玩儿了吗？」

王福生默然地低着頭。

「你為甚麼不說話呢?」蕭澗秋的口氣稍微急迫了一些。

王福生的眼淚快要流出來了,他擦了擦眼睛。

55 蕭澗秋又轉而溫和地說:「好了。以後不要再遲到了,啊。去坐吧!」

王福生被解脫似地坐到自己的位子上。他以敬佩,感激的目光看着這位新老師。蕭澗秋卻已轉身,在黑板上繼續寫字了。

第十八景

下午五點多鐘。錢正興提着一大包禮物,走進陶家的廳堂。

陶媽媽迎了出來,「啊呀!你怎麼來了?」

錢正興將禮物放到桌子上。「伯母,這是家父從杭州帶來的,就算我孝敬伯母的一點小意思吧!」

5 陶媽媽欣喜而又客氣地說:「不敢當,不敢當!你們留着自己吃吧!」

「伯母,您千萬不要見外。」錢正興的態度十分懇切。

「那怎麼好意思呢?」陶媽媽已有接納的表示了。她向下房叫道:「吳媽!」

吳媽在外面答應着。

10 「泡杯茶來。」陶媽媽接着轉向錢正興說:「陶嵐不在家,給蕭先生還書去了。」她又指着椅子,「錢先生,你坐嘛!」

「好。」錢正興心神不寧地坐了下來。

第十九景

學校已經放學。陶嵐拿着那本哲學書愉快地走進校門。操場上,有一羣學生和蕭澗秋正在打着籃球。陶嵐走到操場邊出神地看着。眼前的蕭澗秋突然年輕了許多,甚至露出幾分天真的稚氣。忽然,球滾到了陶嵐跟前,陶嵐替他們拾了起來又拋還給他們。蕭澗秋發現了她,就將手中的球扔給別

王福生默然地低着头。

「你为什么不说话呢？」萧涧秋的口气稍微急迫了一些。

王福生的眼泪快要流出来了，他擦了擦眼睛。

55　萧涧秋又转而温和地说：「好了。以后不要再迟到了，啊。去坐吧！」

王福生被解脱似地坐到自己的位子上。他以敬佩，感激的目光看着这位新老师。萧涧秋却已转身，在黑板上继续写字了。

第十八景

下午五点多钟。钱正兴提着一大包礼物，走进陶家的厅堂。

陶妈妈迎了出来，「啊呀！你怎么来了？」

钱正兴将礼物放到桌子上。「伯母，这是家父从杭州带来的，就算我孝敬伯母的一点小意思吧！」

5　陶妈妈欣喜而又客气地说：「不敢当，不敢当！你们留着自己吃吧！」

「伯母，您千万不要见外。」钱正兴的态度十分恳切。

「那怎么好意思呢？」陶妈妈已有接纳的表示了。她向下房叫道：「吴妈！」

吴妈在外面答应着。

10　「泡杯茶来。」陶妈妈接着转向钱正兴说：「陶岚不在家，给萧先生还书去了。」她又指着椅子，「钱先生，你坐嘛！」

「好。」钱正兴心神不宁地坐了下来。

第十九景

学校已经放学。陶岚拿着那本哲学书愉快地走进校门。操场上，有一群学生和萧涧秋正在打着篮球。陶岚走到操场边出神地看着。眼前的萧涧秋突然年轻了许多，甚至露出几分天真的稚气。忽然，球滚到了陶岚跟前，陶岚替他们拾了起来又抛还给他们。萧涧秋发现了她，就将手中的球扔给别

5　人，連跑帶跳地到了陶嵐的面前。兩人並肩走進花木新生的校園，在含苞待放的桃李樹中穿行。

　　　　陶嵐說：「你和他們在一起玩得真高興！簡直年輕多了。」

　　　　「跟天真純潔的孩子們在一起，使我感到非常地愉快。」

　　　　「除此以外，就再沒有使你愉快的嗎？」陶嵐反問道。

10　　　「那倒不是。我在這兒所遇到的一切，都很順利。這兒給了我一種平安而質樸的感覺。」

　　　　陶嵐卻搖了搖頭說：「這可不盡然。質樸裏面藏着奸刁，平安的下面伏着紛擾。」

　　　　蕭澗秋微微驚奇地看了他一眼，然後慢慢地說：「怎麼，你談起哲學來
15　了？也許是我這幾年奔波得厭倦了。乍一到鄉鎮，有一種新鮮的感覺。」

　　　　陶嵐笑了笑。「我卻羨慕你有東奔西跑的自由，就像籠子裏的小鳥羨慕大雁一樣。」

　　　　蕭澗秋苦笑着說：「我不是大雁，我只是一隻孤雁。」

　　　　陶嵐深深地看他一眼，似要撫慰他孤單的悲涼。

20　　　蕭澗秋卻補充道：「我的意思是說，孤雁常常離羣。」

　　　　陶嵐低下頭，微微有一些不高興。「你為甚麼要解釋？」

　　　　「這不是解釋啊。」蕭澗秋看了她一眼，默默地跟她走着。

　　　　梅枝從他們頭上掠過，花瓣飄落在他們身上。

　　　　走近客房時，陶嵐站住說：「我不上去了，請你借一本關於教育的書給
25　我。」

　　　　「好啊！」蕭澗秋走上樓幾步又回身問道：「欸，你要看教育的書做甚麼？」

　　　　陶嵐又開始活躍起來。「哥哥還沒有告訴你嗎？」

　　　　「沒有啊。」

30　　　「以後，我在學校裏要教課了！」

　　　　蕭澗秋覺得有些奇怪。「哦？」

5　人，连跑带跳地到了陶岚的面前。两人并肩走进花木新生的校园，在含苞待放的桃李树中穿行。

　　　陶岚说：「你和他们在一起玩得真高兴！简直年轻多了。」

　　　「跟天真纯洁的孩子们在一起，使我感到非常地愉快。」

　　　「除此以外，就再没有使你愉快的吗？」陶岚反问道。

10　　　「那倒不是。我在这儿所遇到的一切，都很顺利。这儿给了我一种平安而质朴的感觉。」

　　　陶岚却摇了摇头说：「这可不尽然。质朴里面藏着奸刁，平安的下面伏着纷扰。」

　　　萧涧秋微微惊奇地看了他一眼，然后慢慢地说：「怎么，你谈起哲学来了？也许是我这几年奔波得厌倦了。乍一到乡镇，有一种新鲜的感觉。」

15　　　陶岚笑了笑。「我却羡慕你有东奔西跑的自由，就像笼子里的小鸟羡慕大雁一样。」

　　　萧涧秋苦笑着说：「我不是大雁，我只是一只孤雁。」

　　　陶岚深深地看他一眼，似要抚慰他孤单的悲凉。

20　　　萧涧秋却补充道：「我的意思是说，孤雁常常离群。」

　　　陶岚低下头，微微有一些不高兴。「你为什么要解释？」

　　　「这不是解释啊。」萧涧秋看了她一眼，默默地跟她走着。

　　　梅枝从他们头上掠过，花瓣飘落在他们身上。

　　　走近客房时，陶岚站住说：「我不上去了，请你借一本关于教育的书给

25　我。」

　　　「好啊！」萧涧秋走上楼几步又回身问道：「欸，你要看教育的书做什么？」

　　　陶岚又开始活跃起来。「哥哥还没有告诉你吗？」

　　　「没有啊。」

30　　　「以后，我在学校里要教课了！」

　　　萧涧秋觉得有些奇怪。「哦？」

「在這以前，我哥哥讓我擔任一點課。我說我是在家休養的。現在，他不要我教，我倒偏要教！哥哥拿我也沒有辦法。」她說到最後一句時，臉上掠過一片紅暈。

35   蕭澗秋說：「好，我馬上給你找去。」

第二十景

在西村文嫂家。桌子上放着一盞冒煙的油燈。蕭澗秋坐在小凳子上摟着采蓮幫她剝橘子皮，一家人對他已經毫不陌生了。

采蓮說：「蕭伯伯，你吃。」

「我不吃。」

5   「你吃，你吃！」

蕭澗秋就依了她。「好，好，我吃。」假裝吃了一口。

文嫂抱着阿寶，溫柔地問：「像蕭先生這樣的人，怎麼連個家都還沒有呢？」

「有家倒不自由。我從小失去了父母，多少年來一個人也就慣了。」

10   文嫂關心地說：「像蕭先生這樣的好人，應該有個好的家呀！」

蕭澗秋知道自己是無法給她說清這個道理的，就隨便地答道：「也許將來會有的吧。」又問采蓮：「你還想吃嗎？不要緊。」

文嫂卻說：「不，蕭先生，別再給她吃了，她是沒個夠的。這幾隻你帶回去吧！」

15   「我就是給他們買的嘛！好，我該走了。采蓮上學的事情，就這麼定了。」

「又給你添麻煩了。」文嫂感激地說。

「沒有甚麼。」蕭澗秋說着走了出去。

「在这以前，我哥哥让我担任一点课。我说我是在家休养的。现在，他不要我教，我倒偏要教！哥哥拿我也没有办法。」她说到最后一句时，脸上掠过一片红晕。

35　　　　萧涧秋说：「好，我马上给你找去。」

第二十景

在西村文嫂家。桌子上放着一盏冒烟的油灯。萧涧秋坐在小凳子上搂着采莲帮她剥橘子皮，一家人对他已经毫不陌生了。

采莲说：「萧伯伯，你吃。」

「我不吃。」

5　　　「你吃，你吃！」

萧涧秋就依了她。「好，好，我吃。」假装吃了一口。

文嫂抱着阿宝，温柔地问：「像萧先生这样的人，怎么连个家都还没有呢？」

「有家倒不自由。我从小失去了父母，多少年来一个人也就惯了。」

10　　　文嫂关心地说：「像萧先生这样的好人，应该有个好的家呀！」

萧涧秋知道自己是无法给她说清这个道理的，就随便地答道：「也许将来会有的吧。」又问采莲：「你还想吃吗？不要紧。」

文嫂却说：「不，萧先生，别再给她吃了，她是没个够的。这几只你带回去吧！」

15　　　「我就是给他们买的嘛！好，我该走了。采莲上学的事情，就这么定了。」

「又给你添麻烦了。」文嫂感激地说。

「没有什么。」萧涧秋说着走了出去。

第二十一景

這是一個新鮮幽麗的早晨。陽光為大地鍍上了金色，空氣是新鮮而甜蜜的，田野中的青苗好像頓然長了幾寸。橋下的流水悠悠地流着，小魚已經在清澈的水底爭食了。

文嫂拉着采蓮來至橋頭。

看到蕭澗秋從對面走來，采蓮叫道：「蕭伯伯！」

蕭澗秋答應着。

文嫂為采蓮整了整衣服說：「采蓮，你要聽蕭伯伯的話啊，好好念書。記得嗎？」

「記得。」采蓮笑了笑回答。

「好，我們走吧！」蕭澗秋抱起了采蓮。

「蕭伯伯，學校裏有橘子樹嗎？媽媽說有的。」

蕭澗秋哄着她道：「學校裏甚麼都有。一會兒你就看見了，啊。」就抱着采蓮，要走上橋去。

采蓮原是喜悅的，一時卻變得要哭出來。口中叫着「媽媽！」媽媽也答應着。

蕭澗秋轉向文嫂說：「你先回去吧。你在這兒她是不肯走的。」

「好，那我走了。媽媽晚上來接你，啊。」文嫂半轉身地邊走邊說。「采蓮，下來自個兒走，別讓蕭伯伯抱着了。」

采蓮聽了就說：「蕭伯伯，讓我自個兒下來走吧。」

「好。」

蕭澗秋牽着采蓮的手離開橋頭，慢步跨登着階石，一面哄着她說：「學校裏可好玩兒着呢。有大皮球，還有很多小朋友做遊戲，玩兒老鷹捉小雞。我帶你跟他們一塊兒玩兒去，好吧？」

采蓮聽着又變得高興起來。

第二十一景

　　这是一个新鲜幽丽的早晨。阳光为大地镀上了金色，空气是新鲜而甜蜜的，田野中的青苗好像顿然长了几寸。桥下的流水悠悠地流着，小鱼已经在清澈的水底争食了。

　　文嫂拉着采莲来至桥头。

　　看到萧涧秋从对面走来，采莲叫道：「萧伯伯！」

　　萧涧秋答应着。

　　文嫂为采莲整了整衣服说：「采莲，你要听萧伯伯的话啊，好好念书。记得吗？」

　　「记得。」采莲笑了笑回答。

　　「好，我们走吧！」萧涧秋抱起了采莲。

　　「萧伯伯，学校里有橘子树吗？妈妈说有的。」

　　萧涧秋哄着她道：「学校里什么都有。一会儿你就看见了，啊。」就抱着采莲，要走上桥去。

　　采莲原是喜悦的，一时却变得要哭出来。口中叫着「妈妈！」妈妈也答应着。

　　萧涧秋转向文嫂说：「你先回去吧。你在这儿她是不肯走的。」

　　「好，那我走了。妈妈晚上来接你，啊。」文嫂半转身地边走边说。「采莲，下来自个儿走，别让萧伯伯抱着了。」

　　采莲听了就说：「萧伯伯，让我自个儿下来走吧。」

　　「好。」

　　萧涧秋牵着采莲的手离开桥头，慢步跨登着阶石，一面哄着她说：「学校里可好玩儿着呢。有大皮球，还有很多小朋友做游戏，玩儿老鹰捉小鸡。我带你跟他们一块儿玩儿去，好吧？」

　　采莲听着又变得高兴起来。

第二十二景

　　教務室。陶嵐坐在一張新設的長桌前全神貫注地準備功課。坐在她側後的錢正興，不時地看着她，嘴裏哼着不成曲調的歌曲，好像表示自己也很懂得音樂似的。坐在遠處的方謀偷眼看着他，心裏忍不住想笑。

　　陶校長一跨進門就對陶嵐說：「妹妹，你怎麼不吃早點就來了？」

5　　「我不餓。」陶嵐輕輕回答。

　　陶校長有一些焦急。「那怎麼行呢？你怎麼能支持到中午呢？」

　　「哦，我這裏有糖。」錢正興立刻搭腔。

　　陶校長說：「不用，不用，你留着吃吧！」

　　錢正興從抽屜拿出來一包精緻的糖，殷勤地送到陶嵐桌子上。「不，
10　不。我還有呢。這是家父從杭州帶回來的。你吃一點兒吧。」

　　陶嵐推卻道：「謝謝你，我不吃。」

　　「既然錢先生送來了，你就吃一點兒吧！」陶校長一半是為了愛護妹妹的身體，一半是對錢正興的禮貌。

　　「我不吃嘛！」

15　　「隨你的便吧！」陶校長十分無可奈何。

　　方謀一旁嬉笑着說：「欸，密斯陶是備課心切啊，已經到了廢寢忘食的程度了。」

　　錢正興喪氣地坐了下去。

　　陶校長一時尷尬地站着，勉強添了一句，「哼，她就是這個脾氣。」

20　　蕭澗秋帶着采蓮進來，屋內的僵局為此打破，大家圍攏着采蓮問長問短。蕭澗秋指着各位老師叫采蓮向他們招呼，采蓮一一喚着陶校長、方老師、錢老師、陶老師。

　　陶嵐向采蓮問道：「你叫甚麼名字啊？」

　　「李采蓮。」

25　　陶嵐隨手拿過那包糖塞到采蓮的手裏。「來，吃糖吧！這是錢老師送給你的。」

　　錢正興不得不強裝着笑臉說：「吃吧！吃吧！」

第二十二景

　　教务室。陶岚坐在一张新设的长桌前全神贯注地准备功课。坐在她侧后的钱正兴，不时地看着她，嘴里哼着不成曲调的歌曲，好像表示自己也很懂得音乐似的。坐在远处的方谋偷眼看着他，心里忍不住想笑。

　　陶校长一跨进门就对陶岚说：「妹妹，你怎么不吃早点就来了？」

5　　「我不饿。」陶岚轻轻回答。

　　陶校长有一些焦急。「那怎么行呢？你怎么能支持到中午呢？」

　　「哦，我这里有糖。」钱正兴立刻搭腔。

　　陶校长说：「不用，不用，你留着吃吧！」

　　钱正兴从抽屉拿出来一包精致的糖，殷勤地送到陶岚桌子上。「不，

10　不。我还有呢。这是家父从杭州带回来的。你吃一点儿吧。」

　　陶岚推却道：「谢谢你，我不吃。」

　　「既然钱先生送来了，你就吃一点儿吧！」陶校长一半是为了爱护妹妹的身体，一半是对钱正兴的礼貌。

　　「我不吃嘛！」

15　　「随你的便吧！」陶校长十分无可奈何。

　　方谋一旁嬉笑着说：「欸，密斯陶是备课心切啊，已经到了废寝忘食的程度了。」

　　钱正兴丧气地坐了下去。

　　陶校长一时尴尬地站着，勉强添了一句，「哼，她就是这个脾气。」

20　　萧涧秋带着采莲进来，屋内的僵局为此打破，大家围拢着采莲问长问短。萧涧秋指着各位老师叫采莲向他们招呼，采莲一一唤着陶校长、方老师、钱老师、陶老师。

　　陶岚向采莲问道：「你叫什么名字啊？」

　　「李采莲。」

25　　陶岚随手拿过那包糖塞到采莲的手里。「来，吃糖吧！这是钱老师送给你的。」

　　钱正兴不得不强装着笑脸说：「吃吧！吃吧！」

「澗秋，你看，眉目之間倒長得很像志豪。」陶校長看着采蓮的面貌說。

30 方謀也跟着稱贊起來：「啊！長得很漂亮啊。將來咱們芙蓉鎮又多了一隻孔雀。」

陶嵐聽到這些話就拉着采蓮的手向外走去。「走，我帶你玩兒去。」

采蓮卻回頭叫了一聲「蕭伯伯！」並且伸出了另一隻手要蕭伯伯一起去。於是他倆各拉着采蓮的一隻手走了出去。

35 錢正興呆呆地看着他們的背影。

第二十三景

陶家廂房。鋼琴的蓋板映着燈光。

蕭澗秋輕輕地推門而入。他以為主人在吃晚飯，不便前去打擾。他走到鋼琴前坐下，將琴蓋打開。正預備彈時，隱約聽到了哭聲。

不多時陶校長從裏房走了出來。他見了蕭澗秋就嘆了一口氣道：「澗
5 秋！我妹妹隨便說話，真難辦！現在弄得我處處為難！」

蕭澗秋莫名其妙地看着他。

陶校長接着說：「唉！我妹妹，她自己曾經隨便說過。只要有人肯出錢，每年拿三千塊錢讓她到國外去跑三年，她回來之後，就跟這個人結婚。錢正興本來就想娶我妹妹。他聽到這個話之後，就跑來找我母親，向我母親表示，他願意出錢讓妹妹出國。不過條件稍微修改一下，就是先結婚，後陪
10 我妹妹出國。我母親竟答應了。好，今天錢家派了媒人來商量訂婚的日期，她就大吵大鬧到現在。」

第二十四景

陶嵐的房間。陶嵐伏在床上抽泣着。

陶媽媽坐在一旁，無可奈何地勸道：「要到外國的事情，當初也是你說的。。。。」

「涧秋，你看，眉目之间倒长得很像志豪。」陶校长看着采莲的面貌说。

30　方谋也跟着称赞起来：「啊！长得很漂亮啊。将来咱们芙蓉镇又多了一只孔雀。」

陶岚听到这些话就拉着采莲的手向外走去。「走，我带你玩儿去。」

采莲却回头叫了一声「萧伯伯！」并且伸出了另一只手要萧伯伯一起去。于是他俩各拉着采莲的一只手走了出去。

35　钱正兴呆呆地看着他们的背影。

第二十三景

陶家厢房。钢琴的盖板映着灯光。

萧涧秋轻轻地推门而入。他以为主人在吃晚饭，不便前去打扰。他走到钢琴前坐下，将琴盖打开。正预备弹时，隐约听到了哭声。

不多时陶校长从里房走了出来。他见了萧涧秋就叹了一口气道：「涧
5　秋！我妹妹随便说话，真难办！现在弄得我处处为难！」

萧涧秋莫名其妙地看着他。

陶校长接着说：「唉！我妹妹，她自己曾经随便说过。只要有人肯出钱，每年拿三千块钱让她到国外去跑三年，她回来之后，就跟这个人结婚。钱正兴本来就想娶我妹妹。他听到这个话之后，就跑来找我母亲，向我母亲
10　表示，他愿意出钱让妹妹出国。不过条件稍微修改一下，就是先结婚，后陪我妹妹出国。我母亲竟答应了。好，今天钱家派了媒人来商量订婚的日期，她就大吵大闹到现在。」

第二十四景

陶岚的房间。陶岚伏在床上抽泣着。

陶妈妈坐在一旁，无可奈何地劝道：「要到外国的事情，当初也是你说的。。。。」

陶嵐抬起頭來帶氣地說：「那我是說着玩兒的！你卻當真了。」

5　「你不小了。還這麼任性。終身大事，怎麼能當兒戲呢？」陶媽媽對女兒的責備也是輕聲輕語的。

陶嵐猛然坐了起來，態度倔強。「就算我真的說了，他並沒有同意這樣做。」

「先出去，後出去，還不是一樣？」

10　「媽，你怎麼這麼糊塗！」陶嵐哭了起來。

第二十五景

在廂房裏。陶慕侃繼續向蕭澗秋訴說着。

「。。。現在卻讓我去辦，這雖然不是一件離婚的案子，可是實際上比離婚案還難！唉！錢正興一聽到這個消息，就首先會提出辭退教務。這倒沒有甚麼，可是他的父親是本地一位有地位的士紳。他愛面子，決不會同意這
5　麼辦。澗秋，你是個精明的人，你代我想想辦法！」

這時候蕭澗秋向他看了一眼，幾乎疑心這位誠實的朋友有意刺他。可是他還是鎮靜地答道：「那，只有拖延了，讓對方冷淡下去。」

陶慕侃仍感到為難。「拖延，拖延，我代她拖延，而妹妹偏不拖延！你叫我怎麼辦？」

10　蕭澗秋忽然紅了臉，轉為取笑地說：「那只好為難你作哥哥的了！」

陶媽媽滿面愁容地走進來，蕭澗秋叫了一聲「伯母。」

她見了蕭澗秋仍舊很客氣。「蕭先生，讓你笑話了。」又轉向陶慕侃說：「你還是勸勸她吧！」

「我去也沒有用。」陶慕侃繞了半個圈，忽然想起甚麼似地說：「欸，澗
15　秋，還是你去勸勸她吧，她是相信你的。」

蕭澗秋受刺般地一驚，急忙答道：「不行，不行！我能說些甚麼呢？」說着就拿起琴譜要走。

「蕭先生，你就幫着勸勸吧！」陶媽媽幾乎在懇求他。

陶岚抬起头来带气地说：「那我是说着玩儿的！你却当真了。」

「你不小了。还这么任性。终身大事，怎么能当儿戏呢？」陶妈妈对女儿的责备也是轻声轻语的。

陶岚猛然坐了起来，态度倔强。「就算我真的说了，他并没有同意这样做。」

「先出去，后出去，还不是一样？」

「妈，你怎么这么糊涂！」陶岚哭了起来。

第二十五景

在厢房里。陶慕侃继续向萧涧秋诉说着。

「。。。现在却让我去办，这虽然不是一件离婚的案子，可是实际上比离婚案还难！唉！钱正兴一听到这个消息，就首先会提出辞退教务。这倒没有什么，可是他的父亲是本地一位有地位的士绅。他爱面子，决不会同意这么办。涧秋，你是个精明的人，你代我想想办法！」

这时候萧涧秋向他看了一眼，几乎疑心这位诚实的朋友有意刺他。可是他还是镇静地答道：「那，只有拖延了，让对方冷淡下去。」

陶慕侃仍感到为难。「拖延，拖延，我代她拖延，而妹妹偏不拖延！你叫我怎么办？」

萧涧秋忽然红了脸，转为取笑地说：「那只好为难你作哥哥的了！」

陶妈妈满面愁容地走进来，萧涧秋叫了一声「伯母。」

她见了萧涧秋仍旧很客气。「萧先生，让你笑话了。」又转向陶慕侃说：「你还是劝劝她吧！」

「我去也没有用。」陶慕侃绕了半个圈，忽然想起什么似地说：「欸，涧秋，还是你去劝劝她吧，她是相信你的。」

萧涧秋受刺般地一惊，急忙答道：「不行，不行！我能说些什么呢？」说着就拿起琴谱要走。

「萧先生，你就帮着劝劝吧！」陶妈妈几乎在恳求他。

陶慕侃也接着，「對，對。來，來。去吧，去吧。」同時把蕭澗秋手中的
琴譜拿走。

蕭澗秋還沒來得及回答，就被陶慕侃拉着走進陶嵐的房間。

第二十六景

當陶嵐聽到哥哥説「妹妹，蕭先生來了！」時，她急忙地坐了起來，背
過身去拭着淚，整理自己的頭髮。陶慕侃示意母親一同退出。陶嵐慢慢轉過
頭來看了他一眼，蕭澗秋卻不好意思地低下頭來。兩人一時無話可説。

最後還是陶嵐突破了寂靜，低聲地問道：「你還是每天早上去接采蓮
嗎？」

「是的。」

「你要認她作你的乾女兒嗎？」

「誰説的？」蕭澗秋奇怪地看着她。

陶嵐卻笑了笑，不願特別認真告訴他。「那就別問了。」

「根本沒有這回事啊。」

陶嵐嘆了一口氣，淡淡地説：「蕭先生，我們這兒的消息是傳得很快
的。」

「怎麼？」蕭澗秋全然不懂。

陶嵐卻苦笑了一下説：「沒甚麼。」

第二十七景

又是一個早晨。蕭澗秋站在橋頭等候着采蓮的到來，還不時地向西村
那邊兒眺望着。路上沒有她母女的影子。

王福生挑着一擔柴，從另一條路上走來，停在橋下。蕭澗秋起初沒有認
出這就是他的學生。當王福生放下擔子向他鞠躬，口中叫着「蕭老師！」
時，他才微微一驚。

「王福生？」他又忙上前溫和地問：「你每天這樣做嗎？」

陶慕侃也接着，「对，对。来，来。去吧，去吧。」同时把萧涧秋手中的
20　琴谱拿走。

萧涧秋还没来得及回答，就被陶慕侃拉着走进陶岚的房间。

第二十六景

当陶岚听到哥哥说「妹妹，萧先生来了！」时，她急忙地坐了起来，背
过身去拭着泪，整理自己的头发。陶慕侃示意母亲一同退出。陶岚慢慢转过
头来看了他一眼，萧涧秋却不好意思地低下头来。两人一时无话可说。

最后还是陶岚突破了寂静，低声地问道：「你还是每天早上去接采莲
5　吗？」

「是的。」

「你要认她作你的干女儿吗？」

「谁说的？」萧涧秋奇怪地看着她。

陶岚却笑了笑，不愿特别认真告诉他。「那就别问了。」

10　「根本没有这回事啊。」

陶岚叹了一口气，淡淡地说：「萧先生，我们这儿的消息是传得很快
的。」

「怎么？」萧涧秋全然不懂。

陶岚却苦笑了一下说：「没什么。」

第二十七景

又是一个早晨。萧涧秋站在桥头等候着采莲的到来，还不时地向西村
那边儿眺望着。路上没有她母女的影子。

王福生挑着一担柴，从另一条路上走来，停在桥下。萧涧秋起初没有认
出这就是他的学生。当王福生放下担子向他鞠躬，口中叫着「萧老师！」
5　时，他才微微一惊。

「王福生？」他又忙上前温和地问：「你每天这样做吗？」

「是的。」

「家裏的生活就靠你嗎？」

「不，有爸爸。因為學費沒交齊，我得幫助爸爸多做一點兒。」王福生似乎有些羞愧地低下了頭。

蕭澗秋向他身後的路上看了一看問：「哦。你爸爸呢？」

「還在山上砍柴呢。他怕我遲到，先讓我把這擔送到柴市去。」王福生指着橋下河邊的柴市。

「好的，你趕快去吧！」

王福生又鞠了躬，挑起擔子向柴市走去。

蕭澗秋目送他到柴市，然後轉身望着西村。路上仍無她母女的影子，他有些焦慮起來，決定到西村去一趟。

第二十八景

西村。文嫂坐在屋裏默默地流着淚。采蓮也是剛哭過的樣子，正呆呆地看着媽媽。

這時蕭澗秋彎腰跨進門來。文嫂連忙轉過臉去背着他擦乾眼淚。采蓮高興地撲到他身上叫了一聲「蕭伯伯！」

蕭澗秋抱住采蓮問：「采蓮，你怎麼不去上學？」

文嫂忙替她回答：「蕭先生，我不想再讓采蓮上學了。家裏，阿寶沒人照顧。」

蕭澗秋看着她有些懷疑。「她怎麼能照顧阿寶呢？我看這不是理由。」他又轉向采蓮問：「采蓮，是你自己不願意去上學了嗎？」

采蓮看着媽媽不敢回答。

蕭澗秋性急地向文嫂問：「這究竟是怎麼回事啊？」

文嫂竭力地掩飾內心的痛苦，溫和地說：「說實在的，蕭先生，每天讓你來回地跑，我們心裏不安哪！」

「這有甚麼呢？我可以藉此出外走一走，呼吸一點兒新鮮的空氣啊。」

「不！」文嫂固執地，「不能為了采蓮讓你受累。」

「是的。」

「家里的生活就靠你吗？」

「不，有爸爸。因为学费没交齐，我得帮助爸爸多做一点儿。」王福生似乎有些羞愧地低下了头。

萧涧秋向他身后的路上看了一看问：「哦。你爸爸呢？」

「还在山上砍柴呢。他怕我迟到，先让我把这担送到柴市去。」王福生指着桥下河边的柴市。

「好的，你赶快去吧！」

王福生又鞠了躬，挑起担子向柴市走去。

萧涧秋目送他到柴市，然后转身望着西村。路上仍无她母女的影子，他有些焦虑起来，决定到西村去一趟。

第二十八景

西村。文嫂坐在屋里默默地流着泪。采莲也是刚哭过的样子，正呆呆地看着妈妈。

这时萧涧秋弯腰跨进门来。文嫂连忙转过脸去背着他擦干眼泪。采莲高兴地扑到他身上叫了一声「萧伯伯！」

萧涧秋抱住采莲问：「采莲，你怎么不去上学？」

文嫂忙替她回答：「萧先生，我不想再让采莲上学了。家里，阿宝没人照顾。」

萧涧秋看着她有些怀疑。「她怎么能照顾阿宝呢？我看这不是理由。」他又转向采莲问：「采莲，是你自己不愿意去上学了吗？」

采莲看着妈妈不敢回答。

萧涧秋性急地向文嫂问：「这究竟是怎么回事啊？」

文嫂竭力地掩饰内心的痛苦，温和地说：「说实在的，萧先生，每天让你来回地跑，我们心里不安哪！」

「这有什么呢？我可以借此出外走一走，呼吸一点儿新鲜的空气啊。」

「不！」文嫂固执地，「不能为了采莲让你受累。」

蕭澗秋對文嫂提出的這條理由有些相信了。「如果僅僅是因為這個，那我可以讓一個大同學在橋頭等着她，他是順路的。」

「那。。。」文嫂本不想同意，卻又說不出別的理由來。

「好，天不早了。采蓮，我們走吧！」

「蕭先生。。。」

蕭澗秋沒等文嫂說話，就拉着采蓮走了出去。

門外遠遠的幾個中年婦女對着蕭澗秋的背影指指戳戳，竊竊私議着。

屋裏剩下文嫂一個人時，她的眼淚又流了出來。

第二十九景

在采蓮上學的路上。蕭澗秋拉着采蓮的手，邊走邊問：「是你跟媽媽淘氣了吧？」

「沒有。」

「那你媽媽為甚麼要哭呢？」

采蓮結結巴巴地說：「今天早上我出去玩兒去了。那些小孩兒罵我，我就回家告訴媽媽，媽媽就哭了。」

「他們罵你甚麼呢？」

「他們罵我有個野爸爸。」

蕭澗秋像受了雷擊似地震了一下，腦子嗡嗡地作響。他默默地走着，凝視着遠處的天邊。

果然，天邊湧起了烏雲。

第三十景

天氣陰沈，下着細雨，夜幕將要落下了。蕭澗秋在客房前廊簷下踱來踱去，就好似在西湖邊上徘徊一樣。

陶嵐打着傘走來，蕭澗秋停住腳步用目光迎着她。

萧涧秋对文嫂提出的这条理由有些相信了。「如果仅仅是因为这个，那我可以让一个大同学在桥头等着她，他是顺路的。」

「那。。。」文嫂本不想同意，却又说不出别的理由来。

「好，天不早了。采莲，我们走吧！」

20　「萧先生。。。」

萧涧秋没等文嫂说话，就拉着采莲走了出去。

门外远远的几个中年妇女对着萧涧秋的背影指指戳戳，窃窃私议着。

屋里剩下文嫂一个人时，她的眼泪又流了出来。

第二十九景

在采莲上学的路上。萧涧秋拉着采莲的手，边走边问：「是你跟妈妈淘气了吧？」

「没有。」

「那你妈妈为什么要哭呢？」

5　采莲结结巴巴地说：「今天早上我出去玩儿去了。那些小孩儿骂我，我就回家告诉妈妈，妈妈就哭了。」

「他们骂你什么呢？」

「他们骂我有个野爸爸。」

萧涧秋像受了雷击似地震了一下，脑子嗡嗡地作响。他默默地走着，凝

10　视着远处的天边。

果然，天边涌起了乌云。

第三十景

天气阴沉，下着细雨，夜幕将要落下了。萧涧秋在客房前廊檐下踱来踱去，就好似在西湖边上徘徊一样。

陶岚打着伞走来，萧涧秋停住脚步用目光迎着她。

陶嵐微笑地看了他一眼，好像在説，「你的心思我已經知道了。」她站
在樓下叫道：「蕭先生！我哥哥讓我來請你到我們家去吃晚飯。」

「不用了，學校裏馬上就要開飯了。」

陶嵐調皮地帶着要挾的口氣説：「那麼，是不是要讓我回去，讓哥哥再
來請你啊？」

蕭澗秋無可奈何地笑了一笑，就從房門口取了一把傘，隨着陶嵐一起
走出校門。

雨點打在傘上，響出寂寞的調子。

陶嵐看了他一眼説：「你今天好像有甚麼心事。」

「是嗎？我自己倒不覺得。」蕭澗秋勉強地笑着。

「是因為錢正興的事嗎？」

「我根本没注意他。」蕭澗秋否認着，但又問道：「怎麼，他辭職了？」

陶嵐冷漠地説：「哼，他今天派人送封信給我哥哥，説他要辭掉中學的
職務。原因完全是由於我，還關係到你。」

「關係到我？」蕭澗秋隨口問道。

「可是哥哥不讓我告訴你。」

一個過路的人從對面走來，狐疑地看着他們倆走過去。

陶嵐不知不覺地將自己的雨傘落下靠近了蕭澗秋。「我本來答應哥哥不
告訴你的，可是我還得告訴你。錢正興的信上説，我已經愛上你了。他説你
是個完全不懂得『愛』的人。他還説，悔不該他的家庭有地位，又有錢。要
是他也窮得和你一樣，我就會愛上他了。」陶嵐説到每個「愛」字的時候，已
經吃吃地説不出來，這時她更加臉紅地低着頭。

蕭澗秋幾乎感覺到身體要炸裂了，一時説不出話來，兩眼凝視着迷濛
的街道。

兩人停住了腳步。陶嵐抬起頭來，焦慮地含着眼淚説：「我求你，無論
如何不要煩惱。」

蕭澗秋皺起了眉頭，苦笑着。「看來，我在芙蓉鎮是住不長了。」

陶岚微笑地看了他一眼，好像在说，「你的心思我已经知道了。」她站
在楼下叫道：「萧先生！我哥哥让我来请你到我们家去吃晚饭。」

「不用了，学校里马上就要开饭了。」

陶岚调皮地带着要挟的口气说：「那么，是不是要让我回去，让哥哥再
来请你啊？」

萧涧秋无可奈何地笑了一笑，就从房门口取了一把伞，随着陶岚一起
走出校门。

雨点打在伞上，响出寂寞的调子。

陶岚看了他一眼说：「你今天好像有什么心事。」

「是吗？我自己倒不觉得。」萧涧秋勉强地笑着。

「是因为钱正兴的事吗？」

「我根本没注意他。」萧涧秋否认着，但又问道：「怎么，他辞职了？」

陶岚冷漠地说：「哼，他今天派人送封信给我哥哥，说他要辞掉中学的
职务。原因完全是由于我，还关系到你。」

「关系到我？」萧涧秋随口问道。

「可是哥哥不让我告诉你。」

一个过路的人从对面走来，狐疑地看着他们俩走过去。

陶岚不知不觉地将自己的雨伞落下靠近了萧涧秋。「我本来答应哥哥不
告诉你的，可是我还得告诉你。钱正兴的信上说，我已经爱上你了。他说你
是个完全不懂得『爱』的人。他还说，悔不该他的家庭有地位，又有钱。要
是他也穷得和你一样，我就会爱上他了。」陶岚说到每个「爱」字的时候，已
经吃吃地说不出来，这时她更加脸红地低着头。

萧涧秋几乎感觉到身体要炸裂了，一时说不出话来，两眼凝视着迷濛
的街道。

两人停住了脚步。陶岚抬起头来，焦虑地含着眼泪说：「我求你，无论
如何不要烦恼。」

萧涧秋皱起了眉头，苦笑着。「看来，我在芙蓉镇是住不长了。」

「你別這麼說！」陶嵐激動得幾乎要哭出來，頓了一下囁嚅地說：「都怪我不好！哥哥再三囑咐我不要告訴你的。可是不知怎麼的，在你的面前就像在上帝面前一樣，一點不能隱瞞。我知道說了你會煩惱。可是，這有甚麼辦法？」

35　　蕭澗秋淡淡地笑了笑。「你放心吧！對於錢正興，我並不介意。」

「那就好。」陶嵐似乎得到寬慰，高興了一些。兩人進了陶家的大門。

第三十一景

陶家的客廳。晚餐已經安排好了。陶慕侃、蕭澗秋、陶嵐分坐在一張小八仙桌的三面。蕭澗秋的面前只放着一隻小杯，因為誠實的陶慕侃知道他是不會喝酒的。可是這一次蕭澗秋端起杯子自己喝了起來。

陶慕侃奇怪而又高興地說：「欸，澗秋，你的酒量不小啊！你看，你臉
5　上還一點沒有甚麼呢，你往常騙了我！來，來，來！今天晚上我們要盡興地喝一喝，換個大杯子！」

陶嵐阻止道：「哥哥！」

陶慕侃一面替蕭澗秋秋換了大杯，一面念出句詩：「『人生有酒須當醉，莫使金樽空對月。』[1] 欸！來！」

10　　陶嵐多次向蕭澗秋做眼色，蕭澗秋卻一杯一杯地喝。這時她禁不住地說道：「哥哥，他是不會喝酒的，他這是在麻醉自己！」

「是！麻醉！」陶慕侃毫未介意，又念了句詩：「『何以解憂？唯有杜康。』[2] 來！」

「哥哥！」陶嵐擔着心思，露出了愁容，呆呆地看着蕭澗秋手中的酒
15　杯。

蕭澗秋卻向她說：「嵐，你放心吧！我不會拿酒當藥喝的，我為甚麼要麻醉自己呢？我只想讓自己振奮一些，勇敢一些。」他說完舉起大杯一飲而盡。

「對！來！」陶校長說。

「你别这么说！」陶岚激动得几乎要哭出来，顿了一下嗫嚅地说：「都怪我不好！哥哥再三嘱咐我不要告诉你的。可是不知怎的，在你的面前就像在上帝面前一样，一点不能隐瞒。我知道说了你会烦恼。可是，这有什么办法？」

35　　萧涧秋淡淡地笑了笑。「你放心吧！对于钱正兴，我并不介意。」

「那就好。」陶岚似乎得到宽慰，高兴了一些。两人进了陶家的大门。

第三十一景

陶家的客厅。晚餐已经安排好了。陶慕侃、萧涧秋、陶岚分坐在一张小八仙桌的三面。萧涧秋的面前只放着一只小杯，因为诚实的陶慕侃知道他是不会喝酒的。可是这一次萧涧秋端起杯子自己喝了起来。

陶慕侃奇怪而又高兴地说：「欸，涧秋，你的酒量不小啊！你看，你脸

5　上还一点没有什么呢，你往常骗了我！来，来，来！今天晚上我们要尽兴地喝一喝，换个大杯子！」

陶岚阻止道：「哥哥！」

陶慕侃一面替萧涧秋秋换了大杯，一面念出句诗：「『人生有酒须当醉，莫使金樽空对月。』¹ 欸！来！」

10　陶岚多次向萧涧秋做眼色，萧涧秋却一杯一杯地喝。这时她禁不住地说道：「哥哥，他是不会喝酒的，他这是在麻醉自己！」

「是！麻醉！」陶慕侃毫未介意，又念了句诗：「『何以解忧？唯有杜康。』² 来！」

「哥哥！」陶岚担着心思，露出了愁容，呆呆地看着萧涧秋手中的酒

15　杯。

萧涧秋却向她说：「岚，你放心吧！我不会拿酒当药喝的，我为什么要麻醉自己呢？我只想让自己振奋一些，勇敢一些。」他说完举起大杯一饮而尽。

「对！来！」陶校长说。

第三十二景

　　廂房。蕭澗秋的兩隻大手像十個錘頭似地猛力擊着琴鍵，他精神奮發地彈出了勇敢的旋律。陶嵐開始為他的精神變異而難過，為他端來了水果。後來她也逐漸被音樂感染了，也振奮了起來。鋼琴的聲音延續着。

第三十三景

　　蕭澗秋昂首闊步地跑至橋頭，又大步地越過拱橋向西村走去。

　　河邊路上，文嫂拉着采蓮走來。她遠遠地看見了蕭先生，便停住了腳步，讓采蓮跑上去。蕭澗秋也跑步迎接，一把將采蓮抱起，向遠處的文嫂揮了揮手，轉身跑向學校。

第三十四景

　　學校的操場上。蕭澗秋領着男生，陶嵐領着女生，雙方在激烈而愉快地比賽籃球。

　　教務室裏，幾位教師在窗口竊竊私議着。

　　「簡直是不成體統。」

　　「欸，這是文明的表現嘛！」方謀說。

第三十五景

　　蕭澗秋與陶嵐已經回到客房裏。他倆都顯得有些疲乏，但精神上卻很興奮，像激戰後的勝利者。

　　陶嵐說：「欸，好熱啊！」一面理着頭髮。

　　蕭澗秋抽下手巾放入臉盆內對陶嵐說：「來，洗洗臉吧！」

　　「你洗吧，我就回家了。」陶嵐口渴地喝着熱茶，她臉上的汗越發多了。

第三十二景

厢房。萧涧秋的两只大手像十个锤头似地猛力击着琴键，他精神奋发地弹出了勇敢的旋律。陶岚开始为他的精神变异而难过，为他端来了水果。后来她也逐渐被音乐感染了，也振奋了起来。钢琴的声音延续着。

第三十三景

萧涧秋昂首阔步地跑至桥头，又大步地越过拱桥向西村走去。

河边路上，文嫂拉着采莲走来。她远远地看见了萧先生，便停住了脚步，让采莲跑上去。萧涧秋也跑步迎接，一把将采莲抱起，向远处的文嫂挥了挥手，转身跑向学校。

第三十四景

学校的操场上。萧涧秋领着男生，陶岚领着女生，双方在激烈而愉快地比赛篮球。

教务室里，几位教师在窗口窃窃私议着。

「简直是不成体统。」

「欸，这是文明的表现嘛！」方谋说。

第三十五景

萧涧秋与陶岚已经回到客房里。他俩都显得有些疲乏，但精神上却很兴奋，像激战后的胜利者。

陶岚说：「欸，好热啊！」一面理着头发。

萧涧秋抽下手巾放入脸盆内对陶岚说：「来，洗洗脸吧！」

「你洗吧，我就回家了。」陶岚口渴地喝着热茶，她脸上的汗越发多了。

蕭澗秋將擰乾了的手巾遞給她，說：「給你。」

陶嵐也就不客氣地接了過來擦臉。

蕭澗秋靠她很近，他睜大兩眼，一瞬不瞬地看着她。柔嫩的面孔，這時

10 兩頰起了紅色，長長的睫毛襯在黑黑的眼珠四周。蕭澗秋感到自己的心胸

也在起伏着。

陶嵐感到不好意思。「你為甚麼這樣地看着我？」

「因為，我還從來還沒有這樣看過你呢。」

陶嵐睜着一雙大眼調皮地看着他。「給你。」

15 蕭澗秋接過手巾，隨即返身至臉盆架前洗臉。

這時阿榮送來一份郵件。「蕭先生！」

蕭澗秋接過來說：「謝謝你啊！」

陶嵐問是甚麼。

蕭澗秋答：「雜誌。上海一個朋友寄來的。」隨即將郵件拆開，露出雜

20 誌《新青年》的字樣。

兩人聚精會神地看着，討論着。

第三十六景

蕭澗秋正走上樓梯回到自己的房間去時，就聽到陶嵐在樓下叫着「澗

秋！」於是又轉身下樓迎着她。

陶嵐興奮地説：「我昨天一夜沒睡，把它都看完了。」

「你認為怎麼樣？」

5 「我還不能完全同意你的看法。」

「好。那我們繼續討論吧。」

「好吧。」

兩人就又開始討論起來。

萧涧秋将拧干了的手巾递给她，说：「给你。」

陶岚也就不客气地接了过来擦脸。

萧涧秋靠她很近，他睁大两眼，一瞬不瞬地看着她。柔嫩的面孔，这时
10　两颊起了红色，长长的睫毛衬在黑黑的眼珠四周。萧涧秋感到自己的心胸
也在起伏着。

陶岚感到不好意思。「你为什么这样地看着我？」

「因为，我还从来还没有这样看过你呢。」

陶岚睁着一双大眼调皮地看着他。「给你。」

15　萧涧秋接过手巾，随即返身至脸盆架前洗脸。

这时阿荣送来一份邮件。「萧先生！」

萧涧秋接过来说：「谢谢你啊！」

陶岚问是什么。

萧涧秋答：「杂志。上海一个朋友寄来的。」随即将邮件拆开，露出杂
20　志《新青年》的字样。

两人聚精会神地看着，讨论着。

第三十六景

萧涧秋正走上楼梯回到自己的房间去时，就听到陶岚在楼下叫着「涧
秋！」于是又转身下楼迎着她。

陶岚兴奋地说：「我昨天一夜没睡，把它都看完了。」

「你认为怎么样？」
5　「我还不能完全同意你的看法。」

「好。那我们继续讨论吧。」

「好吧。」

两人就又开始讨论起来。

第三十七景

　　蕭澗秋和陶嵐走進蕭澗秋的客房。蕭澗秋一進門就拾起了地上的一封信。

　　陶嵐注視着這封信，有些奇怪地問：「誰來的信？」

　　「不知道。」蕭澗秋說。

　　陶嵐從蕭澗秋手裏拿過來看。「還是一首詩呢！」

　　「哦？」蕭澗秋驚訝地問。

　　「『芙蓉芙蓉二月開，一個教師外鄉來。』」她念不下去了。

　　蕭澗秋接過來念道：「『芙蓉芙蓉二月開，一個教師外鄉來。兩眼炯炯如惡鷹，內有一副好心裁。左手抱着小寡婦，右手想把芙蓉採。此人若不驅逐了，吾鄉風化安在哉！』」

　　蕭澗秋立刻臉轉蒼白，全身震動地將紙揉成一團，說：「真卑鄙！」

　　陶嵐氣憤地搶過紙來。「你給我，我找哥哥去。」

　　陶嵐說着就要往外走，蕭澗秋卻攔阻了她。「哦，不！何必去給他增添煩惱呢？」

　　「我們一定要徹查一下！」

　　「查出來又有甚麼用啊？他要是個光明正大的人，就不會寫這種東西了！」蕭澗秋在屋中走了兩步，坐在床邊。「看來，我非在你們芙蓉鎮被暗箭射死不可！」

　　陶嵐噙住眼淚說：「你別這麼說。澗秋，我要跟你好！我要他們看着我們好，讓他們笑罵吧！讓他們忌妒吧！讓他們在石壁上碰死。你是個意志堅強的人，應該拿出勇氣來！」

　　「是啊！我們是無所顧惜。可是，我所擔心的是文嫂。沒有人同情她，還不斷地用流言蜚語這樣地傷害她。在這樣的境遇裏，叫她怎麼辦呢？」

　　陶嵐也找不出安慰他的話。他倆沈默了一會兒。

　　「真太殘忍了。」蕭澗秋發出了感嘆。

　　站在窗口的陶嵐，偶然發現校園的樹叢裏呆呆地站着個孩子，她忙向蕭澗秋說：「欸，你看，那不是采蓮嗎？」

第三十七景

萧涧秋和陶岚走进萧涧秋的客房。萧涧秋一进门就拾起了地上的一封信。

陶岚注视着这封信，有些奇怪地问：「谁来的信？」

「不知道。」萧涧秋说。

陶岚从萧涧秋手里拿过来看。「还是一首诗呢！」

「哦？」萧涧秋惊讶地问。

「『芙蓉芙蓉二月开，一个教师外乡来。』」她念不下去了。

萧涧秋接过来念道：「『芙蓉芙蓉二月开，一个教师外乡来。两眼炯炯如恶鹰，内有一副好心裁。左手抱着小寡妇，右手想把芙蓉采。此人若不驱逐了，吾乡风化安在哉！』」

萧涧秋立刻脸转苍白，全身震动地将纸揉成一团，说：「真卑鄙！」

陶岚气愤地抢过纸来。「你给我，我找哥哥去。」

陶岚说着就要往外走，萧涧秋却拦阻了她。「哦，不！何必去给他增添烦恼呢？」

「我们一定要彻查一下！」

「查出来又有什么用啊？他要是个光明正大的人，就不会写这种东西了！」萧涧秋在屋中走了两步，坐在床边。「看来，我非在你们芙蓉镇被暗箭射死不可！」

陶岚噙住眼泪说：「你别这么说。涧秋，我要跟你好！我要他们看着我们好，让他们笑骂吧！让他们忌妒吧！让他们在石壁上碰死。你是个意志坚强的人，应该拿出勇气来！」

「是啊！我们是无所顾惜。可是，我所担心的是文嫂。没有人同情她，还不断地用流言蜚语这样地伤害她。在这样的境遇里，叫她怎么办呢？」

陶岚也找不出安慰他的话。他俩沉默了一会儿。

「真太残忍了。」萧涧秋发出了感叹。

站在窗口的陶岚，偶然发现校园的树丛里呆呆地站着个孩子，她忙向萧涧秋说：「欸，你看，那不是采莲吗？」

蕭澗秋順着她的手看去，很快決斷地答道：「欸，是她。」

29　他急忙奔向校園，陶嵐也跟了出去。

第三十八景

采蓮看見蕭澗秋和陶嵐就哭了起來。

蕭澗秋蹲下身子摟住她問道：「采蓮，你今天早上怎麼没來上學啊？」

「媽媽叫我不要告訴蕭伯伯，叫我來上學。弟弟病了，燒得很厲害。媽媽不讓蕭伯伯知道。」

5　　蕭澗秋慢慢地站了起來。采蓮看着他，好像自己做錯了事似地要哭出來。

陶嵐將她抱在身邊，向蕭澗秋说：「讓阿榮借個體溫表來，我們一塊兒去看看吧。」

「我簡直不敢去了。」

10　「為甚麼？」陶嵐問。

蕭澗秋呆立着答：「社會上的閑話太多了。」

第三十九景

清香園茶館，煙霧繚繞，人聲嘈雜。方謀與錢正興分坐在靠窗的一張茶桌兩邊，正在品茗閑話。

「阿謀，學校裏邊對我的辭職有甚麼議論嗎？啊？」錢正興問道。

方謀说：「欸，密斯脱錢，自從你走了以後，校中同仁都感到非常寂
5　寞，所以我們大家都盼望你回來。」

錢正興像個勝利者般地笑了笑，然後又凜然地说：「哼，姓蕭的不走，我決不回去！」

這時，旁邊桌上的客人們也在議論着：「欸，那個姓蕭的是誰啊？」

「就是那個芙蓉鎮中學的教師嘛。」

10　「哦，我知道。」

萧涧秋顺着她的手看去，很快决断地答道：「欸，是她。」

他急忙奔向校园，陶岚也跟了出去。

第三十八景

采莲看见萧涧秋和陶岚就哭了起来。

萧涧秋蹲下身子搂住她问道：「采莲，你今天早上怎么没来上学啊？」

「妈妈叫我不要告诉萧伯伯，叫我来上学。弟弟病了，烧得很厉害。妈妈不让萧伯伯知道。」

萧涧秋慢慢地站了起来。采莲看着他，好像自己做错了事似地要哭出来。

陶岚将她抱在身边，向萧涧秋说：「让阿荣借个体温表来，我们一块儿去看看吧。」

「我简直不敢去了。」

「为什么？」陶岚问。

萧涧秋呆立着答：「社会上的闲话太多了。」

第三十九景

清香园茶馆，烟雾缭绕，人声嘈杂。方谋与钱正兴分坐在靠窗的一张茶桌两边，正在品茗闲话。

「阿谋，学校里边对我的辞职有什么议论吗？啊？」钱正兴问道。

方谋说：「欸，密斯脱钱，自从你走了以后，校中同仁都感到非常寂寞，所以我们大家都盼望你回来。」

钱正兴像个胜利者般地笑了笑，然后又凛然地说：「哼，姓萧的不走，我决不回去！」

这时，旁边桌上的客人们也在议论着：「欸，那个姓萧的是谁啊？」

「就是那个芙蓉镇中学的教师嘛。」

「哦，我知道。」

錢正興又得意地笑了笑。

方謀嬉笑道：「依我看來，這位江湖落魄者所喜愛的不是孔雀，而是野鴨。」

「野鴨？」錢正興不解地問。

「哎！就是西村的那位年輕的寡婦嘛！」方謀為此比喻而自鳴得意地笑了起來。

附近幾張桌子的茶客都為他們的談笑所吸引。

第四十景

西村。文嫂抱着孩子坐在床沿，陶嵐也坐在旁邊為孩子試體溫。蕭澗秋站在她們面前。三人的目光都集中在昏迷狀態的孩子身上。

「甚麼時候發燒的？」陶嵐問文嫂。

「從昨天起，越來越厲害了。」

「你應該早一點兒請個醫生來看一看。」蕭澗秋非常關心。

「我總以為他自己會好的，中午陳奶奶來看了一次，覺得孩子燒得厲害，她就幫我請醫生去了。」

陶嵐從孩子身上拿出體溫表，到亮處察看。蕭澗秋也走了過去。

這時候陳奶奶——就是船上所看見的那位老婦人——帶進一位年老的中醫，說：「文嫂，先生請來了。」

當他看見蕭澗秋與陶嵐在看體溫表時，馬上就不高興地對陳奶奶說：「你們已經請人了，那。。。？」老醫生說着返身要走。

陳奶奶連忙解釋：「不，他們不是醫生。」

蕭澗秋就插言道：「請你不要誤會，我們是芙蓉鎮中學的教師。」

醫生將眼鏡拉下，向蕭澗秋注視着。「哦，你就是蕭先生！久仰，久仰。」

當老醫生的目光移到陶嵐身上的時候，她不耐煩地說：「請你快給孩子看病吧。」

老醫生又向蕭澗秋瞥了一眼後，才去為孩子按脈。

钱正兴又得意地笑了笑。

方谋嬉笑道：「依我看来，这位江湖落魄者所喜爱的不是孔雀，而是野鸭。」

「野鸭？」钱正兴不解地问。

「咹！就是西村的那位年轻的寡妇嘛！」方谋为此比喻而自鸣得意地笑了起来。

附近几张桌子的茶客都为他们的谈笑所吸引。

第四十景

西村。文嫂抱着孩子坐在床沿，陶岚也坐在旁边为孩子试体温。萧涧秋站在她们面前。三人的目光都集中在昏迷状态的孩子身上。

「什么时候发烧的？」陶岚问文嫂。

「从昨天起，越来越厉害了。」

「你应该早一点儿请个医生来看一看。」萧涧秋非常关心。

「我总以为他自己会好的，中午陈奶奶来看了一次，觉得孩子烧得厉害，她就帮我请医生去了。」

陶岚从孩子身上拿出体温表，到亮处察看。萧涧秋也走了过去。

这时候陈奶奶——就是船上所看见的那位老妇人——带进一位年老的中医，说：「文嫂，先生请来了。」

当他看见萧涧秋与陶岚在看体温表时，马上就不高兴地对陈奶奶说：「你们已经请人了，那。。。？」老医生说着返身要走。

陈奶奶连忙解释：「不，他们不是医生。」

萧涧秋就插言道：「请你不要误会，我们是芙蓉镇中学的教师。」

医生将眼镜拉下，向萧涧秋注视着。「哦，你就是萧先生！久仰，久仰。」

当老医生的目光移到陶岚身上的时候，她不耐烦地说：「请你快给孩子看病吧。」

老医生又向萧涧秋瞥了一眼后，才去为孩子按脉。

20　　陶嵐拿着體溫表低聲告訴蕭澗秋：「三十九度八，燒得很厲害。」

「不要是肺炎吧。」蕭澗秋抬起頭看着醫生。

老醫生緊鎖眉頭，按了脈。他慢慢放下孩子的手，故作輕鬆地說：「沒甚麼病，過兩天就會好的。」

「沒有甚麼病啊？」文嫂驚喜地問。

25　　老醫生拿起小布包說：「小孩兒發點兒寒熱，用不着吃藥。」

蕭澗秋幾乎是責問地說：「不吃藥，孩子怎麼能退燒呢？」

老醫生無可奈何地看了他一眼。「好吧！那就吃一服吧！」他坐下打開了布包，取出紙、筆，開起藥方來。

文嫂向蕭澗秋狐疑地問：「蕭先生，看樣子，會沒病嗎？」

30　　蕭澗秋難以回答，隨便說了兩句。「所以我勸你不要着急啊。退了燒，病就會好的。」就走向老醫生去拿藥方單。

文嫂這時正急着要付診療費。陶嵐卻已拿出錢來說：「這裏已經給了。」

老醫生稍稍客氣後，接過陶嵐手中的錢放入衣袋，又向蕭澗秋看了一35　眼，僂着背走出門去。

蕭澗秋拿着藥方單看了一眼，向文嫂說：「哦，我去買藥去。」

文嫂感激地望着他，又要將錢還給陶嵐。

陶嵐推卻了說：「別這樣。」又隱藏住心酸寬慰她：「文嫂，你千萬不要着急。孩子吃了藥就會好的。我明天再來。。。。」她話未說完就已經眼淚40　盈眶了。

「謝謝你啦！陶小姐。」文嫂說着，要送她到門口。

陶嵐不讓她起身就離開了。

第四十一景

陶家。陶嵐跨進了門，顯得非常勞累的樣子。

「你餓了吧？要不，你就先吃吧！」陶媽媽疼愛地說。

「我不餓，哥哥呢？」陶嵐答道。

20　陶岚拿着体温表低声告诉萧涧秋：「三十九度八，烧得很厉害。」

「不要是肺炎吧。」萧涧秋抬起头看着医生。

老医生紧锁眉头，按了脉。他慢慢放下孩子的手，故作轻松地说：「没什么病，过两天就会好的。」

「没有什么病啊？」文嫂惊喜地问。

25　老医生拿起小布包说：「小孩儿发点儿寒热，用不着吃药。」

萧涧秋几乎是责问地说：「不吃药，孩子怎么能退烧呢？」

老医生无可奈何地看了他一眼。「好吧！那就吃一服吧！」他坐下打开了布包，取出纸、笔，开起药方来。

文嫂向萧涧秋狐疑地问：「萧先生，看样子，会没病吗？」

30　萧涧秋难以回答，随便说了两句。「所以我劝你不要着急啊。退了烧，病就会好的。」就走向老医生去拿药方单。

文嫂这时正急着要付诊疗费。陶岚却已拿出钱来说：「这里已经给了。」

老医生稍稍客气后，接过陶岚手中的钱放入衣袋，又向萧涧秋看了一35　眼，偻着背走出门去。

萧涧秋拿着药方单看了一眼，向文嫂说：「哦，我去买药去。」

文嫂感激地望着他，又要将钱还给陶岚。

陶岚推却了说：「别这样。」又隐藏住心酸宽慰她：「文嫂，你千万不要着急。孩子吃了药就会好的。我明天再来。。。」她话未说完就已经眼泪40　盈眶了。

「谢谢你啦！陶小姐。」文嫂说着，要送她到门口。

陶岚不让她起身就离开了。

第四十一景

陶家。陶岚跨进了门，显得非常劳累的样子。

「你饿了吧？要不，你就先吃吧！」陶妈妈疼爱地说。

「我不饿，哥哥呢？」陶岚答道。

「他剛才回來了一下，又匆匆忙忙地到學校去了。下午是王鎮長派人找
他去的。」

陶嵐愣了一下。她猜測着王鎮長找她哥哥的原因。

陶媽媽看着女兒說：「怎麼，你不舒服嗎？」

「不，我累了。」陶嵐說着走進自己的臥房，躺倒在床上。

陶媽媽擔憂地跟了進來，低聲地問陶嵐：「學校裏出了甚麼事了嗎？」

「沒有甚麼事兒。哥哥對你說甚麼了嗎？」

「他光是皺着眉頭，甚麼也沒說。」陶媽媽輕輕地嘆了一口氣。「甚麼事
情，你們都不肯對我說。」

「媽媽，你放心吧。沒甚麼了不起的事兒。」陶嵐說完有些不耐煩地翻
身朝裏。

第四十二景

西村。蕭澗秋和采蓮坐在小桌前玩弄着藥包裹帶來的小方紙塊。上面
有畫有字，如麥冬、半夏、桂枝之類。蕭澗秋就以此教采蓮認字。文嫂坐在
床邊，因看護孩子太勞累而打盹兒。阿寶已經服下了藥，正在昏睡着，頭上
敷着一條濕毛巾。

一時阿寶突然哭出聲來。文嫂欣喜地叫了幾聲阿寶，繼而對走過來的
蕭澗秋說：「你的法子真靈！阿寶都有兩天沒哭出聲兒來了。」又看着兒子
叫了一聲。

「小弟弟，你好些了吧？」蕭澗秋將那條毛巾取下，又重新濕了水再為
他敷上，以此來降低阿寶的體溫。

文嫂感激地看着。「蕭先生，你對我們的恩德太大了！救活了我們母子
三個人的性命，怎樣才能報答你呢？」

蕭澗秋強笑着，似有些難以為情。「不要說這樣的話了。只要都能夠好
好地活下去，就是大家的幸福了。」他將濕毛巾敷在阿寶頭上，看了一下窗
外的天色，又說：「時間不早了，我該走了。」

「他刚才回来了一下，又匆匆忙忙地到学校去了。下午是王镇长派人找他去的。」

陶岚愣了一下。她猜测着王镇长找她哥哥的原因。

陶妈妈看着女儿说：「怎么，你不舒服吗？」

「不，我累了。」陶岚说着走进自己的卧房，躺倒在床上。

陶妈妈担忧地跟了进来，低声地问陶岚：「学校里出了什么事了吗？」

「没有什么事儿。哥哥对你说什么了吗？」

「他光是皱着眉头，什么也没说。」陶妈妈轻轻地叹了一口气。「什么事情，你们都不肯对我说。」

「妈妈，你放心吧。没什么了不起的事儿。」陶岚说完有些不耐烦地翻身朝里。

第四十二景

西村。萧涧秋和采莲坐在小桌前玩弄着药包里带来的小方纸块。上面有画有字，如麦冬、半夏、桂枝之类。萧涧秋就以此教采莲认字。文嫂坐在床边，因看护孩子太劳累而打盹儿。阿宝已经服下了药，正在昏睡着，头上敷着一条湿毛巾。

一时阿宝突然哭出声来。文嫂欣喜地叫了几声阿宝，继而对走过来的萧涧秋说：「你的法子真灵！阿宝都有两天没哭出声儿来了。」又看着儿子叫了一声。

「小弟弟，你好些了吧？」萧涧秋将那条毛巾取下，又重新湿了水再为他敷上，以此来降低阿宝的体温。

文嫂感激地看着。「萧先生，你对我们的恩德太大了！救活了我们母子三个人的性命，怎样才能报答你呢？」

萧涧秋强笑着，似有些难以为情。「不要说这样的话了。只要都能够好好地活下去，就是大家的幸福了。」他将湿毛巾敷在阿宝头上，看了一下窗外的天色，又说：「时间不早了，我该走了。」

15 「不，就在這裏吃了晚飯走吧！沒有甚麼菜，我就給你燒兩個雞蛋。」文嫂説着就要走向灶台。

蕭澗秋連忙攔阻道：「不用了，天黑了，路就不好走了。」

采蓮抱住蕭澗秋的腿説：「蕭伯伯，你別走了，就在我們家住吧！」

蕭澗秋發窘地喃喃地説：「采蓮，蕭伯伯明天再來看你，啊。」

20 采蓮仍舊不懂事。「我不讓你走！我不讓你走！」

文嫂臉色微紅地低下頭。又對采蓮説：「采蓮，蕭伯伯還有事情。聽媽媽的話，啊。」

采蓮仍舊鬧着，「我不嘛，我不嘛！」並且緊緊抱着蕭澗秋的腿不放，弄得他僵窘非常。

25 恰巧，阿榮這時推門進來解救了他。「蕭先生，陶校長到處找你。」

蕭澗秋由僵窘轉為詫異。「甚麼事啊？」

「不知道，請你馬上到他家裏去一趟。」

蕭澗秋説了聲「好！」就向門外走去，又回頭對文嫂囑咐道：「毛巾要時常給他換一換。可千萬不要讓他受風，啊。」他隨着阿榮走出門去。

第四十三景

陶嵐的房間，陶嵐生氣地坐着。

陶慕侃站在一旁囁嚅地説：「我不過是提醒你注意。我不是個太守舊的人。可是你們的行動太文明了一點兒，學校的同事都看不慣。」

陶嵐卻仍執拗不改。「我偏要和澗秋好。別人，他管得着嗎？」

5 陶慕侃緩和地勸道：「我不是不要你和澗秋好，可是你應該尊重輿論，人言可畏，何況已經傳到鎮長的耳朵裏去了！」

陶嵐激動地站起來説：「我才不管他甚麼鎮長的！笑罵由人笑罵，我行我素！」她説完將椅子上的衣物扔下。

「你也太任性了！」陶慕侃走了出去。

10 陶嵐也不理會，就將房門用力地一關。

15　　　「不，就在这里吃了晚饭走吧！没有什么菜，我就给你烧两个鸡蛋。」文嫂说着就要走向灶台。

　　　萧涧秋连忙拦阻道：「不用了，天黑了，路就不好走了。」

　　　采莲抱住萧涧秋的腿说：「萧伯伯，你别走了，就在我们家住吧！」

　　　萧涧秋发窘地喃喃地说：「采莲，萧伯伯明天再来看你，啊。」

20　　　采莲仍旧不懂事。「我不让你走！我不让你走！」

　　　文嫂脸色微红地低下头。又对采莲说：「采莲，萧伯伯还有事情。听妈妈的话，啊。」

　　　采莲仍旧闹着，「我不嘛，我不嘛！」并且紧紧抱着萧涧秋的腿不放，弄得他僵窘非常。

25　　　恰巧，阿荣这时推门进来解救了他。「萧先生，陶校长到处找你。」

　　　萧涧秋由僵窘转为诧异。「什么事啊？」

　　　「不知道，请你马上到他家里去一趟。」

　　　萧涧秋说了声「好！」就向门外走去，又回头对文嫂嘱咐道：「毛巾要时常给他换一换。可千万不要让他受风，啊。」他随着阿荣走出门去。

第四十三景

　　　陶岚的房间，陶岚生气地坐着。

　　　陶慕侃站在一旁嗫嚅地说：「我不过是提醒你注意。我不是个太守旧的人。可是你们的行动太文明了一点儿，学校的同事都看不惯。」

　　　陶岚却仍执拗不改。「我偏要和涧秋好。别人，他管得着吗？」

5　　　陶慕侃缓和地劝道：「我不是不要你和涧秋好，可是你应该尊重舆论，人言可畏，何况已经传到镇长的耳朵里去了！」

　　　陶岚激动地站起来说：「我才不管他什么镇长的！笑骂由人笑骂，我行我素！」她说完将椅子上的衣物扔下。

　　　「你也太任性了！」陶慕侃走了出去。

10　　　陶岚也不理会，就将房门用力地一关。

第四十四景

廳堂。陶慕侃無可奈何地呆立着。看見蕭澗秋走了進來，就竭力掩飾着內心的不快，迎上去說：「澗秋，你來了！還沒吃晚飯吧？我讓吳媽給你弄來。」

蕭澗秋攔阻道：「不，不用了。你還是先說事情吧，不然我也吃不下。」

5 「好。欸。。。其實，也沒有甚麼了不起的事情。欸，就是。。。」

蕭澗秋非常敏感地接着：「流言蜚語給你增添了麻煩，是不是？」

「不，不，不，我倒是為你受了無辜的誹謗而感到抱歉。」

陶慕侃的話說得非常真誠。蕭澗秋為老朋友的同情心所感動，他低下頭沈思着。

10 陶慕侃一時也說不出話來。他看着坐在桌旁的蕭澗秋，沈吟了一下，很困難地說：「澗秋，我看這幾天你消瘦了許多。欸，我想。。。你是不是。。。到女佛山去休養一個時期，等過了春寒再回來。」

蕭澗秋抬起頭來看了他一下，然後慢慢地答道：「我前幾天就想向你辭職，離開這個地方。因為。。。」

15 蕭澗秋的話未說完，陶慕侃連忙解釋：「你千萬不要誤會，我跟你是訂了三年的約。」

蕭澗秋突然揚起頭來，態度非常果決。「可是我後來改變了主意，我決定忍受下去。就是你趕我走，我也不走了。這樣不清不白地走了，不更要惹人笑罵嗎？」

20 「這就好，這就好。」陶慕侃一面連連點頭，一面卻又為難地想着甚麼。

第四十五景

蕭澗秋走向初一的教室。當快走到時，他放慢了腳步，感覺到自己的心在跳着。他低着頭走進了教室，沒有聽到一點聲音。他抬頭一看，教室內空無一人。他周身的血向上湧，幾乎要昏倒。他竭力地鎮定自己，下意識地走向講台，呆呆地靠着講桌。

第四十四景

厅堂。陶慕侃无可奈何地呆立着。看见萧涧秋走了进来，就竭力掩饰着内心的不快，迎上去说：「涧秋，你来了！还没吃晚饭吧？我让吴妈给你弄来。」

萧涧秋拦阻道：「不，不用了。你还是先说事情吧，不然我也吃不下。」

「好。欸。。。其实，也没有什么了不起的事情。欸，就是。。。」

萧涧秋非常敏感地接着：「流言蜚语给你增添了麻烦，是不是？」

「不，不，不，我倒是为你受了无辜的诽谤而感到抱歉。」

陶慕侃的话说得非常真诚。萧涧秋为老朋友的同情心所感动，他低下头沉思着。

陶慕侃一时也说不出话来。他看着坐在桌旁的萧涧秋，沉吟了一下，很困难地说：「涧秋，我看这几天你消瘦了许多。欸，我想。。。你是不是。。。到女佛山去休养一个时期，等过了春寒再回来。」

萧涧秋抬起头来看了他一下，然后慢慢地答道：「我前几天就想向你辞职，离开这个地方。因为。。。」

萧涧秋的话未说完，陶慕侃连忙解释：「你千万不要误会，我跟你是订了三年的约。」

萧涧秋突然扬起头来，态度非常果决。「可是我后来改变了主意，我决定忍受下去。就是你赶我走，我也不走了。这样不清不白地走了，不更要惹人笑骂吗？」

「这就好，这就好。」陶慕侃一面连连点头，一面却又为难地想着什么。

第四十五景

萧涧秋走向初一的教室。当快走到时，他放慢了脚步，感觉到自己的心在跳着。他低着头走进了教室，没有听到一点声音。他抬头一看，教室内空无一人。他周身的血向上涌，几乎要昏倒。他竭力地镇定自己，下意识地走向讲台，呆呆地靠着讲桌。

5　　　王福生從遠處走來。當他看見老師已經站在講台上，他頓了一下，低着頭走進教室。他向老師鞠了一躬，羞愧地說：「蕭老師，我又遲到了。」

　　蕭澗秋激動得幾乎流出淚來。「不，今天你是第一個。」

　　王福生這才發現教室內是空空的，他以疑問的目光看着蕭先生。

　　蕭澗秋勉強地微笑着，「我來給你一個人上課。去坐吧。」

10　　陶嵐領着十幾個學生回來了。她擁着他們，叫他們快走。

　　學生一個一個從側門進去，又悄悄坐到自己的位置上。陶嵐從窗外看到了蕭澗秋站在講台上，臉上浮現出寬慰的笑容。

　　蕭澗秋發現了窗外的陶嵐，感激地看了她一眼。他在黑板上寫了《苛政猛於虎》，就開始講課。

15　　「同學們，今天我們講第二十三課，《苛政猛於虎》。。。。」

第四十六景

校園裏。蕭澗秋講課的聲音從教室內傳出來。

　　「。。。有一次，孔子帶着他的幾個學生經過泰山的邊上，看見有一位婦人跪在一個墳墓面前，非常悲哀地哭着。孔子就問這位婦人說：『你為甚麼一個人躲在這兒痛哭呢？』這位婦人就回答說：『過去啊，我丈夫的父親

5　在這兒被猛虎吃掉。後來呢，我丈夫也被猛虎吃掉。我的兒子又被猛虎。。。』」

　　陶校長回來了。他遠遠地聽到初一班上正在上課，就奇怪地向這邊走來看一眼。教室裏的情況使他又驚又喜。

　　他悄悄地叫了妹妹一聲說：「是你找來的？」

10　　陶嵐迎上來問：「怎麼，交涉得怎麼樣？」

　　「毫無結果。他們說，這是家長們抗議的表示。」

　　「胡說！」陶嵐氣憤地說。「剛才我到同學們家裏去了，有的家長不知道接到甚麼人的通知，說老師病了，放假一天！」

5　　　王福生从远处走来。当他看见老师已经站在讲台上，他顿了一下，低着头走进教室。他向老师鞠了一躬，羞愧地说：「萧老师，我又迟到了。」

　　　萧涧秋激动得几乎流出泪来。「不，今天你是第一个。」

　　　王福生这才发现教室内是空空的，他以疑问的目光看着萧先生。

　　　萧涧秋勉强地微笑着，「我来给你一个人上课。去坐吧。」

10　　　陶岚领着十几个学生回来了。她拥着他们，叫他们快走。

　　　学生一个一个从侧门进去，又悄悄坐到自己的位置上。陶岚从窗外看到了萧涧秋站在讲台上，脸上浮现出宽慰的笑容。

　　　萧涧秋发现了窗外的陶岚，感激地看了她一眼。他在黑板上写了《苛政猛于虎》，就开始讲课。

15　　　「同学们，今天我们讲第二十三课，《苛政猛于虎》。。。。」

第四十六景

　　　校园里。萧涧秋讲课的声音从教室内传出来。

　　　「。。。有一次，孔子带着他的几个学生经过泰山的边上，看见有一位妇人跪在一个坟墓面前，非常悲哀地哭着。孔子就问这位妇人说：『你为什么一个人躲在这儿痛哭呢？』这位妇人就回答说：『过去啊，我丈夫的父亲
5　在这儿被猛虎吃掉。后来呢，我丈夫也被猛虎吃掉。我的儿子又被猛虎。。。。』」

　　　陶校长回来了。他远远地听到初一班上正在上课，就奇怪地向这边走来看一眼。教室里的情况使他又惊又喜。

　　　他悄悄地叫了妹妹一声说：「是你找来的？」

10　　　陶岚迎上来问：「怎么，交涉得怎么样？」

　　　「毫无结果。他们说，这是家长们抗议的表示。」

　　　「胡说！」陶岚气愤地说。「刚才我到同学们家里去了，有的家长不知道接到什么人的通知，说老师病了，放假一天！」

「哦？這很明白嘛！背後有人跟我們作對，手段很卑鄙。」

15　　陶嵐驕傲地笑了起來。「哼，可是今天我們得勝了！」

陶校長像有所醒悟地說：「唔，為了神聖的教育，為了我跟澗秋的友誼，我不能再顧及其他。」

「你——你這才是我的好哥哥呢！」陶嵐從來沒有對哥哥這樣親密過。

兄妹二人邊說邊向教務處走去。

第四十七景

1　　蕭澗秋邊走邊唱地帶着學生上樓，發作文給學生。

第四十八景

蕭澗秋從橋頭走下來，遇見了對面走來的陶嵐，就問道：「嵐，你甚麼時候來的？」

陶嵐看了蕭澗秋一眼，慢慢地在亭邊坐下來。

蕭澗秋又接着問：「出了甚麼事了？」

5　　陶嵐沈重地說：「孩子死了。」

「死了？」他驚駭地看着她。

「兩個鐘頭以前，我到她家裏，已經是孩子喘着最後一口氣的時候。孩子的喉嚨被堵塞住，眼睛不會看他母親。我緊緊地拉住了孩子的手，眼看着。。。」

第四十九景

西村。文嫂在屋內整理東西，采蓮呆立在一旁。她將阿寶穿過的破小衣服丟在地下，又將采蓮的衣服放在桌上。她沒有哭，眼內是枯乾的，連一些隱閃的滋潤的淚光也沒有。她毫無精神地整理着。

「哦？这很明白嘛！背后有人跟我们作对，手段很卑鄙。」

15　　陶岚骄傲地笑了起来。「哼，可是今天我们得胜了！」

陶校长像有所醒悟地说：「唔，为了神圣的教育，为了我跟涧秋的友谊，我不能再顾及其他。」

「你——你这才是我的好哥哥呢！」陶岚从来没有对哥哥这样亲密过。

兄妹二人边说边向教务处走去。

第四十七景

1　　萧涧秋边走边唱地带着学生上楼，发作文给学生。

第四十八景

萧涧秋从桥头走下来，遇见了对面走来的陶岚，就问道：「岚，你什么时候来的？」

陶岚看了萧涧秋一眼，慢慢地在亭边坐下来。

萧涧秋又接着问：「出了什么事了？」

5　　陶岚沉重地说：「孩子死了。」

「死了？」他惊骇地看着她。

「两个钟头以前，我到她家里，已经是孩子喘着最后一口气的时候。孩子的喉咙被堵塞住，眼睛不会看他母亲。我紧紧地拉住了孩子的手，眼看着。。。」

第四十九景

西村。文嫂在屋内整理东西，采莲呆立在一旁。她将阿宝穿过的破小衣服丢在地下，又将采莲的衣服放在桌上。她没有哭，眼内是枯干的，连一些隐闪的滋润的泪光也没有。她毫无精神地整理着。

蕭澗秋悄悄地走了進來。

文嫂仰頭一望，隨即又低下頭去，沒有說話。繼而伏在桌子上哭泣起來。

蕭澗秋遠遠地站着。後來走到桌邊，似想了許久才想起一句話來。「過去的事情。。。都已經過去了。你不要再去想了。」

文嫂好像沒有聽見，也不說話，仍舊抽泣着。

蕭澗秋又低聲地說：「文嫂，你要多為將來想一想。」

於是文嫂抬起頭來緩緩地答道：「先生，我。。。正在想。。。」

他以極和婉的聲音向她發問：「你是怎麼想的呢？」

文嫂異常平靜。「我應該這樣。我的路。。。走完了。」

「你怎麼這麼想呢？也許我的話說得重了一點兒。這樣小的一個孩子，已經死了，也就算了。你作母親的，就是陪了他去又有甚麼用處呢？文嫂，我們活着，就要和運命苦鬥下去，決不能退讓！你千萬要聽我的話才好啊！」他不覺提高了聲音。

文嫂聽了止不住湧出淚來，半哭着：「先生，我感謝你的恩德。我以前總希望等阿寶長大了來報答你。現在孩子去了，我的法子也完了！」她擦着淚。

「你不要再說這樣的話了，你應該多為采蓮想一想啊！」

「采蓮。。。」她向女孩子看了一看。「你能收她做個丫頭嗎？」

蕭澗秋抱住采蓮，有些發怒。「你怎麼能說出這樣的話來呢？阿寶死了，可是為了采蓮，你也應該好好地活下去呀！」

「可是，活下去，你叫我怎麼。。。？」

蕭澗秋在屋內走了一個圈，忍不住地說：「文嫂，你還年輕，你可以。。。改嫁。」

文嫂猛然抬起頭來，她似乎從沒有聽到過婦人可以有這樣的念頭。

「文嫂，聽我的話吧。日子總會好起來的。只要能。。。找個相當的人。。。」他說不下去了。看到文嫂驚恐的反應，使他感到自己在貞節的婦人面前說錯了話。他將臉轉向一邊，不敢再看她。

文嫂癡癡地想着甚麼，慢慢地低下頭來。

萧涧秋悄悄地走了进来。

文嫂仰头一望，随即又低下头去，没有说话。继而伏在桌子上哭泣起来。

萧涧秋远远地站着。后来走到桌边，似想了许久才想起一句话来。「过去的事情。。。都已经过去了。你不要再去想了。」

文嫂好像没有听见，也不说话，仍旧抽泣着。

萧涧秋又低声地说：「文嫂，你要多为将来想一想。」

于是文嫂抬起头来缓缓地答道：「先生，我。。。正在想。。。」

他以极和婉的声音向她发问：「你是怎么想的呢？」

文嫂异常平静。「我应该这样。我的路。。。走完了。」

「你怎么这么想呢？也许我的话说得重了一点儿。这样小的一个孩子，已经死了，也就算了。你作母亲的，就是陪了他去又有什么用处呢？文嫂，我们活着，就要和运命苦斗下去，决不能退让！你千万要听我的话才好啊！」他不觉提高了声音。

文嫂听了止不住涌出泪来，半哭着：「先生，我感谢你的恩德。我以前总希望等阿宝长大了来报答你。现在孩子去了，我的法子也完了！」她擦着泪。

「你不要再说这样的话了，你应该多为采莲想一想啊！」

「采莲。。。」她向女孩子看了一看。「你能收她做个丫头吗？」

萧涧秋抱住采莲，有些发怒。「你怎么能说出这样的话来呢？阿宝死了，可是为了采莲，你也应该好好地活下去呀！」

「可是，活下去，你叫我怎么。。。？」

萧涧秋在屋内走了一个圈，忍不住地说：「文嫂，你还年轻，你可以。。。改嫁。」

文嫂猛然抬起头来，她似乎从没有听到过妇人可以有这样的念头。

「文嫂，听我的话吧。日子总会好起来的。只要能。。。找个相当的人。。。」他说不下去了。看到文嫂惊恐的反应，使他感到自己在贞节的妇人面前说错了话。他将脸转向一边，不敢再看她。

文嫂痴痴地想着什么，慢慢地低下头来。

第五十景

太陽已經西墜。蕭澗秋拖着自己長長的影子獨自在河邊路上走着。文嫂憂愁哭泣的面容不時地映在他的眼前。

「。。。改嫁?。。。我感謝你的恩德。。。。采蓮。。。你能收她做個丫頭嗎?。。。」

5   蕭澗秋一路胡思亂想着,不知不覺地回到了校中。

第五十一景

客房内。書桌上放着一盞玻璃罩的煤油燈,蕭澗秋在八行的信紙上只寫了一個頭:「親愛的嵐,」後面的兩行寫上又塗去了。濕潤的毛筆擱在一
3 旁,他再也寫不下去了。

第五十二景

校園裏。皎潔的月光透過樹上的枝葉,投下稀疏的斑影。蕭澗秋在池邊徘徊着,有如當年他在西湖邊上一樣的情景。

陶嵐輕輕地走進蕭澗秋的客房來,她在門口猶豫了一下就走到桌前看那張信紙。她凝視了一下,走至窗前向校園深處尋視着,喊着:「澗秋!我
5 就下來!」

陶嵐隨即跑向蕭澗秋,高興地問:「澗秋,你在給我寫信嗎?怎麼又不寫下去了呢?」

蕭澗秋低着頭慢慢地說:「我寫不下去。」

「這有甚麼?你心裏怎麼想的,就怎麼說好了。」陶嵐坐在池邊的石塊
10 上,說到後一句聲音特別小,頭也低了下來。「我已經在你面前了,能對我說嗎?」

第五十景

太阳已经西坠。萧涧秋拖着自己长长的影子独自在河边路上走着。文嫂忧愁哭泣的面容不时地映在他的眼前。

「。。。改嫁？。。。我感谢你的恩德。。。。采莲。。。你能收她做个丫头吗？。。。」

5　　萧涧秋一路胡思乱想着，不知不觉地回到了校中。

第五十一景

客房内。书桌上放着一盏玻璃罩的煤油灯，萧涧秋在八行的信纸上只写了一个头：「亲爱的岚，」后面的两行写上又涂去了。湿润的毛笔搁在一
3　旁，他再也写不下去了。

第五十二景

校园里。皎洁的月光透过树上的枝叶，投下稀疏的斑影。萧涧秋在池边徘徊着，有如当年他在西湖边上一样的情景。

陶岚轻轻地走进萧涧秋的客房来，她在门口犹豫了一下就走到桌前看那张信纸。她凝视了一下，走至窗前向校园深处寻视着，喊着：「涧秋！我
5　就下来！」

陶岚随即跑向萧涧秋，高兴地问：「涧秋，你在给我写信吗？怎么又不写下去了呢？」

萧涧秋低着头慢慢地说：「我写不下去。」

「这有什么？你心里怎么想的，就怎么说好了。」陶岚坐在池边的石块
10　上，说到后一句声音特别小，头也低了下来。「我已经在你面前了，能对我说吗？」

蕭澗秋没有回話。

「要是你覺得還是寫信方便的話，那你就寫吧。」她說完轉身要走。

「不！」蕭澗秋挽留着她。

15　「那你就說吧。」陶嵐瞪大眼看着他。

蕭澗秋又頓了一下，似為難地說：「我相信你是會同意，也會諒解的，因為你和我具有同樣的思想。」

陶嵐已經感覺到不是她所希望的了。她淡淡地說：「你說吧！」

「關於采蓮和她的母親，我們必須用根本的方法來救濟她們。」他頓息

20　了一下才接着說：「我決定娶她，讓她做我的妻子。」

陶嵐像遭到霹靂似地周身有些發抖。「怎麼，你真的是這麼想的嗎？」

「是的。她。。。她現在絕望得很。」蕭澗秋没有敢看她，只低聲地說：「我實在想不出比這更好的辦法來。嵐，原諒我吧！如果你同意的話，我準備明天就去對她說。」

25　「你愛她嗎？」陶嵐呆立着。

「唔。」蕭澗秋面對着陶嵐點頭。

「不！你這是同情，不是愛！」陶嵐說完就再也抑制不住地跑去了。

蕭澗秋追上幾步，叫着陶嵐，呆望着她跑去的身影。他心裏想着，「真是節外生枝，枝外又生節地永遠弄不清楚。」

第五十三景

蕭澗秋跨進自己的房門，意想不到地愣住了。

錢正興從屋角陰暗處的椅子上站起來，他笑容可掬地說：「對不起，蕭先生，打擾了。」

「你找我有甚麼事嗎？」蕭澗秋詫異地問。

5　「没有甚麼，想找你隨便聊聊。」錢正興不客氣地自己坐了下來。

蕭澗秋坐到錢正興對面看着他。「錢先生，你有甚麼消息要告訴我嗎？」

「消息？」錢正興抬起頭來反問。

萧涧秋没有回话。

「要是你觉得还是写信方便的话，那你就写吧。」她说完转身要走。

「不！」萧涧秋挽留着她。

15　「那你就说吧。」陶岚睁大眼看着他。

萧涧秋又顿了一下，似为难地说：「我相信你是会同意，也会谅解的，因为你和我具有同样的思想。」

陶岚已经感觉到不是她所希望的了。她淡淡地说：「你说吧！」

「关于采莲和她的母亲，我们必须用根本的方法来救济她们。」他顿息

20　了一下才接着说：「我决定娶她，让她做我的妻子。」

陶岚像遭到霹雳似地周身有些发抖。「怎么，你真的是这么想的吗？」

「是的。她。。。她现在绝望得很。」萧涧秋没有敢看她，只低声地说：「我实在想不出比这更好的办法来。岚，原谅我吧！如果你同意的话，我准备明天就去对她说。」

25　「你爱她吗？」陶岚呆立着。

「唔。」萧涧秋面对着陶岚点头。

「不！你这是同情，不是爱！」陶岚说完就再也抑制不住地跑去了。

萧涧秋追上几步，叫着陶岚，呆望着她跑去的身影。他心里想着，「真是节外生枝，枝外又生节地永远弄不清楚。」

第五十三景

萧涧秋跨进自己的房门，意想不到地愣住了。

钱正兴从屋角阴暗处的椅子上站起来，他笑容可掬地说：「对不起，萧先生，打扰了。」

「你找我有什么事吗？」萧涧秋诧异地问。

5　「没有什么，想找你随便聊聊。」钱正兴不客气地自己坐了下来。

萧涧秋坐到钱正兴对面看着他。「钱先生，你有什么消息要告诉我吗？」

「消息？」钱正兴抬起头来反问。

「比如說，外界的輿論啊。」

10　錢正興笑了笑說：「有甚麼輿論呢？我們鎮上的人對蕭先生，那是很敬重的。雖然蕭先生到我們這裏還不到兩個月，可是蕭先生的大名連一般孩子們都知道了。」

蕭澗秋抑制住怒火，故意附和着：「哼，照你這樣說，我在這兒生活得很愉快了。」

15　「假如蕭先生以為在這兒生活得很愉快，我倒希望蕭先生能夠永遠住下去。」

「住下去，能嗎？」

「當然可以。」錢正興假笑地道。「所以我想問一問，蕭先生有心要組織一個家庭嗎？」

20　「你這是甚麼意思？」

「沒甚麼，隨便問問。」

蕭澗秋冷笑了一聲。「那，你就不必問了。」

「哼，你何必瞞我呢？」錢正興嘴邊浮起冷笑。「外界都說你愛上了西村的文嫂。」

25　「我另有所愛！」蕭澗秋帶着幾分憤怒地說。

錢正興卻又故作不知地問：「那，是誰呢？」

「陶慕侃的妹妹！陶嵐！陶嵐！」

錢正興的臉上顯出一副失望的表情。他低下頭，凝視着自己的腳尖。

蕭澗秋似乎出了點兒氣，得勝似地看着他，向外走去。

30　錢正興急忙站起來，阻止道：「你不要走！」自己又走到蕭澗秋的面前懇求：「蕭先生，你不是常常說要同情可憐的人嗎？你同情我一點兒好不好？你把陶嵐讓給我吧。」

蕭澗秋沒好氣地說：「真無聊！」就走出門外。

錢正興追出去哀求：「蕭先生！蕭先生！蕭先生，我請求你！蕭先生，
35　我一生的痛苦與幸福，都關係在你的身上。你只要同意了，我一定要報答你。你假如要和文嫂結婚，我願意。。。我願意。。。幫助你一千塊錢。」

「比如说，外界的舆论啊。」

钱正兴笑了笑说：「有什么舆论呢？我们镇上的人对萧先生，那是很敬重的。虽然萧先生到我们这里还不到两个月，可是萧先生的大名连一般孩子们都知道了。」

萧涧秋抑制住怒火，故意附和着：「哼，照你这样说，我在这儿生活得很愉快了。」

「假如萧先生以为在这儿生活得很愉快，我倒希望萧先生能够永远住下去。」

「住下去，能吗？」

「当然可以。」钱正兴假笑地道。「所以我想问一问，萧先生有心要组织一个家庭吗？」

「你这是什么意思？」

「没什么，随便问问。」

萧涧秋冷笑了一声。「那，你就不必问了。」

「哼，你何必瞒我呢？」钱正兴嘴边浮起冷笑。「外界都说你爱上了西村的文嫂。」

「我另有所爱！」萧涧秋带着几分愤怒地说。

钱正兴却又故作不知地问：「那，是谁呢？」

「陶慕侃的妹妹！陶岚！陶岚！」

钱正兴的脸上显出一副失望的表情。他低下头，凝视着自己的脚尖。

萧涧秋似乎出了点儿气，得胜似地看着他，向外走去。

钱正兴急忙站起来，阻止道：「你不要走！」自己又走到萧涧秋的面前恳求：「萧先生，你不是常常说要同情可怜的人吗？你同情我一点儿好不好？你把陶岚让给我吧。」

萧涧秋没好气地说：「真无聊！」就走出门外。

钱正兴追出去哀求：「萧先生！萧先生！萧先生，我请求你！萧先生，我一生的痛苦与幸福，都关系在你的身上。你只要同意了，我一定要报答你。你假如要和文嫂结婚，我愿意。。。我愿意。。。帮助你一千块钱。」

蕭澗秋受到侮辱似地睜大了眼睛。「不要說了！你給我走開！」說完就大步離去。

39　錢正興慢慢地走了出去。

第五十四景

校園裏。王福生對采蓮說：「你自己去吧，啊。」

兩人又互相說了「再見」。

蕭澗秋從自己的屋裏出來。在散遊着許多學生中看到采蓮就叫道：「采蓮！」

5　「蕭伯伯！」采蓮叫了一聲就跑到他身邊。

蕭澗秋稍稍奇怪地問：「你怎麼來了？」

「媽媽讓我來上學，還給我換了新衣裳。」采蓮高興地指着身上的半新上衣。

「媽媽還哭嗎？」

10　「不哭了。」

上課的預備鈴響了。

蕭澗秋與采蓮分手道：「好，那你先上課去吧。回頭，我中午跟你一塊兒去看媽媽去，啊。」

采蓮答應着。

第五十五景

教務處。方謀正在跟幾位教師高聲談論着。

「如果革命軍按期北伐的話，不出一年哪，江浙一帶必有大戰。」

一位教師接着：「依我看，江西是首當其衝。孫傳芳的兵是不堪一擊的。」

5　「如果江西守不住的話，那江浙一帶也就難保了。咱們芙蓉鎮。。。」

另一位教師看見蕭澗秋從門外走進，叫了一聲「蕭先生！」

萧涧秋受到侮辱似地睁大了眼睛。「不要说了！你给我走开！」说完就大步离去。

39　　钱正兴慢慢地走了出去。

第五十四景

校园里。王福生对采莲说：「你自己去吧，啊。」

两人又互相说了「再见」。

萧涧秋从自己的屋里出来。在散游着许多学生中看到采莲就叫道：「采莲！」

5　　「萧伯伯！」采莲叫了一声就跑到他身边。

萧涧秋稍稍奇怪地问：「你怎么来了？」

「妈妈让我来上学，还给我换了新衣裳。」采莲高兴地指着身上的半新上衣。

「妈妈还哭吗？」

10　　「不哭了。」

上课的预备铃响了。

萧涧秋与采莲分手道：「好，那你先上课去吧。回头，我中午跟你一块儿去看妈妈去，啊。」

采莲答应着。

第五十五景

教务处。方谋正在跟几位教师高声谈论着。

「如果革命军按期北伐的话，不出一年哪，江浙一带必有大战。」

一位教师接着：「依我看，江西是首当其冲。孙传芳的兵是不堪一击的。」

5　　「如果江西守不住的话，那江浙一带也就难保了。咱们芙蓉镇。。。」

另一位教师看见萧涧秋从门外走进，叫了一声「萧先生！」

　　　方謀對大家說：「欸，你看，正好蕭先生來了。蕭先生，我看，還是請你發表高論吧。」

　　　「對。」大家應和着。

10　　「蕭先生，你看，廣州政府軍準備興師北伐了。」

　　　「哦。」蕭澗秋手中拿着報紙答應着，卻沒有加入談話。他彷彿一滴油不能融於水一般。

　　　「唐先生，你說孫傳芳會不會死守江浙？」

　　　「他想守也守不住。」

15　　「這幫軍閥太腐敗，也太不得人心了。」

　　　沒一會兒，陶校長也出來了。他對蕭澗秋說：「澗秋，來。我問你一樁事情。」

　　　大家立刻靜了下來。

　　　陶校長繼續說：「昨天晚上妹妹哭了一夜，我問母親為甚麼。母親說，

20　妹妹說從此不嫁人了，因為蕭先生要結婚。這豈不是怪事嗎？你要結婚，而妹妹又說從此不嫁人了，這究竟是怎麼回事？」

　　　方謀等人的目光一齊投向蕭澗秋。

　　　他有些尷尬地回答：「我自己也不知道。」

　　　方謀立刻向陶校長問：「那麼，蕭先生預備同誰結婚呢？」

25　　「你問他吧。」陶校長回答。

　　　於是方謀隨即轉向蕭澗秋。

　　　他就說：「請你去問將來吧。」

　　　教師們一笑。

　　　方謀說：「回答得真妙啊！」

30　　陶校長接着感嘆道：「我這個作哥哥的給弄得個莫名其妙。」

　　　「不用奇怪了，未來自然會告訴你們的。至於現在，我自己也不十分清楚。」蕭澗秋臉上露出不悅的神色，各人一時默然。

　　　陶校長又緩和地勸道：「老朋友，我看你最近態度，有些個異樣。這樣作事要失敗的。這是我妹妹的脾氣，你為甚麼要學她呢？」

35　　「也許要失敗。也許正是因為要失敗，所以我才這樣作的。」

　　方谋对大家说：「欸，你看，正好萧先生来了。萧先生，我看，还是请你发表高论吧。」

　　「对。」大家应和着。

10　　「萧先生，你看，广州政府军准备兴师北伐了。」

　　「哦。」萧涧秋手中拿着报纸答应着，却没有加入谈话。他仿佛一滴油不能融于水一般。

　　「唐先生，你说孙传芳会不会死守江浙？」

　　「他想守也守不住。」

15　　「这帮军阀太腐败，也太不得人心了。」

　　没一会儿，陶校长也出来了。他对萧涧秋说：「涧秋，来。我问你一桩事情。」

　　大家立刻静了下来。

　　陶校长继续说：「昨天晚上妹妹哭了一夜，我问母亲为什么。母亲说，20　妹妹说从此不嫁人了，因为萧先生要结婚。这岂不是怪事吗？你要结婚，而妹妹又说从此不嫁人了，这究竟是怎么回事？」

　　方谋等人的目光一齐投向萧涧秋。

　　他有些尴尬地回答：「我自己也不知道。」

　　方谋立刻向陶校长问：「那么，萧先生预备同谁结婚呢？」

25　　「你问他吧。」陶校长回答。

　　于是方谋随即转向萧涧秋。

　　他就说：「请你去问将来吧。」

　　教师们一笑。

　　方谋说：「回答得真妙啊！」

30　　陶校长接着感叹道：「我这个作哥哥的给弄得个莫名其妙。」

　　「不用奇怪了，未来自然会告诉你们的。至于现在，我自己也不十分清楚。」萧涧秋脸上露出不悦的神色，各人一时默然。

　　陶校长又缓和地劝道：「老朋友，我看你最近态度，有些个异样。这样作事要失败的。这是我妹妹的脾气，你为什么要学她呢？」

35　　「也许要失败。也许正是因为要失败，所以我才这样作的。」

「全不懂，全不懂！」陶校長搖着頭。

各人心裏都聚集着疑團，推究着芙蓉鎮裏的奇聞。

正在這個時候，阿榮領着西村的陳奶奶來找蕭澗秋。

「蕭先生，有人找你。」

40　蕭澗秋立刻緊張地迎上去問：「甚麼事啊？」

那位老婦人的嘴唇只是打顫，好不容易才説出話來。「蕭先生，快！采蓮的媽媽。。。吊死了！」老婦人向四周看了看。「蕭先生，采蓮在哪兒？快找她，好哭她媽媽幾聲。」

蕭澗秋這時才清醒過來。「哦，不用了吧！好，我跟你去一趟！」

45　老婦人應着。

蕭澗秋又轉向陶校長説：「慕侃，放學的時候請你把采蓮帶到你家裏去吧。」

陶校長答應着：「好，你快去吧。」

「好。」蕭澗秋等不及跟老婦人一道走，逕直地向文嫂家跑去。

50　在文嫂家中，蕭澗秋在她床前站立了片刻，緩緩地放下了蚊帳。

第五十六景

黃昏，陶家廳堂。陶嵐的琴聲飄蕩到庭院中。采蓮在一旁呆呆地看着，手裏拿着紅橘。

蕭澗秋拖着疲乏的身子跨進大門，輕步走進了廂房。他惟恐驚動她們似地輕輕地在門邊的一張凳子上坐下。琴聲替他吐出了悲哀與惆悵。

5　不知甚麼時候她們發現了他。陶嵐的琴聲停止了。

采蓮撲到蕭澗秋的面前説：「蕭伯伯！我要回家，我要媽媽！」

蕭澗秋抱住孩子，撫摸着她的頭，慢慢地説：「你媽媽。。。出遠門去了。以後，你就跟着陶先生吧！我們采蓮。。。是最聽話的孩子。」

陶嵐強忍着自己的眼淚。

「全不懂，全不懂！」陶校长摇着头。

各人心里都聚集着疑团，推究着芙蓉镇里的奇闻。

正在这个时候，阿荣领着西村的陈奶奶来找萧涧秋。

「萧先生，有人找你。」

40　萧涧秋立刻紧张地迎上去问：「什么事啊？」

那位老妇人的嘴唇只是打颤，好不容易才说出话来。「萧先生，快！采莲的妈妈。。。吊死了！」老妇人向四周看了看。「萧先生，采莲在哪儿？快找她，好哭她妈妈几声。」

萧涧秋这时才清醒过来。「哦，不用了吧！好，我跟你去一趟！」

45　老妇人应着。

萧涧秋又转向陶校长说：「慕侃，放学的时候请你把采莲带到你家里去吧。」

陶校长答应着：「好，你快去吧。」

「好。」萧涧秋等不及跟老妇人一道走，径直地向文嫂家跑去。

50　在文嫂家中，萧涧秋在她床前站立了片刻，缓缓地放下了蚊帐。

第五十六景

黄昏，陶家厅堂。陶岚的琴声飘荡到庭院中。采莲在一旁呆呆地看着，手里拿着红橘。

萧涧秋拖着疲乏的身子跨进大门，轻步走进了厢房。他惟恐惊动她们似地轻轻地在门边的一张凳子上坐下。琴声替他吐出了悲哀与惆怅。

5　不知什么时候她们发现了他。陶岚的琴声停止了。

采莲扑到萧涧秋的面前说：「萧伯伯！我要回家，我要妈妈！」

萧涧秋抱住孩子，抚摸着她的头，慢慢地说：「你妈妈。。。出远门去了。以后，你就跟着陶先生吧！我们采莲。。。是最听话的孩子。」

陶岚强忍着自己的眼泪。

第五十七景

陶家廳堂。晚餐已經佈置好。

陶慕侃提着酒壺要為蕭澗秋斟酒，蕭澗秋卻以手蓋杯。「我不喝。」

「你明明是有酒量的，今天為甚麼又不喝了呢？」陶慕侃仍欲斟酒，蕭澗秋微笑地搖搖頭藏起酒杯。

陶嵐卻在一旁勸道：「你喝吧！喝醉了也好，也許你會舒暢一些。」她從哥哥手裏拿過酒壺為他斟滿了一杯，也為自己斟上一些。「來。」兩人舉杯對飲。

從門外走進兩位教師。一位年紀比較大，另一位就是方謀。他不客氣地說：「我們想加入你們喝一杯酒啊。」

「好，好。來吧，來吧！歡迎，歡迎！」陶慕侃急忙答道。

陶嵐將酒杯放下，進內房去了。兩位客人不客氣地坐了下來。陶慕侃為他們一一斟酒。

「不，不，不。我已經吃過了。」那位老教師向陶慕侃謙讓着。

「哪裏，哪裏，喝杯酒嘛！來，來。請坐，請坐。」陶慕侃招呼着客人。

「謝謝，謝謝。」

「聽說蕭先生酒量不小啊。今天咱們得好好地較量較量，啊。」方謀說。

「我哪能是你們的對手啊？」

「方先生。」陶慕侃遞上了碗和筷子。

「唔，好，好，好。」

「隨便用一點。」陶慕侃繼續招呼着。

那位老教師說：「剛才我們從街上來，家家都在談論西村的事情。誰都說文嫂應當作節婦論。」

陶慕侃同意道：「唔，她是個正派人。社會逼得她活不下去！」

方謀也附和着：「是啊！采蓮母親的突然自殺啊，竟使每個人聽了以後都很敬佩。可真是妻殉其夫，母殉其子啊！」又轉向蕭澗秋繼續說：「欸，蕭先生，我跟你說句心裏話。以前哪，很多人誤會你，可是現在我知道，他們全都明白了。」

第五十七景

陶家厅堂。晚餐已经布置好。

陶慕侃提着酒壶要为萧涧秋斟酒，萧涧秋却以手盖杯。「我不喝。」

「你明明是有酒量的，今天为什么又不喝了呢？」陶慕侃仍欲斟酒，萧涧秋微笑地摇摇头藏起酒杯。

陶岚却在一旁劝道：「你喝吧！喝醉了也好，也许你会舒畅一些。」她从哥哥手里拿过酒壶为他斟满了一杯，也为自己斟上一些。「来。」两人举杯对饮。

从门外走进两位教师。一位年纪比较大，另一位就是方谋。他不客气地说：「我们想加入你们喝一杯酒啊。」

「好，好。来吧，来吧！欢迎，欢迎！」陶慕侃急忙答道。

陶岚将酒杯放下，进内房去了。两位客人不客气地坐了下来。陶慕侃为他们一一斟酒。

「不，不，不。我已经吃过了。」那位老教师向陶慕侃谦让着。

「哪里，哪里，喝杯酒嘛！来，来。请坐，请坐。」陶慕侃招呼着客人。

「谢谢，谢谢。」

「听说萧先生酒量不小啊。今天咱们得好好地较量较量，啊。」方谋说。

「我哪能是你们的对手啊？」

「方先生。」陶慕侃递上了碗和筷子。

「唔，好，好，好。」

「随便用一点。」陶慕侃继续招呼着。

那位老教师说：「刚才我们从街上来，家家都在谈论西村的事情。谁都说文嫂应当作节妇论。」

陶慕侃同意道：「唔，她是个正派人。社会逼得她活不下去！」

方谋也附和着：「是啊！采莲母亲的突然自杀啊，竟使每个人听了以后都很敬佩。可真是妻殉其夫，母殉其子啊！」又转向萧涧秋继续说：「欸，萧先生，我跟你说句心里话。以前哪，很多人误会你，可是现在我知道，他们全都明白了。」

蕭澗秋問：「那是為甚麼呢？」

30　「欸，這事情不是很清楚嗎？要是你們。。。要是你們。。。有甚麼的話，那她孩子死了，這不正是一個好機會嗎？那她為甚麼要自殺呢？由此可見，你和文嫂是完全清白的。」

蕭澗秋不快地哼了一聲。

方謀繼續下去：「欸，誰都知道啊，你是他們的恩人啊！來！蕭先生，

35　我要敬你一杯。現在我們鎮上無論是男女老幼都想見一見你啊！」

蕭澗秋自我謅諷地說：「那可以讓學校把我拿出去展覽，讓大家來參觀吧！」

陶慕侃打岔道：「方先生，不談這些。來，乾了這杯。」

方謀紅起臉，吃吃地解釋：「你不要誤會，我是完全敬佩你的話。像你

40　這樣煞費苦心地去救濟他們，實在是令人佩服。可是，這樣的結果是你蕭先生料想不到的。」

蕭澗秋再也抑制不住自己的激怒，他沈痛地說：「我沒有想到，我沒有救活他們，反而害死了他們！我更沒有想到，有人背後冷言冷語，現在卻居然為我來舉杯喝彩了！」他站起來向方謀道：「來！我謝謝你的好意！」他說

45　完就舉杯飲酒。

方謀膽怯地看着他。

「小人之心，小人之口！」蕭澗秋激怒地將酒杯放下，杯中的餘酒灑在桌上。

第五十八景

蕭澗秋躺在床上病着。

陶嵐輕輕地推門進來，關心地問道：「現在覺得怎麼樣？」

「我真像。。。做了一場惡夢！」蕭澗秋答道。

「過去的事情，就不要再想它了。」陶嵐勸慰着。

5　蕭澗秋緊緊握住她的手，停了一下，說：「嵐，我對不起你。」

「何必說這些呢？」陶嵐嬌羞地轉過頭去。

萧涧秋问：「那是为什么呢？」

「欸，这事情不是很清楚吗？要是你们。。。要是你们。。。有什么的话，那她孩子死了，这不正是一个好机会吗？那她为什么要自杀呢？由此可见，你和文嫂是完全清白的。」

萧涧秋不快地哼了一声。

方谋继续下去：「欸，谁都知道啊，你是他们的恩人啊！来！萧先生，我要敬你一杯。现在我们镇上无论是男女老幼都想见一见你啊！」

萧涧秋自我嘲讽地说：「那可以让学校把我拿出去展览，让大家来参观吧！」

陶慕侃打岔道：「方先生，不谈这些。来，干了这杯。」

方谋红起脸，吃吃地解释：「你不要误会，我是完全敬佩你的话。像你这样煞费苦心地去救济他们，实在是令人佩服。可是，这样的结果是你萧先生料想不到的。」

萧涧秋再也抑制不住自己的激怒，他沉痛地说：「我没有想到，我没有救活他们，反而害死了他们！我更没有想到，有人背后冷言冷语，现在却居然为我来举杯喝彩了！」他站起来向方谋道：「来！我谢谢你的好意！」他说完就举杯饮酒。

方谋胆怯地看着他。

「小人之心，小人之口！」萧涧秋激怒地将酒杯放下，杯中的余酒洒在桌上。

第五十八景

萧涧秋躺在床上病着。

陶岚轻轻地推门进来，关心地问道：「现在觉得怎么样？」

「我真像。。。做了一场恶梦！」萧涧秋答道。

「过去的事情，就不要再想它了。」陶岚劝慰着。

萧涧秋紧紧握住她的手，停了一下，说：「岚，我对不起你。」

「何必说这些呢？」陶岚娇羞地转过头去。

兩人沈默了一下。

陶嵐又問：「你在想甚麼？」

「沒甚麼。我有點兒不舒服。」

10　　陶嵐站起來說：「我去拿點兒藥來。」

蕭澗秋阻止道：「欸，不用了。那桌子上就有，在裏邊那個抽屜裏。」

王福生悄悄地走了進來，向老師鞠了一躬，叫道：「蕭老師。」又向陶嵐鞠了一躬，叫道：「陶老師。」

蕭澗秋奇怪地問：「王福生，你怎麼不去上課去啊？」

15　　「聽說老師病了，我來看看您。」

蕭澗秋拉住他的手，說：「不要緊的。明天早上我就可以跟你們上課去了。」

王福生難過地低下頭來。

「你怎麼了？」

20　　「我以後不能再上學了。」

「為甚麼？是不是因為交不起學費啊？」蕭澗秋會意地問。

王福生又低下頭，一時說不出話來。

「有關學費的事，我可以跟陶校長說一說。」

陶嵐用決定的口吻向蕭澗秋說：「我讓哥哥免了他的學費就是了。」

25　　王福生以感激的目光看着他們二人，卻慢慢地回答道：「不用了。昨天爸爸上山，把腿摔斷了。以後家裏的生活就要靠我了。」

蕭澗秋和陶嵐兩人聽了，一時說不出話來。王福生含淚向他們各鞠了一躬，推門出去。

蕭澗秋凝視他走去的背影，激動地撫着頭，發出悲憤的聲音。

第五十九景

1　　蕭澗秋在徘徊。

两人沉默了一下。

陶岚又问：「你在想什么？」

「没什么。我有点儿不舒服。」

陶岚站起来说：「我去拿点儿药来。」

萧涧秋阻止道：「欸，不用了。那桌子上就有，在里边那个抽屉里。」

王福生悄悄地走了进来，向老师鞠了一躬，叫道：「萧老师。」又向陶岚鞠了一躬，叫道：「陶老师。」

萧涧秋奇怪地问：「王福生，你怎么不去上课去啊？」

「听说老师病了，我来看看您。」

萧涧秋拉住他的手，说：「不要紧的。明天早上我就可以跟你们上课去了。」

王福生难过地低下头来。

「你怎么了？」

「我以后不能再上学了。」

「为什么？是不是因为交不起学费啊？」萧涧秋会意地问。

王福生又低下头，一时说不出话来。

「有关学费的事，我可以跟陶校长说一说。」

陶岚用决定的口吻向萧涧秋说：「我让哥哥免了他的学费就是了。」

王福生以感激的目光看着他们二人，却慢慢地回答道：「不用了。昨天爸爸上山，把腿摔断了。以后家里的生活就要靠我了。」

萧涧秋和陶岚两人听了，一时说不出话来。王福生含泪向他们各鞠了一躬，推门出去。

萧涧秋凝视他走去的背影，激动地抚着头，发出悲愤的声音。

第五十九景

萧涧秋在徘徊。

第六十景

陶嵐的臥房。陶嵐剛將采蓮哄睡着，正半躺在床沿就燈閱讀。

門外傳來陶慕侃的聲音：「妹妹，睡了嗎？」

陶嵐起身開了門，陶慕侃和蕭澗秋出現在面前。

陶慕侃對蕭澗秋說：「你在這兒坐一會兒。我去給你準備點兒夜宵。」

5　「不用了。我就要回學校去了。」

「多坐一會兒。」陶慕侃挽留着。

陶嵐見了蕭澗秋，又驚又喜地問：「怎麼，你好些了嗎？」

「我完全好了。」蕭澗秋邊說邊走進房來。「我來看看采蓮。」

他們互相深情地看了一眼，蕭澗秋走到床邊。

10　陶嵐輕聲地說：「她剛才哭了很久，好容易才把她哄着了。」

蕭澗秋輕輕地撫摩着采蓮的頭。「可憐的孩子，她還蒙在鼓裏呢。」又轉向陶嵐說：「恐怕我一時顧不了她。以後，全部的責任都委託給你了。」

「你這甚麼意思？」陶嵐不安地問。

蕭澗秋笑了笑。「我這幾天氣悶得很。想到女佛山去休息幾天。慕侃已
15　經答應了。」

「也好。那我陪你一塊兒去。」陶嵐堅決地表示着，她的眼眶有些濕潤
了。

蕭澗秋想了想說：「不必了吧！我三五天就會回來的。」

「澗秋，無論如何，我不能讓你一個人去。」陶嵐堅持着。

20　「我一個人去，更自由一些。」蕭澗秋又轉而意味深長地說：「嵐，等着
吧！我們會有長長的未來的！」

第六十一景

輪船碼頭在鎮的東頭，有二三里路。蕭澗秋提着輕便的小皮箱，大步地
走着。他一路看着田野村落的景色。早晨乳白色的薄雲透着金色的陽光。遠
3　山和田野連成一片翠綠。一陣陣微風吹來，使他感到清新而舒暢。

第六十景

陶岚的卧房。陶岚刚将采莲哄睡着，正半躺在床沿就灯阅读。

门外传来陶慕侃的声音：「妹妹，睡了吗？」

陶岚起身开了门，陶慕侃和萧涧秋出现在面前。

陶慕侃对萧涧秋说：「你在这儿坐一会儿。我去给你准备点儿夜宵。」

5　　「不用了。我就要回学校去了。」

「多坐一会儿。」陶慕侃挽留着。

陶岚见了萧涧秋，又惊又喜地问：「怎么，你好些了吗？」

「我完全好了。」萧涧秋边说边走进房来。「我来看看采莲。」

他们互相深情地看了一眼，萧涧秋走到床边。

10　　陶岚轻声地说：「她刚才哭了很久，好容易才把她哄着了。」

萧涧秋轻轻地抚摩着采莲的头。「可怜的孩子，她还蒙在鼓里呢。」又转向陶岚说：「恐怕我一时顾不了她。以后，全部的责任都委托给你了。」

「你这什么意思？」陶岚不安地问。

萧涧秋笑了笑。「我这几天气闷得很。想到女佛山去休息几天。慕侃已

15　经答应了。」

「也好。那我陪你一块儿去。」陶岚坚决地表示着，她的眼眶有些湿润了。

萧涧秋想了想说：「不必了吧！我三五天就会回来的。」

「涧秋，无论如何，我不能让你一个人去。」陶岚坚持着。

20　　「我一个人去，更自由一些。」萧涧秋又转而意味深长地说：「岚，等着吧！我们会有长长的未来的！」

第六十一景

轮船码头在镇的东头，有二三里路。萧涧秋提着轻便的小皮箱，大步地走着。他一路看着田野村落的景色。早晨乳白色的薄云透着金色的阳光。远

3　山和田野连成一片翠绿。一阵阵微风吹来，使他感到清新而舒畅。

第六十二景

　　學校的客房裏。陶嵐與哥哥一同看着蕭澗秋留下的信。

　　信紙上寫着：「。。。我一踏進芙蓉鎮，就像掉進了是非的漩渦。我幾乎在這漩渦裏溺死。文嫂的自殺，王福生的退學，像兩根鐵棒猛擊了我的頭腦，使我暈旋，也使我清醒。從此終止了我的徘徊，找到了一條該走的道路。我將投身到時代的洪流中去。。。。」

　　「欸，他跟我說是到女佛山去嘛。怎麼，他甚麼都没帶。」陶慕侃的口氣也不十分堅信。「妹妹，你。。。」

　　「我找他去。」她説着就衝了出去，快步下樓，跑上橋頭。。。。

　　　　　　　　　劇終

第六十二景

学校的客房里。陶岚与哥哥一同看着萧涧秋留下的信。

信纸上写着：「。。。我一踏进芙蓉镇，就像掉进了是非的漩涡。我几乎在这漩涡里溺死。文嫂的自杀，王福生的退学，像两根铁棒猛击了我的头脑，使我晕旋，也使我清醒。从此终止了我的徘徊，找到了一条该走的道路。我将投身到时代的洪流中去。。。。」

「欸，他跟我说是到女佛山去嘛。怎么，他什么都没带。」陶慕侃的口气也不十分坚信。「妹妹，你。。。」

「我找他去。」她说着就冲了出去，快步下楼，跑上桥头。。。。

剧终

生词

shēngcí

Vocabulary

生词

第一景

1 陰曆　　　阴历　　　yīnlì　　　　　N: lunar calendar
　　陽曆　　　　阳历　　yánglì　　　　N: solar calendar

　　梅花　　　　　　　méihuā　　　　N: plum blossom

　　落　　　　　　　　luò　　　　　　V: to fall; to drop; *cf.* 7.51, 61.2

　　瓣　　　　　　　　bàn　　　　　　N: petal, segment, section

　　柳樹　　　　柳树　　liǔshù　　　　N: willow tree

　　吐　　　　　　　　tǔ　　　　　　V: to shoot forth; to sprout

　　嫩　　　　　　　　nèn　　　　　　SV: tender; delicate

　　芽　　　　　　　　yá　　　　　　N: bud; sprout; shoot

　　異常　　　　异常　　yìcháng　　　SV (A): unusual; abnormal

　　和暖；暖和　　　　hé'nuǎn; nuǎnhuo　SV: pleasantly warm;
　　　　　　　　　　　　　　　　　　　和: *cf.* 53.13, 55.9

2 女佛山　　　　　　Nǔfó shān　　　PN: （地名）

　　至　　　　　　　　zhì　　　　　　V: 到: to; to arrive, reach

　　芙蓉鎮　　　芙蓉镇　Fúróng zhèn　　PN: （地名）"Hibiscus Town"
　　芙蓉　　　　　　　fúróng　　　　　N: cottonrose hibiscus; lotus
　　鎮　　　　　镇　　zhèn　　　　　　N: town; *cf.* 25.7, 45.3

　　班輪　　　　班轮　　bānlún　　　　N: regular ship service
　　輪船　　　　轮船　　lúnchuán　　　N: steamship; steamboat

　　平靜　　　　平静　　píngjìng　　　SV: calm; quiet; tranquil
　　靜　　　　　静　　jìng　　　　　　SV: still; quiet; calm

56

内河		nèihé	N: inland waterway; river
内		nèi	L: inner; inside
行駛	行驶	xíngshǐ	V: to go; to travel (said of vehicles of transport); 行: *cf.* 1.4, 7.52, 43.7
統艙	统舱	tǒngcāng	N: steerage (the cheapest passenger accomodations); 統/统: *cf.* 1.7, 34.4
艙	舱	cāng	N: ship's hold; cabin
擠滿	挤满	jǐmǎn	RV: to be full, jam-packed
擠	挤	jǐ	V/SV: to crowd; to cram; to squeeze in
大多（數）	大多（数）	dàduō (shù)	N: 多數；多半 多数；多半

3	生意		shēngyì	N: business; 生: *cf.* 5.18, 7.45, 7.50, 11.3, 17.30, 19.5, 40.5, 52.29
	客商		kèshāng	N: 商人; businessman; 商: *cf.* 23.11
	朝香		cháoxiāng	VO: to make a pilgrimage to a temple; 朝: 41.14
	老太婆		lǎotàipó	N: old woman
4	談論	谈论	tánlùn	V: to discuss; to talk about
	行情		hángqíng	N: market prices; 行: *cf.* 1.2, 5.4, 7.52, 9.55, 19.6, 43.7; 情: *cf.* 2.16, 13.5, 42.12, 53.28, 60.9
	與	与	yǔ	C: 跟; and: *EX 1.VI; cf.* 5.19
	菩薩	菩萨	púsà	N: Buddha; bodhisattva
	瓜子		guāzi	N: melon seeds
	其中		qízhōng	L Ph: in/ among/ of them; there; of/ in which: *EX 1.I*
5	叫賣	叫卖	jiàomài	V: to hawk; to sell using a cry or chant; 叫: *cf.* 7.7, 8.3, 14.12, *EX 5.VII*
6	人羣	人群	rénqún	N: crowd
	羣	群	qún	M: group, flock
	顯得	显得	xiǎnde	V: to look; to seem; to appear

調和	调和	tiáohé	SV: to suit well; to fit in; to blend in V: to blend, mix well; to mediate, temper, reconcile; 調/调: *cf.* 8.1, 13.6, 30.7; 和: *cf.* 53.13, 55.9
青年		qīngnián	N: young person
年齡	年龄	niánlíng	N: age
7 嗶嘰	哔叽	bìjī	N: serge (type of fabric)
裝	装	zhuāng	N: outfit; uniform; dress; costume; *cf.* 11.47, 20.6
足		zú	N: foot; *cf.* 5.7, 12.53
深統皮鞋	深统皮鞋	shēntǒng píxié	N: boots; lit., "deep-tubed leather shoes"; 統/统: *cf.* 1.2, 34.4; 皮: *cf.* 30.7
深		shēn	SV: deep; penetrating; profound
路途		lùtú	N: road; journey
風塵	风尘	fēngchén	N: hardships of travel; travel fatigue
8 腿		tuǐ	N: leg
旁		páng	L: 邊 边
皮箱		píxiāng	N: leather suitcase; 皮: *cf.* 30.7
幾乎	几乎	jīhū	A: almost; practically; nearly; *cf.* 4.7, 7.14
貼	贴	tiē	V: to glue; to stick
等		děng	P: etc., and so on; *cf.* 27.1, 55.49
托運標簽 托運	托运标签 托运	tuōyùnbiāoqiān tuōyùn	N: luggage tag; destination tag V: to check (baggage) for shipment; 運/运: *cf.* 9.53, 49.16
標簽	标签	biāoqiān	N: tag; label
煙霧	烟雾	yānwù	N: steam and smoke
9 嗡嗡		wēngwēng	ON: drone; hum; buzz
使		shǐ	V: (causative) to make; to cause to; *cf.* 31.9

氣悶	气闷	qìmèn	SV: lit., (to feel that) the air is stifling, oppressive: to feel stifled, oppressed, claustrophobic
頭昏	头昏	tóuhūn	V: to be dizzy, giddy; 昏: *cf.* 56.1
無法	无法	wúfǎ	V: 没法子; to have no way; to be unable [VO]
無	无	wú	V: 没有
轉身 轉	转身 转	zhuǎnshēn zhuǎn	VO: to turn around (one's body) V: to turn
盡力（地） 盡力	尽力（地） 尽力	jìnlì (de) jìnlì	A: with all one's might; to one's utmost VO/SV: to do all one can; to do one's best
將	将	jiāng	CV: 把; to take or use sth. to V; *cf.* 30.1
扭		niǔ	V: to turn, to twist (the head or body)
向		xiàng	CV: facing; toward V: to face; to turn toward; to side with
10 緊挨 緊	紧挨 紧	jǐn'āi jǐn	V: to be right next to A/SV: tightly; closely V: to tighten
模樣	模样	móyàng; múyàng	N: appearance; look
胖子		pàngzi	N: fatso; fat guy
打盹（兒）	打盹（儿）	dǎdǔn(r)	VO: to doze off; to nap
肥碩	肥硕	féishuò	SV: (of body) large and firm-fleshed
腦袋	脑袋	nǎodài	N: head
不時（地）	不时（地）	bùshí (de)	A: frequently; often; at any time
11 磕碰		kēpèng	V: to knock against; to bump
肩頭	肩头	jiāntóu	N: shoulder
忍受		rěnshòu	V: to bear; to endure; 受: *cf.* 7.44, 11.43, 17.8, 25.16, 28.15
抽身 抽		chōushēn chōu	VO: to pull away; to withdraw oneself V: to draw out; to pull out; to take out (from in between); *cf.* 24.1

第二景

1	當（｡｡｡｡ 的時候）	当（｡｡｡｡ 的时候）	dāng (. . . de shí hou)	CV Ph: when . . . ; the moment . . . ; just as . . . ; 當／当: cf. 5.2, 5.3, 11.37, 18.5, 24.4, 49.29, 55.3, 57.23; 候: cf. 27.1
	踏上		tàshàng	RV: to step onto
	船頭	船头	chuántóu	N: bow or prow of a boat
	輕鬆 　輕	轻松 　轻	qīngsōng qīng	SV: relieved; relaxed SV: light, soft, gentle
	許多	许多	xǔduō	SV: many; much; a lot
	貪婪	贪婪	tānlán	SV (A): avaricious; greedy; as if starved
	吸		xī	V: to inhale; to breathe in
	清新		qīngxīn	SV: clear and fresh
	空氣	空气	kōngqì	N: air; atmosphere
2	望		wàng	V: to gaze into the distance at; cf. 2.18, 39.5, 53.28
	岸		àn	N: shore; bank
	自然		zìrán	SV/N/A: natural
	景色		jǐngsè	N: view; scenery; landscape
	滾	滚	gǔn	V: to roll
	俯身		fǔshēn	V: to bend (the body) over [VO]
	拾起		shíqǐ	RV: to pick up (from the ground); 拾: cf. 17.35
3	眼秀頰紅	眼秀颊红	yǎnxiù jiáhóng	SV: lit., to have beautiful eyes and red cheeks
	頰	颊	jiá	N: cheeks
	交給	交给	jiāogěi	V: to hand sb. sth.; to give; 交: cf. 9.1, 46.10
	同時	同时	tóngshí	MA: at the same time; simultaneously; 同: cf. 26.2, 55.24
	靠近		kàojìn	V/CV: to be close to; to be near; 靠: cf. 27.8, 45.4

	船舷		chuánxián	N: side of the boat
4	欄杆	栏杆	lán'gān	N: railing
	婦人	妇人	fùrén	N: married woman
	破舊	破旧	pòjiù	SV: old and shabby
	夾襖	夹袄	jiá'ǎo	N: lined jacket; 夾/夹: cf. 5.3
	滿面愁容； 愁容滿面 愁容 面容	满面愁容； 愁容满面	mǎnmiàn chóuróng; chóuróng mǎnmiàn chóuróng miànróng	SV (A): to have a face full of worry; to look extremely distressed N: worried look; anxious expression N: face; 容: cf. 11.42, 60.10
	凝視 視	凝视 视	níngshì shì	V: to stare; to gaze fixedly V: to to look at; to watch; to regard
5	瞧出 瞧		qiáochū qiáo	RV: 看出; able to tell by looking V: 看; to look at
	極度 極	极度 极	jídù jí	N/A: extreme (degree) N/A: extreme
	悲哀		bēi'āi	N/SV: grief; sorrow
	懷裏 懷	怀里 怀	huáilǐ huái	L Ph: in (sb.'s) arms N: bosom; chest
6	睡熟		shuìshóu; shuìshú	RV: to be sound asleep
7	膝		qī; xī	N: knee
	珍惜		zhēnxī; zhēnxí	V (A): to treasure; to value
	玩弄		wánnòng	V: to play with; 弄: see 23.5
	熱切地	热切地	rèqiè de	A: fervently; earnestly
9	奶奶		nǎinai	N/APP: (respectful term for) an elderly woman; term for paternal grandmother; "Granny"
	要 VE 就 VE		yào VE jiù VE	PAT: VE if you want to VE; 要: cf. 12.53, 30.7; 就: cf. 60.1
10	啊		ā	P: (phrase-final: used to seek agreement) ". . . , ok?" Cf. 4.17, 4.23, 7.8, 22.30

11	乘客	chéngkè	N: passenger
	道	dào	V: to say; *cf.* 5.4, 55.49, 62.4
	孫女（兒） 孙女（儿）	sūnnǚ(r)	N: granddaughter
12	鄰居 邻居	línjū	N: neighbor; 居: *cf.* 57.43
13	哦	ò	P: (interjection expressing understanding or sudden realization) "Oh!" *Cf.* 19.31
14	革命軍 革命军	Gémìng jūn	PN: Revolutionary Army soldier; army established by Dr. Sun Yat-sen (1866-1925), the first President of the Republic of China, to fight the regional warlords in his campaign to re-unify China
	打仗	dǎzhàng	VO: to fight in a battle; to go to war
	打死	dǎsǐ	RV: to be killed; lit., to be beaten to death
	死	sǐ	V: to die; *cf.* 55.13 SV: fixed; rigid
	嗐	hài	P: (interjection expressing regret or sorrow) sigh
	丟下	diūxià	RV: to abandon; to throw away; to cast off
	孤兒寡婦 孤儿寡妇	gū'ér guǎfù	N: widow and orphan
	孤兒 孤儿	gū'ér	N: orphan; lit., solitary child
	寡婦 寡妇	guǎfù	N: widow
15	往後 往后	wǎnghòu; wànghòu	MA: 以後 以后 [CVO]
	日子	rìzi	N: 生活
	可	kě	A: indeed; certainly; really (emphatic); *cf.* 4.15, 5.14, 7.7, 11.26, 12.34, 43.6, 53.2, 57.31
16	為 N（所）V 为 N（所）V	wéi N (suǒ) V	PAT: (passive construction) to be V-ed by N: *EX 1.II;* 為/为: *cf.* 11.14, 13.6, 22.12, 22.20, 23.5, 36.4, 42.12; 所: *cf.* 7.52, 19.10, 37.22, 46.16

強烈	强烈	qiángliè	SV: strong; intense; violent
同情心 同情		tóngqíng xīn tóngqíng	N: sympathy V: to sympathize with; to have sympathy for; 同: *cf.* 26.2, 55.24; 情: *cf.* 1.4, 7.41, 46.8, 52.2
驅駛	驱驶	qūshǐ	V: to spur; to urge; to prompt
目光		mùguāng	N: gaze; the look in one's eyes; lit., the light in one's eyes; 光: *see* 4.2; *cf.* 4.6, 7.2, 11.34, 17.9, 37.16, 41.11
17 探索		tànsuǒ	V/N: to investigate; to try to find out
根由		gēnyóu	N: cause; origin; 由: *see* 30.17; *cf.* 5.18, 43.7
呆呆地 呆		dāidāi de dāi	A: woodenly; dumbstruck; blankly SV/A: wooden; stupid
18 似乎		sìhū	MA: to seem as if; seemingly; 似: *see* 5.23
白嫩		báinèn	SV: fair; delicate (complexion); 白: *cf.* 9.37; 嫩: *see* 1.1
安慰		ānwèi	V: to comfort; to console SV: to be comforted and consoled
內心		nèixīn	N: lit., inner heart: deep in one's heart; 內: *see* 1.2
酸痛		suāntòng	N/SV: pain; heartache
絕望	绝望	juéwàng	N: utter despair; hopelessness VO/SV: to have lost all hope 望: *cf.* 2.2, 17.3, 27.2
仍（然）		réng(rán)	A: still; continuing as before
癡癡地	痴痴地	chīchī de	A: dumbly; in a dull-witted manner; idiotically
19 微笑 微		wēixiào; wéixiào wēi; wéi	V/N: smile SV/A: slight; minute; tiny; abstruse; subtle

第三景

1	渡頭	渡头	dùtóu	N: dock

第四景

1	教師	教师	jiàoshī	N: teacher; instructor; 師/师: *cf.* 12.24, 55.10
	跨		kuà	V: to step; to stride
	陶		Táo	PN: （姓）
	老式		lǎoshì	AT: old-style; old-fashioned
	家庭		jiātíng	N: family; household
2	廊簷	廊檐	lángyán	N: eaves of the gallery
	朱		zhū	AT: (bound form) vermillion red
	柱		zhù	N: column
	久遠	久远	jiǔyuǎn	SV: long and far-reaching; eternal
	日光		rìguāng	N: sunlight; rays of the sun
	光		guāng	N: light; *cf.* 4.6, 7.2, 11.34, 17.9, 37.16, 41.11
	曬	晒	shài	V: to be exposed to the sun
	穿過	穿过	chuān'guò	RV: to cut through; to cross
	庭院		tíngyuàn	N: courtyard
	廳堂	厅堂	tīngtáng	N: main hall
3	陳設	陈设	chénshè	V/N: to furnish; to decorate; 陳/陈: *cf.* 40.6
	設	设	shè	V: to lay out; to arrange
	紅木	红木	hóngmù	N: redwood
	家具		jiājù	N: furniture; 具: *cf.* 52.17
	壁		bì	N: wall

幅		fú	M: "piece" (used for paintings, cloth, etc.)
淡墨 山水（畫）	淡墨 山水（画）	dànmò shānshuǐ (huà)	N: landscape (painting) done in light ink
寬敞	宽敞	kuānchǎng	SV: spacious; roomy
4 而		ér	C: and: *EX 3.VI; cf.* 9.28, 11.14, 12.42, 17.55, 25.8, 42.5, 57.43
幽靜	幽静	yōujìng	SV: quiet and secluded; peaceful; 靜/静: *see* 1.2
5 校長 —— 長	校长 —— 长	xiàozhǎng —— zhǎng	N: school principal; headmaster; N: chief of ——; *cf.* 7.7, 22.20, 60.20
陶嵐	陶岚	Táo Lán	PN:（人名）
約	约	yuē	A: approximately; around; *cf.* 23.3, 44.16
美貌		měimào	SV/N: beautiful (of women)
6 隨便	随便	suíbiàn	CVO: lit., following one's convenience: as one pleases; casually; randomly; carelessly; 隨/随: *see* 4.16 SV: easy-going; casual; informal; careless; wanton; arbitrary VO: to do as another pleases
編織	编织	biānzhī	V: to knit; to weave; to plait; 織/织: *cf.* 53.18
毛線	毛线	máoxiàn	N: yarn
（好）像 N/VE 似的/地		(hǎo)xiàng N/VE shìde	PAT: to seem like an N/ to seem as if VE-ing: *EX 1.III;* 好: *cf.* 5.18, 37.19, 55.43; 似: *see* 5.23
N/VE 似的/地		N/VE shìde	A: like an N/ as if to VE: *EX 1.III*
無聊	无聊	wúliáo	SV: bored; boring [VO]; 無/无: *see* 1.9
消磨		xiāomó	V: to fritter away; to idle away; 消: *cf.* 25.3

時光	时光	shíguāng	N: time; 光: *cf.* 2.16, 4.1, 7.2, 11.34, 17.9, 21.1, 37.16, 41.11
7 衣着		yīzhuó	N: dress; attire; apparel
錢正興	钱正兴	Qián Zhèngxīng	PN: （人名）興/兴: *cf.* 5.2, 9.11, 9.22, 12.20, 31.5, 35.2, 55.10
親切	亲切	qīnqiè	SV: intimate; close to; warm
帶幾分 SV	带几分 SV	dài jǐfēn SV	VO: to be somewhat SV; 帶/带: *cf.* 55.2; 幾/几: *cf.* 1.8
8 扭捏		niǔniē	SV: bashful; 扭: *see* 1.9
9 紈綺子弟	纨绮子弟	wánkù zǐdì	N: profligate son of the rich; dandy
厭惡	厌恶	yànwù	V: to abhor; to be disgusted to detest
惡	恶	wù	V: to hate; to detest; 惡: *cf.* 37.9, 58.3
感覺	感觉	gǎnjué	N/V: feeling; sensation
隨即	随即	suíjí	MA: promptly; immediately; 隨/随: *see* 4.16
11 老臉皮	老脸皮	lǎo liǎnpí	SV/N: brazen; not easily embarrassed; tough-skinned; 皮: *cf.* 30.7
方謀	方谋	Fāng Móu	PN: （人名）方: *cf.* 7.18, 25.7, 34.1, 40.28, 40.31, 42.1
故意（地）		gùyì (de)	A: intentionally; on purpose
欸		èi	P: (interjection: used to attract attention) "hey"; *cf.* 9.15, 9.17
密斯		mìsi	APP: (transliteration for) "Miss"; 密: *cf.* 46.18
12 （腳）步	（脚）步	(jiǎo)bù	N: (foot) steps; pacing
睜	睁	zhēng	V: to widen; to open (the eyes)
13 緊接	紧接	jǐnjiē	V: to immediately follow; 緊/紧: *see* 1.10
接		jiē	V: to continue; to take over
14 搖頭	摇头	yáotóu	VO: to shake one's head

翩然		piānrán	A: lightly; gliding
V 入		V rù	RV: V into
入		rù	V: to enter in

15 無可奈何　　无可奈何　　wúkě nàihé

SV (A): lit., to be unable to do anything: to be helpless, powerless; to have no alternative [VO]: *EX 1.V*

無可 V　　无可 V　　wúkě V

PAT: 没法 V; lit., to have no way to V [VO]; 無/无: *see* 1.9; 可: *cf.* 2.15

奈何　　　　　　　　nàihé

SE: (emphatic) 怎麼辦？
怎么办？
"What can one do?!" [VO]; 何: *see* 5.13

看 N 一眼　　　　kàn N yìyǎn

VO: to take a glance at N (眼 acts as a measure word for "look"); 看: *cf.* 40.18, 42.3

不快意（地）　　búkuàiyì (de)
不快　　　　　búkuài

A: unhappily; with displeasure
SV/N: unhappy; displeased; 快: *cf.* 27.14

16 隨　　　随　　suí

CV/V: along with; following

偷眼看　　　tōuyǎn kàn

V: to steal a glance; 看: *cf.* 40.18, 42.3

暗自　　　　ànzì

A: inwardly; to oneself; secretly

好笑　　　　hǎoxiào

SV: funny; amusing; 好: *cf.* 5.18, 37.19, 55.43

卻　　　却　　què

A: yet; however; nevertheless: *EX 1.IV*; *cf.* 22.11

17 啊　　　a

P: (phrase-final: marks the sentence topic, effecting a pause to call attention to the rest of the sentence) *Cf.* 2.10, 4.23, 7.8, 22.30; 嘛: *cf.* 7.12

18 心不在焉　　xīn búzài yān

SV (A): inattentive; preoccupied; absent-minded: *EX 1.VII*

勉强（地）　　勉强（地）　　miǎnqiáng (de); miǎnqiǎng (de)
勉强　　　　勉强　　miǎnqiáng; miǎnqiǎng

A: in a forced manner; reluctantly; to barely manage to; grudgingly
SV: forced; strained; unconvincing
V: to force

19 面貌　　miànmào

N: face; appearance

慈祥		cíxiáng	SV: kind
20 啦		la	P: 了 + 啊 (phrase-final exclamation mark; expression of doubt) 啊: *see* 4.23, 7.8
21 彬彬有禮	彬彬有礼	bīnbīn yǒulǐ	SV (A): well-mannered; refined and courteous
伯母		bómǔ	APP/N: "Aunt"; lit., wife of father's elder brother: respectful form of address for a woman about the age of, or slightly older than, one's mother
（陶）慕侃		(Táo) Mùkǎn	PN: （人名）
23 啊		a	P: (phrase-final exclamation mark) *Cf.* 2.10, 4.17, 7.8, 22.30
陶媽媽 ── 媽媽	陶妈妈 ── 妈妈	Táo Māmā ── Māmā	PN: （人名）"Auntie Tao" APP: "Auntie ──" (form of address for an older married woman) *cf.* 8.2
讓	让	ràng	V: (causative) to invite; to have sb. do sth.; to cause to; *cf.* 6.9, 21.19, 49.16, 57.13, *EX 5.VII*

第五景

1 市街		shìjiē	N: commercial district
市		shì	N: market
各色		gèsè	N: all kinds; 各: *cf.* 22.34
店鋪	店铺	diànpù	N: store; shop
風味	风味	fēngwèi	N: flavor
規模	规模	guīmó	N: scale; dimensions
狹小		xiáxiǎo	SV: small and narrow
2 伙友		huǒyǒu	N: sales clerk; shop assistant
店櫃	店柜	diànguì	N: shop counter

清閑	清闲	qīngxián	SV: idle
唯有		wéiyǒu	V: 只有
當鋪	当铺	dàngpù	N: pawnshop; 當/当: cf. 2.1, 11.37, 18.5, 24.2, 24.4, 49.29, 52.2, 55.3, 57.23
興隆	兴隆	xīnglóng	SV: prosperous; thriving; 興/兴: cf. 4.7, 9.11, 9.22, 12.20, 31.5, 35.2, 55.10
窮人	穷人	qióngrén	N: poor people
3 夾	夹	jiā	V: to place sth. in between; to sandwich; to carry under one's arm; cf. 2.4
棉衣		miányī	N: cotton-padded clothing
當票	当票	dàngpiào	N: pawn ticket; 當/当: cf. 2.1, 11.37, 18.5, 24.2, 24.4, 49.29, 52.2, 55.3, 57.23
4 街道		jiēdào	N: streets; 道: cf. 2.11, 7.7
行人		xíngrén	N: pedestrian; passerby; 行: cf. 1.4, 7.52, 43.7
稀少		xīshǎo	SV: few; scarce
校役		xiàoyì	N: custodian
阿榮 阿——	阿荣 阿——	Āróng Ā ——	PN:（人名） APP: personal name prefix
擔	担	dān	V: to carry with a shoulder pole; cf. 17.35
網籃	网篮	wǎnglán	N: basket covered with netting
陪		péi	V: (pre-pivotal) to accompany; to escort
蕭澗秋	萧涧秋	Xiāo Jiànqiū	PN:（人名）
6 身材		shēncái	N: figure
以		yǐ	CV: (may also occur after the main verb) with: EX 2.I, 2.II; cf. 7.52, 19.9, 31.12, 40.30, 42.12
渾厚	浑厚	húnhòu	SV: simple and honest

	印象	yìnxiàng	N: impression
7	足足(地)	zúzú (de)	A: fully; *cf.* 1.7, 11.12
8	苦	kǔ	A/SV: bitterly
	跑遍	pǎobiàn	V: to travel all over
	V 遍	V biàn	V: to V completely, all through
9	感到	gǎndào	RV: to feel; to have a sense of
	厭倦　　厌倦	yànjuàn	SV: tired; weary V: to weary of
10	倒(是)	dào(shi)	A: yet, rather, but (contrary to expectations); 倒: *cf.* 12.15, 41.8, 45.3; 是: *cf.* 6.2, 62.2
	世外 桃(花)源	shìwài táo(hūa)yuán	N: lit., peach-blossom spring beyond this world: paradise
11	露出	lòuchū; lùchū	RV: to reveal; to show
	得意	déyì	SV/VO: proud, pleased
	神色	shénsè	N: expression
12	沿	yán	CV/V: along; following N: edge; border
13	如何	rúhé	Q: 怎麼。。。？怎麼樣？ 怎么。。。？怎么样？ *EX 6.IV*
	何	hé	Q: what? *EX 6.IV*
14	可能	kěnéng	SV/MA/N: possible; 可: *cf.* 2.15
16	快樂　　快乐	kuàilè	SV/N: happy; 快: *cf.* 27.14; 樂/乐: *cf.* 13.3, 13.12
	發抖　　发抖	fādǒu	V: to quiver; to shake [VO]
18	面生	miànshēng	SV: lit., to have an unfamiliar face: to be a stranger; 生: *cf.* 1.3, 7.45, 17.30, 40.5, 52.29

不由得。。。		bù yóudé . . .	V/MA: cannot help but . . . ; can only . . . ; 由: see 43.7; *cf.* 2.17, 12.53, 19.16, 30.17, 57.31
好奇		hàoqí	SV: to be full of curiosity; lit., to love the strange and unusual [VO]; 好: *cf.* 4.6, 4.16, 11.42, 37.19, 53.33, 55.7, 55.43, 60.10
好 VE		hào VE	V: to like to VE; to enjoy VE-ing [VO]: *EX 4.I*
注視	注视	zhùshì	V: to look attentively at; to have one's eyes glued to; 視/视: *see* 2.4
19 算了		suànle	SE: to let it pass; to forget it
指點	指点	zhǐdiǎn	V: to point at
指		zhǐ	N/V: lit., finger: to point
與	与	yǔ	CV: 跟: *EX 1.VI*; *cf.* 1.4
議論	议论	yìlùn	V/N: to discuss
呀		ya	P: (phrase-final exclamation mark) 啊 (form that follows vowel endings) *see* 4.23
20 派		pài	V: (causative) to send; to dispatch; to assign; to appoint (sb. to a task); *cf.* 57.24
查		chá	V: to examine; to inspect; to look up
21 引起		yǐnqǐ	RV: to bring out; to evoke; to lead to
羞慚	羞惭	xiūcán	SV: to be ashamed (of)
22 自在		zìzài	SV: at ease; free
垂眼		chuíyǎn	VO: to look down; to lower one's eyes
23 似 VE 地		sì VE de	A: 像 VE 地; as if to VE; to seem to VE: *EX 1.III*
似		sì	V: 像
解釋	解释	jiěshì	V/N: to explain; to interpret
人口		rénkǒu	N: population

面熟		miànshóu; miànshú	SV: to look familiar
24 外鄉	外乡	wàixiāng	N: other places; lit., places outside
尊敬		zūnjìng	V: respect; esteem
表示		biǎoshì	N/V: expression; indication
25 末了		mòliǎo	T: final; end
顯然	显然	xiǎnrán	MA: apparently; evidently
玩笑		wánxiào	N: joke
口吻		kǒuwěn	N: tone of voice
淡淡的/地		dàndàn de	AT/A: weak; slight

第六景

1 領	领	lǐng	V: (pre-pivotal) to lead sb. to do sth.; *cf.* 7.33, 9.38
迎		yíng	V: 歡迎; 欢迎; to welcome; to receive
2 於是	于是	yúshì	C: thereupon; consequently; 於/于: *see* 55.12; *cf.* 45.13; 是: *cf.* 5.10, 7.21, 7.33, 9.5, 17.13, 62.2
連忙(地)	连忙(地)	liánmáng (de)	A: hastening to; at once
3 提起		tíqǐ	RV: to mention; to bring up in conversation; 提: *cf.* 6.10, 49.17
4 連聲(地)	连声(地)	liánshēng (de)	A: (sounding) one after another; repeatedly saying
久仰		jiǔyǎng	SE: lit., "I have long heard your illustrious name." "I'm very pleased to meet you!"; 仰: *cf.* 9.4, 49.5
5 繼續	继续	jìxù	V: to continue; to go on

6	敝		bì	Pn: 我（們）的； 我（们）的；"my/our shabby" (humble, or polite, form of the first person possessive)
	草字		cǎozì	N: (humble term) "name"
7	相互；互相		xiānghù; hùxiāng	A: to each other
9	讓	让	ràng	V: to yield; *cf.* 4.23, 21.19, *EX 5.VII*
10	返回；返		fǎnhuí; fǎn	V: to come/go back; to return
	吩咐		fēnfù; fēnfu	V: to instruct; to direct
	提		tí	V: to carry or lift by a handle; *cf.* 6.3, 17.15, 43.2
	下房		xiàfáng	N: 佣人的房間 佣人的房间
12	答應	答应	dāyìng	V: to answer "yes"; to comply with; to promise; to agree to; *cf.* 18.9; 應／应: *cf.* 57.23
	忙碌	忙碌	mánglù	SV (A)/V: busy; to bustle about
	奔		bēn	V: to run quickly; to hurry; to rush

第七景

1	閑談	闲谈	xiántán	V: to chat
2	光臨	光临	guānglín	N: "illustrious presence" (of guests) V: "to honor (us) with one's presence"; 光: *cf.* 2.16, 4.1, 4.6, 11.34, 21.1, 37.16, 41.11
3	僅	仅	jǐn	A: only; merely: *EX 2.V*
5	同意		tóngyì	V: to agree; to approve; to consent; 同: *cf.* 26.2, 55.24
	按 N（來説）	按 N（来说）	àn N (láishuō)	CV Ph: according to N, . . . ; 按: *cf.* 40.19

時令	时令	shílìng	N: season; 令: *cf.* 17.6, 57.40
6 紫羔		zǐgāo	N: purple lambskin
灰鼠		huīshǔ	N: squirrel fur
7 翻		fān	V: to turn over
長袍	长袍	chángpáo	N: long robe; gown; 長/长: *cf.* 4.5, 17.5, 41.4, 46.11
角		jiǎo	N: corner
哼		hng	P: (interjection expressing contempt or disapproval) "snort"; *cf.* 22.2
難道	难道	nándào	MA: "Do you really mean to say . . . ?" "You can't possibly mean . . . " (rhetorical question construction); 難/难: *cf.* 7.10, 23.5, 40.30, 42.12, 44.11, 55.5; 道: *see* 2.11; *cf.* 5.4, 55.49, 62.4
非。。。 不成/不可		fēi . . . bùchéng/ bùkě	PAT: must . . . ; to insist on . . . (emphatic); 可: *cf.* 2.15
叫		jiào	V: (causative) to have sb. do sth.; to order: *EX 5.VII; cf.* 1.5, 8.3, 14.12
單	单	dān	AT: lit., single (layer): unlined; *cf.* 40.31
8 啊		a	P: (phrase-final: carries a questioning tone) "Do you really think that . . . ?" *Cf.* 2.10, 4.17, 4.23, 7.8, 22.30
啊		á	P: (interjection expressing disbelief and/or seeking agreement from the listener; may appear either before or after the statement in question) "What?!" "You're kidding!" "Come on!" *Cf.* 2.10, 4.17, 4.23, 7.8, 22.30
10 不祥之兆		bùxiáng zhī zhào	N: not a good omen
災難	灾难	zāinàn	N: disaster; catastrophe; 難/难: *cf.* 7.7, 23.5, 40.30, 42.12, 44.11, 55.5

11	意見	意见	yìjiàn; yìjian

N: opinion; view (often understood as differing opinion or objection)

	變化	变化	biànhuà
	變	变	biàn

N: change; 化: *cf.* 37.10
V: to change; to transform

	現象	现象	xiànxiàng

N: phenomena

	至於	至于	zhìyú

CV: as for; with regards to: *EX 2.III;* 至: *see* 1.2; 於/于: *see* 55.12; *cf.* 45.13

12	人間	人间	rénjiān

L Ph: (in) the human world

	嘛		ma

P: (phrase-final: marks the sentence topic, effecting a pause to call attention to the rest of the sentence) *Cf.* 9.31

13	順水推舟	顺水推舟	shùnshuǐ tuīzhōu

V (A): lit., to push the boat with the current: to take advantage of an opportunity [VO]

	順	顺	shùn

CV: along; with
V: to follow along;
to go in the same direction as; to obey
SV: smooth; fitting; in order

	推		tuī

V: to push

	唉		ài

P: (interjection) sigh

	免		miǎn

V: to exempt; to be free of; to avoid

14	近幾年〔/月/天〕來	近几年〔/月/天〕来	jìn jǐ nián [/yuè/ tiān] lái

T: in recent years [/ months/ days]; 幾/几: *cf.* 1.8; 天: *cf.* 9.39, 11.39, 12.39, 42.14, 53.5

	直奉戰爭	直奉战争	Zhí Fèng zhànzhēng
	戰爭	战争	zhànzhēng

PN: Battle between (the warlords of) Héběi and Manchuria, 1922
N: war; 爭/争: *see* 21.3

	甘肅	甘肃	Gānsù

PN: (province name)

	地震		dìzhèn
	震		zhèn

N/V: earthquake; 地 (dì): *cf.* 11.10
V: to shake; to quake; to startle in shock

	河南		Hé'nán

PN: (province name)

	土匪		tǔfěi

N: bandits

15	山東	山东	Shāndōng

PN: (province name)

鬧	闹	nào	V: to suffer from; to have trouble with; *cf.* 23.12
水災	水灾	shuǐzāi	N: flood
厲害	厉害	lìhai	SV/N: severe; fierce; 害: *cf.* 17.39, 37.23, 57.43
16 皇后		huánghòu	N: empress
18 出現	出现	chūxiàn	V/N: to appear; to emerge
大方		dàfang	SV: easy mannered; unaffected; natural; 方: *cf.* 4.11, 14.2, 25.7, 34.1, 40.28, 40.31, 42.1
活潑	活泼	huópo	SV: lively; vivacious
21 還不是。。。	还不是。。。	háibúshì...	PAT: (rhetorical question construction) "Isn't it just a matter of . . . ?"; 是: *cf.* 6.2, 62.2
就是了		jiùshìle	P: (phrase-final) and that's it; that's all there is to it: *EX 2.IV;* 就: *cf.* 60.1; 是: *cf.* 6.2, 62.2
23 香煙	香烟	xiāngyān	N: cigarettes
抱歉		bàoqiàn	SV (A)/V: apologetic; sorry [VO] SE: "Sorry!"
忘記	忘记	wàngjì	V: to forget
招待		zhāodài	V: to entertain; to show hospitality to; 待: *cf.* 8.1, 12.6, 19.5
25 凝思		níngsī	V: to be deep in thought; to think with intense concentration
回憶	回忆	huíyì	V/N: to recall; to recollect
尋找 尋	寻找 寻	xúnzhǎo xún	V: to look for; to seek V: to search; to seek
27 竭力(地)		jiélì (de)	A: to try as hard as one can; to one's utmost
追憶 追	追忆	zhuīyì zhuī	V: to (try to) remember; to call to mind V: to chase; to pursue; to go after

30	原諒	原谅	yuánliàng	V: to forgive; to pardon; 原: *cf.* 12.5, 30.17
	學問	学问	xuéwèn; xuéwen	N: learning; scholarship; erudition
31	請教 　請	请教 　请	qǐngjiào qǐng	V: to request instruction or advice [VO] V: (pre-pivotal) to request; to ask for (a favor)
	指教		zhǐjiào	V: to give advice and pointers; 指: *see* 5.19
33	滔滔地		tāotāo de	A: in a constant flow of words; fluently; eloquently
	簡直（地/是）	简直（地/是）	jiǎnzhí (de/ shì)	A: simply; just; practically: *EX 6.II;* 是: *cf.* 6.2, 62.2
	佔領	占领	zhànlǐng	V: to occupy; to capture; 領/领: *cf.* 6.1, 9.38
	神態	神态	shéntài	N: expression; manner
34	柔媚		róumèi	SV: gentle; soft and lovely
	嬌養	娇养	jiāoyǎng	SV: fragile; delicate; spoiled V: to spoil; to pamper
	習氣	习气	xíqì	N: demeanor; (bad) habit
35	美麗	美丽	měilì	SV: beautiful
38	嬉笑		xīxiào	V: to tease; to laugh
39	脾氣	脾气	píqì; píqi	N: temperament; temper
	V 個 SV	V 个 SV	V ge SV	PAT: (complement of degree construction in which 個/个 acts as a marker of emphasis, exaggerating the resulting state SV) "V to the point of SV"
	理		lǐ	V: to acknowledge; to pay attention to; *cf.* 12.17, 12.53, 35.3
40	面色		miànsè	N: expression; the look on one's face

凝重		níngzhòng	SV: serious; grave
重		zhòng	SV: lit., heavy: important; weighty; stressed; valued; *cf.* 42.8
異樣	异样	yìyàng	SV: peculiar; strange; unusual
感觸	感触	gǎnchù	N: feeling
41 旁若無人	旁若无人	páng ruò wúrén	SV (A): lit., as if no one else were there: self-assured: *EX 2.VII;* 旁: *see* 1.8; 若: *cf.* 37.9; 無/无: *see* 1.9
古怪		gǔguài	SV: eccentric; odd; strange; 怪: *cf.* 14.12
其實	其实	qíshí	MA: actually; in fact
不過。。。	不过。。。	búguò . . .	PAT: nothing more than . . . and that's
罷了	罢了	bàle	all; only . . . and nothing more: *EX 2.V*
人情世故		rénqíng shìgù	N: the ways of the world; 情: *cf.* 2.16, 13.5, 42.12, 53.28, 60.9
42 哲學	哲学	zhéxué	N: philosophy
真正		zhēnzhèng	AT/A: genuine; true; real
做人		zuòrén	V: to conduct oneself properly; to behave as a human being; to be an upright person [VO]
43 知識	知识	zhī shì; zhī shi	N: knowledge; learning
44 似/像 N/VE		sì/xiàng N/VE	PAT: 像; just like N/VE; *cf. EX I.III;*
（一）般		(yì)bān	似: *see* 5.23
N/VE		N/VE	A: in the way of a N/ as if VE-ing
（一）般地		(yì)bān de	
受		shòu	V: to suffer; to be subjected to (marker of passive construction); *cf.* 1.11, 17.8
諷刺	讽刺	fěngcì; fèngcì	V: to mock; to satirize
刺	刺	cì	V: to stab; to prick; to sting N: thorn; splinter
45 閱歷	阅历	yuèlì	N/V: experience; 閱/阅: *cf.* 13.1, 60.1

先生		xiānshēng; 　xiānsheng	N: 老師; 　　老師; 生: *cf.* 1.3, 5.18, 7.50, 11.3, 19.5, 52.29
46 謙遜	谦逊	qiānxùn	SV (A): modest; unassuming
47 信任		xìnrèn	V: to have confidence in; to believe in; to trust; 信: *cf.* 9.56; 任: *see* 17.8
48 （鋼）琴	（钢）琴	(gāng)qín	N: piano
彈	弹	tán	V: to play (an instrument)
50 手指		shǒuzhǐ	N: fingers; 指: *see* 5.19
生疏		shēngshū	SV: out of practice; rusty; unfamiliar; 生: *cf.* 1.3, 7.45, 17.30, 19.5, 40.5, 52.29
51 冷落		lěngluò	V: to treat coldly; to leave (one) out SV: desolate, empty; 落: *cf.* 1.1, 19.23, 39.12, 61.2
忌妒心 　忌妒		jìdù xīn 　jìdù	N: jealousy V: to be jealous
52 行動	行动	xíngdòng	N/V: actions; movements; behavior; 行: *cf.* 1.2, 1.4, 5.4, 9.55, 19.6
在座		zàizuò	V: to be present [VO]
不知所以		bùzhī suǒyǐ	V (A): to not know why [VO]; 所: *cf.* 2.16, 19.10, 37.22, 46.16; 以: *cf.* 5.6, 19.9, 40.30, 42.2, 42.12
53 呈現	呈现	chéngxiàn	V: to emerge; to appear; to show
一片		yípiàn	M: a spreading expanse; sprawl; stretch
沈寂	沉寂	chénjí; chénjì	N/SV: quiet; stillness

第八景

1 案板		ànbǎn	N: cutting board; 案: *cf.* 25.2

各色各樣	各色各样	gèsè gèyàng	N/SV: all kinds; assortment; 各色: *see* 5.1; 各: *cf.* 22.34
待 V		dài V	V: (waiting) to be V-ed; about to V; pending V: *EX 4.II; cf.* 7.23, 12.6
烹調	烹调	pēngtiáo	V: to cook; 調/调: *cf.* 1.6, 13.6, 30.7
2 菜餚	菜肴	càiyáo	N: dishes; foods; main courses
吳媽	吴妈	Wú Mā	PN: （人名）
── 媽	── 妈	── Mā	APP: (form of address for an older, married woman servant) *cf.* 4.23
灶台		zàotái	N: brick stove
打雜	打杂	dǎzá	V: to do odds and ends [VO]
3 叫		jiào	V: to greet elders by calling them the appropriate terms of address; *cf.* 1.5, 7.7, 14.12, *EX 5.VII*
6 粗		cū	SV: coarse; rough; crude
端		duān	V: to carry level in front with both hands (as with a tray)
人家 PN		rénjiā PN	Pn: (expression of respect or status) "that [honorable] personage, PN"; *cf.* 14.12
7 吃不來	吃不来	chībùlái	RV: 吃不習慣; 吃不习惯; cannot eat; to have the food not be to one's accustomed taste; 吃: *cf.* 30.25
8 山珍海味		shānzhēn hǎiwèi	N: delicacies from land and sea
9 碟(子)		dié(zi)	N: plate
投		tóu	V: to throw; to cast
鍋	锅	guō	N: pot; wok
嘎		gā	ON: crackle; snap; sizzle (sound of frying)
10 濺	溅	jiàn	V: to spatter; to splash

| 緞 | 缎 | duàn | N: satin |

第九景

1	吊燈 　吊	吊灯	diàodēng 　diào	N: hanging lamp V: to hang
	燃		rán	V: to light; to ignite; to burn
	耀		yào	V: to illuminate
	交映		jiāoyìng	V: to reflect (lit., on each other); 交: cf. 2.3, 27.9
	映		yìng	V: to reflect; to shine
	淡紅	淡红	dànhóng	SV: pale red
2	八仙桌		bāxiān zhuō	N: old-fashioned square table for eight
	杯箸		bēizhù	N: 酒杯，筷子
	四個碟子	四个碟子	sì ge diézi	N: lit., four dishes: appetizers, usually served in a set of four dishes; see 8.9
	壺	壶	hú	N/M: vessel; jug
3	圍坐 　圍	围坐 　围	wéizuò 　wéi	V: to sit around V/CV: to be around
4	高談闊論	高谈阔论	gāotán kuòlùn	V: to talk freely, loudly, bombastically
	如果 A（的 　話），（就）B	如果 A（的 　话），（就）B	rúguǒ A (de- huà), (jiù) B	PAT: if A, (then) B; 就: cf. 60.1
	信仰		xìnyǎng	N/V: beliefs; convictions; 信: cf. 9.56; 仰: cf. 6.4, 49.5
	失掉 　V 掉 　掉		shīdiào 　V diào 　diào	RV: to lose RV: V away; V until gone V: to drop; to come off; to lose
5	意義	意义	yìyì	N: meaning; sense
	凡（是） 　specified N（都）		fán(shì) 　specified N (dōu)	PAT: Every N that is so specified; in all cases of this specified case of N: EX 2.VI; 是: cf. 6.2, 62.2

救國	救国	jiùguó	VO: to rescue one's country; to save the nation
三民主義	三民主义	Sānmín zhǔyì	PN: The Three Principles of the People (nationalism, democracy and livelihood), as advocated by Dr. Sun Yat-sen in 1905
主義	主义	zhǔyì	N: doctrine; "—ism"

7 倚   yǐ   V: to lean on; to rest against

9 笑嘻嘻   xiào xīxī   SV (A): grinning; all smiles

見識   见识   jiànshi   N: experience; knowlege
V: to get experience; to widen one's knowledge

11 興致勃勃   兴致勃勃   xìngzhì bóbó   SV (A): bursting with enthusiasm; 興/兴: cf. 4.7, 5.2, 35.2, 55.10

手勢   手势   shǒushì   N: gesture

反對   反对   fǎnduì   V: to oppose; to object to; to fight

幹嗎   干吗   gànmá   Q: why; whatever for (emphatic)

12 節制   节制   jiézhì   V/N: to control; to check; to moderate; 節/节: cf. 49.30, 52.29, 57.23

資本   资本   zīběn   N: capital

競爭   竞争   jìngzhēng   V/N: to compete; 爭/争: see 21.3

發展   发展   fāzhǎn   V/N: to develop; to grow; to expand

14 並 + NEG   并 + NEG   bìng + NEG   A: (used in front of the negative 不/没 for emphasis) not in the least, in no way, by no means; cf. 17.13, 19.5, 22.33

排斥   páichì   V: to exclude; to reject

15 欸   éi   P: (interjection that indicates that a thought has suddenly come to mind, sudden realization, or surprise) Cf. 4.11, 9.17

17 罷休   罢休   bàxiū   V: to give up; to let drop

		欸		ěi	P: (interjection expressing objection) *Cf.* 4.11, 9.15
18	高妙		妙	gāomiào / miào	SV: subtle; ingenious; fine SV: clever; subtle; excellent; fine
20	到。。。程度		程度	dào . . . chéngdù / chéngdù	VO: to get to a level of . . . N: level; degree
22	酒興	酒兴		jiǔxìng	N: elation from drinking; 興/兴: *cf.* 4.7, 5.2, 12.20, 35.2, 55.10
24	冷冷地			lěnglěng de	A: coldly
	帶刺	带刺		dàicì	VO (A): lit., to carry thorns: to have bite; to be stinging, barbed; 帶/带: *cf.* 55.2; 刺: *see* 7.44
25	顧	顾		gù	V: to attend to; to take into consideration
	個人主義	个人主义		gèrén zhǔyì	N: individualism
26	攔阻	拦阻		lánzǔ	V (A): to block; to obstruct; to impede
	目前			mùqián	T: at the moment; at present
27	實際	实际		shíjì	SV: realistic; practical
28	一飲而盡	一饮而尽		yìyǐn ér jìn	SE: lit., in one drink, to completely finish: to drink all in one gulp; 而: *cf.* 4.4, 9.28, 12.42, 17.55, 25.8, 42.5, 57.43
	一 V1 而 V2			yì V1 ér V2	PAT: V1-ing, (resulting in) V2: *EX 5.IV*
	僅。。。 而已	仅。。。 而已		jǐn . . . éryǐ	PAT: only . . . and that's all: *EX 3.V*; 僅/仅: *see* 7.3; 而: *cf.* 4.4, 11.14, 12.42, 17.55, 25.8, 42.5, 57.43
	舉	举		jǔ	V: to lift; to raise
	呷			xiā	V: to take a sip
	示意			shìyì	V: lit., to indicate one's intentions (by facial expression or gesture): to signal; to motion [VO]

29	熱氣騰騰	热气腾腾	rèqì téngténg	SV: steaming hot
	火鍋	火锅	huǒguō	N: hot pot; 鍋/锅: *see* 8.9
31	搭腔		dāqiāng	VO: to respond; to answer
	正常		zhèngcháng	SV: normal
	嘛		ma	P: (phrase final) "isn't it obvious?" "Can't you see?" *Cf.* 7.12
36	靜寂； 寂靜	静寂； 寂静	jìngjí; jìngjì; jíjìng; jìjìng	SV/N: quiet; silent; 靜/静: *see* 1.2
37	憂愁	忧愁	yōuchóu	SV (A): worried; anxious
	文嫂 ——嫂		Wén Sǎo —— Sǎo	PN: (人名) "Sister Wen" APP: lit., the wife of one's elder brother: respectful form of address for a friend's wife
	白		bái	A: in vain; for nothing; *cf.* 2.18, 37.11, 44.18, 61.2
	趟		tàng	M: a trip
	撫恤金	抚恤金	fǔxù jīn	N: pension for the family of the disabled or deceased
38	領	领	lǐng	V: to receive; to get; *cf.* 6.1, 7.33
39	孫傳芳	孙传芳	Sūn Chuánfāng	PN: (人名) 1885-1935; warlord operating in the Jiāngsū-Zhèjiāng region, eventually defeated by the Revolutionary Army in 1926 during The Northern Expedition 北伐: *cf.* 55.2; 傳/传: *see* 26.11
	天下		tiānxià	N: area of rule; empire; world; 天: *cf.* 7.14, 12.39, 42.14, 53.5
	革命黨	革命党	Gémìng dǎng	PN: Revolutionary Party, led by Dr. Sun Yat-sen, with headquarters in Guǎngzhōu
	機關	机关	jīguān	N: office; administration
44	皺眉(頭)	皱眉(头)	zhòuméi(tóu)	VO: to knit the eyebrows; to frown

45	師範學院	师范学院	shīfàn xuéyuàn	N: college for teacher training; 師/师: *cf.* 12.24, 55.10
	演講	演讲	yǎnjiǎng	V/N: to lecture; to make a speech
46	李志豪		Lǐ Zhìháo	PN:（人名）
47	家小		jiāxiǎo	N: wife and children
49	感嘆	感叹	gǎntàn	V/N: to sigh with feeling
	有志氣	有志气	yǒu zhìqi	VO/SV: to have high aspirations, ambition
	得志		dézhì	VO/SV: to be successful; to fulfill one's ambitions
50	東奔西跑	东奔西跑	dōngbēn xīpǎo	V: to be busy running all over the place; 奔: *see* 6.12
	考取		kǎoqǔ	RV: to be admitted to a school by passing the entrance exam; 考: *cf.* 13.8; 取: *see* 40.28
	黃埔軍校	黄埔军校	Huángpǔ jūnxiào	PN: Whampoa Military Academy, Guǎngdōng Province; set up to train the Revolutionary Army soldiers
	前途		qiántú	N: future prospects
	竟（然）		jìng(rán)	MA: unexpectedly; surprisingly: *EX 5.III*
51	攻打		gōngdǎ	V: to attack; to assault
	惠州		Huìzhōu	PN:（地名）refers to a military campaign against a warlord of Guǎngdōng province, fought in 1925
	陣亡	阵亡	zhènwáng	V: to be killed in action
52	驚訝	惊讶	jīngyà	SV (A): shocked; astonished; astounded; 驚/惊: *see* 11.47
53	唔		ng	P: (affirmative response) "yes"

五四運動	五四运动	Wǔsì yùndòng	PN: May Fourth Movement, 1919. Initiated by students protesting the Treaty of Versailles which gave possession of the island of Qīngdǎo (Shāndōng Province) to Japan instead of returning it to China; 運/运: cf. 1.8, 49.16
54 批		pī	M: bunch; group
搜查日貨	搜查日货	sōuchá Rìhuò	VO: to search stores for Japanese goods as part of a boycott against Japan (1919)
搜查		sōuchá	V: to search (a person, a house, etc.); 查: see 5.20
55 遊行	游行	yóuxíng	V/N: to march in protest; to demonstrate; 行: cf. 7.52, 43.7; 遊/游: cf. 14.2, 21.22, 54.3
56 點頭	点头	diǎntóu	VO: to nod
嘆氣	叹气	tànqì	VO: to sigh
通信		tōngxìn	VO: to communicate by letter; to correspond; 信: cf. 7.47, 9.4, 11.40, 62.7
57 打斷	打断	dǎduàn	RV: to interrupt; to cut short
話題	话题	huàtí	N: topic of conversation
59 對飲	对饮	duìyǐn	V: to drink facing each other
無心(地)	无心(地)	wúxīn (de)	A: absent-mindedly; in a preoccupied or uninterested manner; 無/无: see 1.9
無心	无心	wúxīn	VO: to be in no mood
增加		zēngjiā	V: to add; to increase
層	层	céng	M: layer; story or floor (of buildings)
負擔	负担	fùdān	N/V: burden; responsibility; 擔/担: see 5.4, cf. 17.35

第十一景

1	低矮		dī'ǎi	SV: low

2	直立		zhílì	V: to stand erect; to stand stiffly; 立: *cf.* 12.5
	躊躇	踌躇	chóuchú	V: to hesitate
	敲		qiāo	V: to knock (of doors); to strike; to beat

| 3 | 遇見
遇 | 遇见 | yùjiàn
yù | V: to meet; to come across; to encounter
V: to meet; to encounter; *cf.* 37.23 |
| | 陌生 | | mòshēng | SV: strange; unfamiliar; 生: *cf.* 1.3, 7.45, 19.3, 17.30, 40.5, 52.29 |

4	順手	顺手	shùnshǒu	CVO/SV: handily; without any extra trouble; 順/顺: see 7.13
	V 住		V zhù	RV: to V fast; to V to a point of control
	溫和	温和	wēnhé	SV (A): gentle; mild; 和: *cf.* 53.13, 55.9

| 6 | 一下(子) | | yíxià(zi) | MA/N: an instant; a moment; all at once; suddenly |
| | 緩 | 缓 | huǎn | V: to take a moment; to recover; to delay; to slow down |

| 7 | 過去 | 过去 | guòqù; guòqu | T: in the past; formerly |

| 9 | 哽咽 | | gěngyè; gěngye | V: to have catches in the voice; to choke with sobs |

| 10 | 不幸 | | búxìng | N/SV/MA: misfortune; unfortunate |
| | 特地 | | tèdì | A: specially; 地 (dì): *cf.* 7.14, 11.33, 25.4 |

| 12 | 一時 | 一时 | yìshí | MA/N: momentarily; temporarily |
| | 手足無措 | 手足无措 | shǒuzú wúcuò | SV: lit., not to know what to do with one's hands and feet: at a loss what to do; flustered [VO]: *EX 3.VII*; 足: *see* 1.7; *cf.* 5.7, 12.53; 無/无: *see* 1.9 |

含淚	含泪	hánlèi	VO: to have tears in one's eyes
含		hán	V: to hold (in the mouth); to contain; to imply; to insinuate
眼淚	眼泪	yǎnlèi	N: tears
14 為 X 而 VE	为 X 而 VE	wèi X ér VE	PAT: because of X, VE; for the sake of X, VE: *EX 3.1;* 為/为: *cf.* 2.16, 13.6, 23.5, 36.4, 42.12; 而: *cf.* 4.4, 9.28, 12.42, 17.55, 25.8, 42.5, 57.43
寒冷		hánlěng	SV: cold
顫抖	颤抖	chàndǒu; zhàndǒu	V: to shiver; to shake
15 掩門	掩门	yǎnmén	VO: to close the door
像樣(子)	像样(子)	xiàngyàng(zi)	SV: presentable; decent; up to standard [VO]
16 灰暗		huī'àn	SV: gray and gloomy
灰塵	灰尘	huīchén	N: dust
17 七穿八孔		qīchuān bākǒng	SV: full of holes; 孔: *cf.* 22.31, 35.9, 46.2
棉被		miánbèi	N: cotton coverlet; quilt; 被: *cf.* 11.34
20 伯伯		bóbo	APP/N: "Uncle"; father's elder brother; respectful form of address for a man about the age of (usually slightly older than) one's father
采蓮	采莲	Cǎilián	PN:（人名）
22 湊近	凑近	còujìn	V: to move close to
26 可惜		kěxī; kěxí	MA/SV: unfortunately; (it's a) pity; (it's) too bad; 可: *cf.* 2.15
31 說不上	说不上	shuōbúshàng	RV: unable to say; hard to tell
33 田地		tiándì	N: fields; farmland; 地 (dì): *cf.* 11.10

34	被 (X) V		bèi (X) V	PAT: (passive construction, used in situations expressing adversity, where the agent X may or may not be named) to be V-ed (by X); *cf.* 11.17
	V 光		V guāng	RV: V until there is nothing left; 光: *cf.* 2.16, 4.1, 4.6, 7.2, 17.9, 21.1, 37.16, 41.11
35	親戚	亲戚	qīnqi	N: relatives
37	沈默	沉默	chénmò	SV: deep in silence
	適當	适当	shìdàng	SV: appropriate; fitting; proper; 當/当: *cf.* 2.1, 5.2, 5.3, 18.5, 24.2, 24.4, 49.29, 52.2, 55.3, 57.23
	踱		duó	V: to pace
39	俗話	俗话	súhuà	N: common saying; proverb
	天無 　絕人之路	天无 　绝人之路	Tiān wú juérén zhī lù	SE: lit., Heaven does not allow for roads that cut people off: Heaven will find us a way; there's always a way out; 天: *cf.* 7.14, 12.39, 42.14, 53.5; 無/无: *see* 1.9
40	相信		xiāngxìn	V: to believe; to have faith in; 信: *cf.* 9.56
	不禁 VE		bùjīn VE	V: cannot help VE-ing; cannot refrain from VE-ing: *EX 3.II*
42	慌亂 亂	慌乱 乱	huāngluàn luàn	SV: panicked; flustered SV/N/A: in chaos, disorder, confusion, turmoil
	好不容易		hǎo bù róngyì	A: with great difficulty; 好: *cf.* 5.18, 37.19, 55.43; 容: *cf.* 2.4, 45.12, 53.2
43	終究	终究	zhōngjiū; zhōngjiù	MA: eventually; in the end: *EX 3.III*; 究: *cf.* 55.37

受委曲		shòu wěiqu	VO/SV: to suffer a wrong or humiliation; 受: *see* 7.44; *cf.* 1.11, 17.8
委曲		wěiqu	N: wrongs; grievances; troubles V: to wrong; to trouble; to inconvenience SV: wronged; to have a grievance; 委: *cf.* 60.12; 曲: *cf.* 13.3, 13.4, 13.6, 13.12, 22.2
44 收住		shōu zhù	RV: to have stopped; to have controlled; to have restrained; 收: *cf.* 11.55, 13.6, 17.35; 住: *see* 11.4
46 此		cǐ	Pr: this: *EX 7.III*
阻止		zǔzhǐ	V (A): to stop; to prevent
止		zhǐ	V: to stop; to halt; to prohibit
不用		búyòng	SE: "It's not necessary"; "There's no need"
47 強裝	强装	qiángzhuāng; qiǎngzhuāng	V: to make an effort to pretend; to force oneself to pretend; 裝: *cf.* 1.7
強 V	强 V	qiáng V; qiǎng V	A: to make an effort to V; to force oneself to V
受驚	受惊	shòujīng	VO (A): to get a shock; to be frightened, startled; 受: *see* 7.44; *cf.* 1.11, 17.8
驚	惊	jīng	V/N: to start; to startle; to be shocked, frightened, alarmed
49 責任	责任	zérèn	N: responsibility; 任: *see* 17.8
50 力量		lìliang	N: power; strength; force
52 見外	见外	jiànwài	SV: to regard as an outsider [VO]
素來	素来	sùlái	A: always (in the past); 素: *cf.* 43.7
敬佩		jìngpèi	V: to admire; to esteem
口袋		kǒudài	N: pocket
53 掏		tāo	V: to pull out; to scoop out
鈔票	钞票	chāopiào	N: paper money; bill
蓋	盖	gài	N/V: cover; lid

55	介意		jièyì	SV: to take offence; to mind [VO]
	收下		shōuxià	RV: to accept; to take 收: *cf.* 11.44, 13.6, 17.35
57	惶恐		huángkǒng	SV: apprehensive; fearful
	感激		gǎnjī; gǎnji	V: to be grateful, thankful (to sb.)
	背影		bèiyǐng	N: the view of sb.'s back or receding figure
	背		bèi	N: back (of body or object) V: to turn one's back to

第十二景

1	（有）如 N/VE 一樣	（有）如 N/VE 一样	(yǒu)rú N/VE yíyàng	PAT: 好像 N/VE 一樣; 好像 N/VE 一样; [VO]; *cf. EX 1.III*
	鶴	鹤	hè	N: crane
	雲	云	yún	N: clouds
	飛翔	飞翔	fēixiáng	V: to fly; to glide in the air
	貪戀	贪恋	tānliàn	V: to hate to leave; to cling to
	田野		tiányě	N: fields; open country
2	雪景		xuějǐng	N: snow scene
	顧盼	顾盼	gùpàn	V: to look around; 顧/顾: *see* 9.25
	跳躍	跳跃	tiàoyuè	V: to jump; to leap; to bound; 躍/跃: *cf.* 19.28
	跳		tiào	V: to jump; to palpitate; to skip (over)
	微妙		wēimiào; wéimiào	SV: obscure and mysterious; subtle; 微: *see* 2.19; 妙: *see* 9.18
	愉悦		yúyuè	N/SV: joy; delight; cheer
4	一手		yìshǒu	A: lit., with one hand: with ease; quickly: *EX 3.IV*

不料。。。		búliào . . .	V: 没想到 . . . ; no one expected that . . .
翻書	翻书	fānshū	VO: to leaf through a book; to flip through a book; 翻: see 7.7
5　立即		lìjí; lìjì	A: immediately; at once; 立: cf. 11.2, 17.6
合攏	合拢	hélǒng	RV: to close up
原處	原处	yuánchù	N: original place; 原: cf. 7.30
6　待		dāi	V: to stay; cf. 7.23, 8.1, 19.5
7　冒昧		màomèi	SV: presumptuous; bold
8　圍巾	围巾	wéijīn	N: scarf; 圍/围: see 9.3
10　來得及	来得及	láidejí	RV: to have time to; to be able to do sth. in time
11　拉		lā	V: to pull, drag, tug
15　倒		dào	V: to pour; cf. 5.10, 41.8, 45.3
17　理科		lǐkē	N: science (as a school subject); 理: cf. 7.39, 12.53, 35.3, 43.10
19　藝術	艺术	yìshù	N/SV: art
數學	数学	shùxué	N: mathematics
偏		piān	A: to just insist on; to just have to
20　感興趣	感兴趣	gǎn xìngqù	SV: to be interested [VO]; 興/兴: cf. 4.7, 5.2, 9.11, 9.22, 35.2, 55.10
22　主人		zhǔrén	N: host; master
24　打官司		dǎ guānsi	VO: to bring a lawsuit; to go to court
律師	律师	lǜshī	N: lawyer; 律: cf. 13.11; 師/师: cf. 4.1, 9.45, 17.8, 55.10
25　狀紙	状纸	zhuàngzhǐ	N: court papers for filing a lawsuit or complaint

	壓迫	压迫	yāpò	V: to oppress
	出庭		chūtíng	VO: to appear in court
	辯護	辩护	biànhù	V: to defend; to argue (a case)
26	書籍	书籍	shūjí	N: books; works; writings; literature
27	遞給	递给	dìgěi	V: to hand over; to pass (sth.) to
30	自供		zìgòng	V: to confess
32	補充	补充	bǔchōng	V: to add; to supplement
34	搓手		cuōshǒu	VO: to rub one's hands together
	可憐	可怜	kělián	SV: poor; pitiful; miserable; wretched V: to pity; 可: cf. 2.15
36	簡短	简短	jiǎnduǎn	SV (A): brief
37	有（一）些 SV		yǒu(yì)xiē SV	VO: to be somewhat SV
39	天真		tiānzhēn	SV (A): innocent; artless; naive; 天: cf. 7.14, 9.39, 11.39, 42.14, 53.5
40	爐	炉	lú	N: stove; furnace
42	驚奇	惊奇	jīngqí	SV (A): amazed; to wonder at; 驚/惊: see 11.47
	不僅 X （而已）， 而（且）Y	不仅 X （而已）， 而（且）Y	bùjǐn X (éryǐ), ér(qiě) Y	PAT: not only X, but also Y: EX 3.V; 僅/仅: see 7.3; 而: see 25.8; cf. 4.4, 9.28, 11.14, 17.55, 42.5
	聰慧	聪慧	cōnghuì	SV: bright; intelligent
43	管		guǎn	V: to manage; to have charge of; cf. 43.7
49	來意	来意	láiyì	N: purpose in coming
50	一大早		yídàzǎo	T: very early in the morning
	位置		wèizhi	N: place; seat
	擺	摆	bǎi	V: to arrange; to place

53	要求		yāoqiú	N/V: request; demand; requirement; 要: *cf.* 2.9, 30.1, 30.7
	求		qiú	V: (pre-pivotal) to request; to entreat; to seek
	滿足	满足	mǎnzú	V: to satisfy; to meet (a requirement); to fulfill SV: to be satisfied; 足: *cf.* 1.7, 11.12; 滿意/满意: *cf.* 17.18
	理由		lǐyóu	N: reason; 理: *cf.* 7.39, 12.17, 35.3, 43.10; 由: *see* 30.17; *cf.* 5.18, 43.7
54	回頭	回头	huítóu	VO: lit., to turn one's head: to turn; *cf.* 54.12
	琴譜	琴谱	qínpǔ	N: (sheets of) piano music; 琴: *see* 7.48
56	返身		fǎnshēn	V: to turn (the body) to go back [VO]
57	目送		mùsòng	V: to watch sb. go; lit., to see sb./sth. off with one's eyes
	拖		tuō	V: to pull; to drag; to haul

第十三景

1	廂房		xiāngfáng	N: side room; wing
	全神貫注	全神贯注	quánshén guànzhù	V (A): to concentrate on with all one's might; to be absorbed in
	貫注	贯注	guànzhù	V: to concentrate on
	閱	阅	yuè	V: to read through; *cf.* 7.45
2	音階	音阶	yīnjiē	N: notes in a musical scale
3	手抄		shǒuchāo	AT: hand-written
	樂譜	乐谱	yuèpǔ	N: music scores; sheets of music; 樂/乐: *cf.* 5.16

	徘徊曲	Páihuái qǔ	PN: (name of a musical composition) 曲: *cf.* 11.43
	徘徊	páihuái	V/N: to pace back and forth; to waver
	抬	tái	V: to lift; to raise
4	作曲家	zuòqǔ jiā	N: composer; 曲: *cf.* 11.43
	作品	zuòpǐn	N: work (of literature, art); 品: *cf.* 17.13, 39.2
5	感情衝動　感情冲动	gǎnqíng chōngdòng	SV: to be (over) excited; to be overwhelmed with emotion
	感情	gǎnqíng	N: emotion; feeling; 情: *cf.* 1.4, 7.41, 46.8, 52.2
	衝動　冲动	chōngdòng	SV: (over) excited; overwhelmed; 衝/冲: *see* 55.3
6	胡亂（地）　胡乱（地）	húluàn (de)	A: carelessly; randomly; 亂/乱: *see* 11.42
	不成其為　不成其为	bùchéng qíwéi	V: 不能把他當作; 不能把他当作; not good enough to be; cannot be considered as: *EX 4.VI;* 為/为: *cf.* 2.16, 11.14, 22.12, 22.20, 23.5, 42.12
	曲調；調（子）　曲调；调（子）	qǔdiào; diào(zi)	N: melody; tune; 曲: *cf.* 11.43 調/调: *cf.* 1.6, 8.1, 30.7
	隨手　随手	suíshǒu	CVO: handily; at hand; conveniently; 隨/随: *see* 4.16
	收起來　收起来	shōu qǐlái	RV: to put away; 收: *cf.* 11.44, 11.55
8	考慮　考虑	kǎolǜ	V: to think over; to consider; 考: *cf.* 9.50
	見笑　见笑	jiànxiào	V: to laugh at; to ridicule; to make fun of [VO]
10	彈奏　弹奏	tánzòu	V: to play (an instrument); 彈/弹: *see* 7.48
11	起初	qǐchū	MA: in the beginning; at first
	指法	zhǐfǎ	N: fingering pattern; 指: *see* 5.19

	旋律		xuánlǜ	N: melody; 律: cf. 12.24
12	感染		gǎnrǎn	V: to affect; to move; to infect
	凝神（地）		níngshén (de)	A: with fixed attention [VO]
	彷彿	仿佛	fǎngfú	MA/V: 好像
	首		shǒu	M: (for songs, pieces of music, poems) cf. 25.3, 33.1, 55.3
	樂曲	乐曲	yuèqǔ	N: musical composition; music; 樂/乐: cf. 5.16; 曲: cf. 11.43
14	喚起	唤起	huànqǐ	RV: to call to mind; to recall; to arouse; 喚/唤: see 22.21
	段		duàn	M: section; segment; part; length; passage; cf. 17.28, 46.14

第十四景

1	西湖		Xīhú	PN: （地名）West Lake: famed tourist spot in Hángzhōu, Zhèjiāng Province
	月色		yuèsè	N: moonlight
	曚曨	曚昽	ménglóng	SV: dim; hazy
	吹蕩	吹荡	chuīdàng	V: lit., to blow and swing: "swinging in the breeze"
	垂柳		chuíliǔ	N: weeping willow
	留髮	留发	liú fǎ; liú fà	VO: to wear one's hair; 留: see 18.5; cf. 62.1
2	遊人	游人	yóurén	N: tourist; 遊/游: see 54.3; cf. 9.55, 21.22
	方苹		Fāng Píng	PN: （人名）方: cf. 7.18, 25.7, 34.1, 40.28, 40.31, 42.1
3	挽着膀子 膀子		wǎnzhe bǎngzi bǎngzi	VO: to be arm in arm; to link arms N: arm

4	V 定		V dìng	RV: V until fixed; V fast
8	自殺		zìshā	V: to kill oneself; to commit suicide
9	多餘 餘	多余 余	duōyú yú	SV: unnecessary; excessive AT/N: remaining; leftover; surplus
	監視	监视	jiānshì	V: to keep watch on; to guard; 視/视: *see* 2.4
	犯人		fànrén	N: criminal; prisoner
11	僵窘 窘		jiāngjiǒng jiǒng	SV: stiff and awkward; ill at ease V: to embarrass SV: to be embarrassed
12	責怪；怪	责怪；怪	zéguài; guài	V: to blame; 怪: *cf.* 7.41
	叫 N（給）VE	叫 N（给）VE	jiào N (gěi) VE	PAT: (passive construction) 讓 N（給）VE: 让 N（给）VE: *EX 5.VII;* 叫: *cf.* 1.5, 7.7, 8.3
	人家		rénjiā	Pn: others; *cf.* 8.6

第十五景

1	突然		tūrán; túrán	MA: suddenly; abruptly
	中斷	中断	zhōngduàn	V: to break off in the middle; to suspend
3	誤會	误会	wùhuì	V/N: to misunderstand; 會/会: *cf.* 35.21, 38.11
4	杭州		Hángzhōu	PN:（地名）city in Zhèjiāng Province
	葛嶺	葛岭	Gélǐng	PN:（地名）
7	傻	傻	shǎ	SV: stupid; dumb
10	風暴	风暴	fēngbào	N: storm; tempest
	開除	开除	kāichú	V: to expel

11	作官		zuòguān	VO: to be an official
	得發	得发	défā	V: to gain position and wealth [VO]
	徬徨	彷徨	pánghuáng	SV/N: pacing back and forth, not knowing what to do; indecisive
12	用力(地)		yònglì (de)	A: forcefully
	用力		yònglì	VO/SV: to exert oneself; to use one's force or strength
16	無意中	无意中	wúyì zhōng	L Ph: lit., in the midst of not having any intentions: unintentionally, accidentally, unwittingly; 無/无: see 1.9
	無意	无意	wúyì	VO: to have no intention; to have no interest in
	暴露		bàolù; pùlù	V: to expose; to reveal
	弱點	弱点	ruòdiǎn	N: weak points
17	克服		kèfú	V: to overcome; to surmount; 服: cf. 40.27, 57.40.
	教育		jiàoyù	N/V: education
19	認真	认真	rènzhēn	SV (A): lit., to take as real: earnest; serious [VO]
	思索		sīsuǒ	V: to think hard; to ponder

第十六景

1	攤(子)	摊(子)	tān(zi)	N: vendor's booth, stall, stand

第十七景

1	鈴	铃	líng	N: bell
	噹	当	dāng	ON: ding-dong

響	响	xiǎng	V: to sound; to make a noise SV: loud; noisy
課堂	课堂	kètáng	N: classroom
2 教務	教务	jiàowù; jiàowu	N: educational administration; *cf.* 25.3
初中 = 初級中學	初级中学	chūzhōng= chūjí zhōngxué	N: junior high school; middle school; lit., beginning levels of middle (i.e., high) school
年級	年级	niánjí	N: grade; year (in school)
3 張望	张望	zhāngwàng	V: to look around; 望: *see* 2.2; *cf.* 2.18, 39.5, 53.28
4 位子		wèizi	N: seat; place
5 肅靜	肃静	sùjìng	SV: solemnly silent; 靜/静: *see* 1.2
級長	级长	jízhǎng	N: class head; class monitor; 長/长: *see* 4.5; *cf.* 7.7, 22.21, 60.20
6 號令	号令	hàolìng	N: verbal command; 令: *see* 57.40; *cf.* 7.5
起立		qǐlì	V: to stand up; 立: *cf.* 12.5
鞠躬		jūgōng	VO: to bow
盯		dīng	V: to fix (one's gaze) on; to stare
7 講台	讲台	jiǎngtái	N: dais; rostrum
8 級任老師	级任老师	jírèn lǎoshī	N: teacher responsible for the class; homeroom teacher; 師/师: *cf.* 12.24, 55.10
能夠	能够	nénggòu	AV: to be able to; to be capable of
接受		jiēshòu	V: to accept; 接: *see* 4.13; 受: *cf.* 1.11, 7.44, 11.43, 25.16, 28.15
聘請	聘请	pìnqǐng	N/V: job offer or invitation
任教 任		rènjiào rèn	VO: to take on a teaching post V: to take on a responsibility, a job; to serve in a position; to appoint to a position

9	光榮	光荣	guāngróng	N/SV: honor; glory; 光: *cf.* 2.16, 4.1, 4.6, 11.34, 21.1, 37.16, 41.11
	幸福		xìngfú	N/SV: good fortune; well-being; happiness
	廣闊	广阔	guǎngkuò	SV: broad; vast
10	淵博	渊博	yuānbó	SV: profound and wide-ranging
11	截住		jiézhù	RV: to cut off; to stop; to intercept; 住: *see* 11.4
13	美德		měidé	N: virtue; moral excellence
	稱得起(是)	称得起(是)	chēngdeqǐ (shì)	RV: to deserve to be called; to be worthy of the name; 是: *cf.* 6.2, 62.2
	品學並茂	品学并茂	pǐn xué bìngmào	SV: equally excellent in both moral character and academic learning; 品: *cf.* 13.4, 39.2; 並/并: *cf.* 9.14, 19.5, 22.33
	值得		zhíde	V/SV: to be worth; to merit; to deserve
	仿效		fǎngxiào	V: to imitate; to follow the example of
	用心(地)		yòngxīn (de)	A: diligently; with concentrated attention
	用心		yòngxīn	VO/SV: to concentrate one's diligence on; to pay great attention to
	求教		qiújiào	VO: to seek instruction; ask for advice; 求: *see* 12.53
14	拍手		pāishǒu	VO: to clap hands; to applaud
15	提示		tíshì	N/V: prompt; 提: *cf.* 6.10, 49.17
	鼓掌		gǔzhǎng	VO: to clap hands; to applaud
16	窘迫		jiǒngpò	SV (A): embarrassed and hard-pressed; caught in a predicament; 窘: *see* 14.11
	點名簿	点名簿	diǎnmíng bù	N: roll book
	點名	点名	diǎnmíng	VO: to do roll call

17	藉此	借此	jiècǐ	CVO: lit., to take this (as an opportunity): to take advantage of this: EX 7.III; 此: see 11.46
18	滿意	满意	mǎnyì	SV (A): satisfied; pleased; 滿足／满足: cf. 12.53
	退出		tuìchū	RV: to withdraw; to retreat; to exit; to quit; 退: cf. 40.26
19	余志雄		Yú Zhìxióng	PN:（人名）
21	黃文平		Huáng Wénpíng	PN:（人名）
24	應聲	应声	yìngshēng	VO: to respond; to answer N: echo; 應／应: cf. 57.23
	林月仙		Lín Yuèxiān	PN:（人名）
25	辮子	辫子	biànzi	N: braid
	綁	绑	bǎng	V: to tie; to bind
28	段王海		Duàn Wánghǎi	PN:（人名）段: cf. 13.14, 46.14
30	王福生		Wáng Fúshēng	PN:（人名）生: cf. 1.3, 5.18, 7.50, 11.3, 19.5, 52.29
	回聲	回声	huíshēng	VO: to respond N: echo
32	復	复	fù	A: to repeat; again
	請假	请假	qǐngjià	VO: to ask for leave; 假: cf. 20.6, 53.15
33	經常	经常	jīngcháng	A: frequently; often
	遲到	迟到	chídào	V: to arrive late
35	收拾		shōushi	V: to put in order; to tidy; to pack; 收: cf. 11.44, 11.55; 拾: cf. 2.2
	早點	早点	zǎodiǎn	N: 早飯 早饭
	擔（子）	担（子）	dàn(zi)	N/M: load carried on a shoulder pole; cf. 5.4, 9.59, 19.32, 31.14, 41.9

鄉村	乡村	xiāngcūn	N: lit., (rural) village: country
氣息	气息	qìxī; qìxí	N: flavor; air; 息: cf. 25.3, 52.19
36 汗		hàn	N: sweat; perspiration
緊張	紧张	jǐnzhāng	SV: nervous; tense; 緊/紧: see 1.10
放慢		fàngmàn	V: to slow down
放		fàng	V: to relax; to release; to set free; to let go
38 悄悄（地）		qiāoqiāo (de)	A: quietly; stealthily
初一		chūyī	N: 初中一年級 初中一年级
39 害怕		hàipà	SV: afraid; scared; 害: cf. 7.15, 37.23, 57.43
41 黑板		hēibǎn	N: blackboard
課文	课文	kèwén	N: lesson text
招手		zhāoshǒu	VO: to beckon; to summon by waving
43 羞愧		xiūkuì	SV (A): ashamed; mortified
49 亮		liàng	SV: (to get) bright, light, shiny
態度	态度	tàidù; tàidu	N: attitude; manner
減低	减低	jiǎndī	RV: to lessen; to lower
52 默然		mòrán	SV (A): silent
53 口氣	口气	kǒuqì	N: tone of voice
稍微（地）		shāowēi (de); shāowéi (de)	A: slightly; a little; 微: see 2.19
急迫		jípò	SV: pressing; urgent
54 擦		cā	V: to wipe
55 轉而	转而	zhuǎn'ér	C: turning; changing to; shifting: EX 7.IV; 轉/转: see 1.9; 而: cf. 4.4, 9.28, 11.14, 12.42, 25.8, 57.43

| 56 | 解脱 | | jiětuō | V: to be freed; 脱: cf. 39.4 |

第十八景

1	禮物	礼物	lǐwù	N: present; gift
3	孝敬		xiàojìng	V: to show filial piety and respect for parents and superiors, often by presenting them with gifts
4	小意思		xiǎoyìsi	N: a small token of regard (e.g. gift)
5	欣喜		xīnxǐ	SV (A): happy; delighted
	不敢當	不敢当	bù gǎndāng	SE: "I don't deserve this"; "you flatter me" (polite response to a compliment); 當/当: cf. 2.1, 5.2, 5.3, 11.37, 24.2, 24.4, 49.29, 52.2, 57.23
	留		liú	V: to keep, reserve, save; cf. 62.1
6	千萬	千万	qiānwàn	A: (emphatic, used in injunctions) "whatever you do"; "by all means"; "be sure to"; "under no circumstances should you"; absolutely
	十分		shífēn	A/N: 100%; completely; fully
	懇切	恳切	kěnqiè	SV: sincere; earnest
7	接納	接纳	jiēnà	V: to accept; 接: see 4.13
9	答應	答应	dāyìng	V: to answer; to respond; cf. 6.12; 應/应: cf. 57.23
10	泡茶		pàochá	VO: to brew tea
12	心神不寧	心神不宁	xīnshén bùníng	SV (A): uneasy; restless

第十九景

1	放學	放学	fàngxué	VO: to have school finish (for the day); 放: *see* 17.36
	愉快		yúkuài	SV (A): happy; cheerful; joyful; 快: *cf.* 27.14
	操場	操场	cāochǎng	N: playground; athletic field
2	出神		chūshén	VO (A): to be absorbed in, spellbound
3	甚至(於)	甚至(于)	shènzhì(yú)	C: even (to the point of): *EX 4.III*; 至: *see* 1.2; 於/于: *see* 55.12; *cf.* 45.13
	稚氣	稚气	zhìqì	N: childishness
	跟前		gēnqián	L Ph: in front of; near (said of people)
4	抛		pāo	V: to throw; to toss
	扔		rēng	V: to throw; to toss
5	連跑帶跳地	连跑带跳地	liánpǎo dàitiào de	A: running and skipping: *EX 4.IV*; 跳: *see* 12.2; 帶/带: *cf.* 55.2
	並肩	并肩	bìngjiān	CVO: shoulder to shoulder; side by side; 並/并: *cf.* 9.14, 17.13, 22.33
	新生		xīnshēng	V: to be newborn; 生: *cf.* 1.3, 5.18, 7.45, 7.50, 11.3, 17.30, 40.5
	含苞待放		hánbāo dàifàng	V: to have buds about to open [VO]: *EX 4.II*; 含: *see* 11.12; 待: *see* 8.1; *cf.* 7.23, 12.6; 放: *see* 17.36
6	桃李		táolǐ	N: peach and plum
	穿行		chuānxíng	V: to pass through; 行: *cf.* 1.4, 7.52, 43.7
8	純潔	纯洁	chúnjié	SV: innocent; pure and clean
9	除此以外		chúcǐ yǐwài	C: aside from this [CV Ph]; 此: *see* 11.46; 以: *cf.* 5.6, 7.52, 31.12, 40.30, 42.2, 42.12
	反問	反问	fǎnwèn	V: to ask a question in reply

10	所 V 的		suǒ V de	PAT: that which one V's (emphasizes object of the V); 所: *cf.* 2.16, 7.52, 37.22, 46.16
	順利	顺利	shùnlì	SV: smooth; without a hitch; to go well; 順/顺: *see* 7.13
	平安		píng'ān	SV: safe and sound; secure; stable; peaceful
11	質樸	质朴	zhípǔ; zhìpǔ	SV: simple; unadorned; unaffected; straightforward
12	不盡然	不尽然	bújìnrán	SV/A: lit., not completely so: not necessarily so, not exactly as supposed
	藏		cáng	V: to hide; to conceal; to store
	奸刁		jiāndiāo	N/SV: wickedness; treachery; villainy
	伏		fú	V: to hide; to conceal; *cf.* 24.1, 35.11
13	紛擾	纷扰	fēnrǎo	N/SV: confusion; disorder; turmoil
15	奔波		bēnbō	V: to be constantly on the run; to be on the go; 奔: *see* 6.12
	乍一		zhàyī	A: suddenly
	鄉鎮	乡镇	xiāngzhèn	N: village; (small) town; 鎮/镇: *see* 1.2; *cf.* 25.7, 45.3
	新鮮	新鲜	xīnxiān	SV: fresh; new; novel
16	羨慕		xiànmù	V: to admire; to envy
	自由		zìyóu	N/SV: freedom; 由: *see* 30.17; *cf.* 5.18, 43.7
	籠子	笼子	lóngzi	N: cage
17	（大）雁		(dà)yàn	N: wild goose
18	孤雁		gūyàn	N: solitary goose (as opposed to the conventional understanding of geese in flocks)
19	撫慰	抚慰	fǔwèi	V: to comfort; to console

	孤單	孤单	gūdān	SV: lonely; friendless; 單/单: see 7.7; cf. 40.31
	悲涼		bēiliáng	N/SV: sad melancholy; mournful desolation
22	默默（地）		mòmò (de)	A: silently
23	掠過	掠过	lüèguò	V: to sweep past; to graze
	飄落	飘落	piāoluò	V: to float down; 落: see 1.1; cf. 7.51, 61.2
24	客房		kèfáng	N: guest quarters
	關於	关于	guānyú	CV: with regard to; concerning; about; on; 於/于: see 55.12; cf. 45.13
28	活躍	活跃	huóyuè	SV: animated; lively; 躍/跃: cf. 12.2
31	哦		ó	P: (interjection expressing surprise) "oh?" Cf. 2.13
32	擔任	担任	dānrèn	V: to take on (a job or responsibilites); 擔/担: see 5.4; cf. 17.35; 任: see 17.8
	休養	休养	xiūyǎng	V: to rest; to recuperate
33	拿 N 沒辦法	拿 N 没办法	ná N méi bànfǎ	PAT: can't do anything about N: EX 4.V
34	紅暈	红暈	hóngyūn; hóngyùn	N: blush; flush
	暈	晕	yūn; yùn	N: mist; halo; cf. 62.4

第二十景

1	盞	盏	zhǎn	M: (for lamps)
	冒煙	冒烟	màoyān	VO: to emit smoke
	凳子		dèngzi	N: stool
	摟	搂	lǒu	V: to hold in one's arms; to hug

2	剝皮	剥皮	bāopí; bōpí	VO: to peel the skin; to shell; to skin; 皮: cf. 30.7
	毫不 SV		háobù SV	A: 一點兒都不 SV: 一点儿都不 SV: *EX 8.II*
6	依		yī	V: to comply with; to listen to;
	假裝 假	假装	jiǎzhuāng jiǎ	V: to pretend; to feign; 裝/装: cf. 1.7 SV/A: false; fake; artificial; *cf.* 17.32, 46.13
7	阿寶	阿宝	Ābǎo	PN:（人名）阿: *see* 5.4
	溫柔	温柔	wēnróu	SV (A): soft and gentle
9	失去		shīqù	V: to lose
	（習）慣 習慣	（习）惯 习惯	(xí)guàn xíguàn	SV: accustomed to; used to N: habit; custom
10	關心	关心	guānxīn	V (A): to be concerned about
17	添		tiān	V: to add to; to increase

第二十一景

1	幽麗	幽丽	yōulì	SV: serene, tranquil beauty
	陽光	阳光	yángguāng	N: sunlight; 光: cf. 4.6, 7.2, 11.34, 17.9, 37.16, 41.11
	鍍金	镀金	dùjīn	VO: to plate with gold
	甜蜜		tiánmì	SV: sweet
2	青苗		qīngmiáo	N: green shoots (of grain, commonly referring to rice)
	頓然（地）	顿然（地）	dùnrán (de)	A: suddenly; abruptly; 頓/顿: cf. 30.31, 52.19
	悠悠（地）		yōuyōu (de)	A: leisurely; slowly; unhurried
3	清澈		qīngchè	SV: clear; limpid

	爭	争	zhēng	V: to strive; to fight for
7	整		zhěng	V: 整理; to adjust; to straighten out
12	哄		hǒng	V: to humor; to coax
14	喜悦		xǐyuè	SV: happy; delighted
18	自個兒	自个儿	zìgěr	Pn: 自己
19	讓	让	ràng	V: to let; to allow; cf. 4.23, 6.9, 49.16, 57.13, EX 5.VII
21	牽手	牵手	qiānshǒu	VO: to hold hands
	登		dēng	V: to go up; to climb; to mount
	階石	阶石	jiēshí	N: stone steps
22	皮球		píqiú	N: rubber ball; 皮: cf. 30.7
	做遊戲	做游戏	zuò yóuxì	VO: to play games
	遊戲	游戏	yóuxì	N/V: game; 遊/游: see 54.3; cf. 9.55, 14.2
	（老）鷹	（老）鹰	(lǎo)yīng	N: hawk; eagle
	捉		zhuō	V: to catch; to capture

第二十二景

1	側後	侧后	cèhòu	L: diagonally behind
2	哼		hēng	V: to hum; cf. 7.7
	歌曲		gēqǔ	N: tune; melody; song; 曲: cf. 11.43
3	忍不住		rěnbúzhù	RV: cannot help; cannnot stop (oneself); 住: see 11.4
6	焦急		jiāojí	SV: anxious; worried
	支持		zhīchí	V/N: to sustain; to hold out

9	抽屜	抽屉	chōutì	N: drawer; 抽: *see* 1.11; *cf.* 24.1
	精緻	精致	jīngzhì	SV: fine; exquisite
	殷勤		yīnqín	SV (A)/N: eagerly attentive; solicitous
11	推卻	推却	tuīquè	V: to refuse; 推: *see* 7.13; 卻/却: *cf.* 4.15
12	既然		jìrán	C: since
	一半(是) X; 一半(是) Y		yíbàn (shì) X; yíbàn (shì) Y	PAT: partly (it's) X and partly (it's) Y; 是: *cf.* 6.2, 62.2
	為了	为了	wèile	V/CV: for the purpose of; in order to; for the sake of; 為/为: *cf.* 2.16, 13.6, 23.5, 36.4, 42.12
	愛護	爱护	àihù	V: to take good care of; to cherish
13	禮貌	礼貌	lǐmào	N: good manners; politeness
16	備課	备课	bèikè	VO: to prepare lessons for class (said of teachers); 備/备: *cf.* 24.6
	。。。心切		...xīnqiè	SV: eager; anxious; with all one's heart; whole-hearted (typically occurs in complement of degree construction)
	廢寢忘食	废寝忘食	fèiqǐn wàngshí	SV: to go without sleep and forget to eat [VOVO]: *EX 4.VII*
18	喪氣	丧气	sàngqì	SV (A): disheartened; discouraged; dejected [VO]
19	尷尬	尴尬	gān'gà	SV (A): embarrassed; awkward
20	僵局		jiāngjú	N: deadlock; impasse
	為此	为此	wèicǐ	CVO: because of this; for this purpose; thus: *EX 7.III*; 為/为: *cf.* 2.16, 13.6, 23.5, 36.4, 42.12; 此: *see* 11.46
	圍攏	围拢	wéilǒng	V: to crowd around; 圍/围: *see* 9.3

問長問短	问长问短	wèncháng wènduǎn	V: 問這個，問那個； 问这个，问那个； to make detailed inquiries [VOVO] 長/长: *cf.* 4.5, 17.5, 41.4, 46.11
21 招呼		zhāohu	V/N: to greet; to say hello; *cf.* 57.14
一一		yīyī	A: one by one; one after another: *EX 6.V*
喚	唤	huàn	V: 叫
25 塞		sāi	V: to fill; to stuff
28 眉目之間 之間	眉目之间 之间	méimù zhījiān zhījiān	L Ph: (facial) features; looks L: between; amongst
30 稱贊	称赞	chēngzàn	V: to praise; to commend
啊		à	P: (interjection expressing approval, delight, pleasure) "Ah!" *Cf.* 2.10, 4.17, 4.23, 7.8
咱們	咱们	zánmen	Pn: (inclusive) we; you and I
31 孔雀		kǒngquè	N: peacock; 孔: *cf.* 11.17, 35.9; 46.2
33 並且	并且	bìngqiě	C: and; besides; moreover; 並/并: *cf.* 9.14, 17.13, 19.5
伸出		shēnchū	RV: to reach out; to extend
34 各		gè	A: each; separately; *cf.* 5.1, 8.1
拉手		lāshǒu	VO: lit., to pull or tug the hand: to hold hands; to shake hands; 拉: *see* 12.11

第二十三景

1 蓋板	盖板	gàibǎn	N: piano keyboard cover; 蓋/盖: *see* 11.53

2	不便 VE		búbiàn VE	V: to be inappropriate, unsuitable to VE: *EX 5.I*
	不便		búbiàn	SV: inconvenient
	打擾	打扰	dǎrǎo	V: to disturb
3	隱約（地）	隐约（地）	yǐnyuē (de)	A: indistinctly; faintly; obscurely; 約: *cf.* 4.5, 44.16
	隱	隐	yǐn	V/A: to hide
5	弄		nòng	V: to do; to handle; to make into a particular condition
	為難	为难	wéinán	SV: to feel awkward or embarrassed V: to make things difficult or awkward for sb.; 為/为: *cf.* 2.16, 11.14, 13.6, 22.12, 22.20, 36.4; 難/难: *cf.* 7.7, 7.10
6	莫名其妙		mòmíng qímiào	SV (A): baffled, bewildered, uncomprending; baffling; incomprehensible, inexplicable; 莫: *see* 31.9; 妙: *see* 9.18
7	曾經 V（過）	曾经 V（过）	céngjīng V (guò)	PAT: to have V-ed before: *EX 5.II*
9	娶		qǔ	V: to take as a wife
10	條件	条件	tiáojiàn	N: conditions; terms
	修改		xiūgǎi	V: to revise; to modify
	改		gǎi	V: to change; to correct; to amend
11	媒人		méirén	N: matchmaker
	商量		shāngliang	V: to consult; to talk over; 商: *cf.* 1.3
	訂婚	订婚	dìnghūn	VO: to get engaged (to be married)
	訂	订	dìng	V: to set; to agree on
	日期		rìqī	N: date
12	大哭大鬧	大哭大闹	dàkū dànào	V: to yell and scream; to have a fit; to throw a tantrum
	鬧	闹	nào	V: to make a scene; *cf.* 7.15 SV: noisy; loud

第二十四景

1	伏		fú	V: to lie face down; *cf.* 19.12, 35.11
	抽泣		chōuqì	V: to sob; 抽: *cf.* 1.11, 22.9
	泣		qì	V: to weep silently
2	勸	劝	quàn	V: (pre-pivotal) to urge; to persuade; to exhort
	當初	当初	dāngchū	T: at first; in the beginning [CVO]; 當/当: *cf.* 5.2, 5.3, 11.37, 18.5, 24.4, 49.29, 55.3, 57.23
4	帶氣地	带气地	dàiqì de	A: angrily; huffily; 帶/带: *cf.* 55.2
	當真	当真	dàngzhēn	V: to take seriously; to take as true [VO]; 當/当: *cf.* 2.1, 5.2, 5.3, 11.37, 18.5, 24.2, 49.29, 52.2, 55.3, 57.23
5	任性		rènxìng	SV: to do as one pleases; willful; headstrong; unrestrained; uninhibited [VO]; 任: *see* 17.8
	終身大事	终身大事	zhōngshēn dàshì	N: great event in one's life (often referring to marriage)
	兒戲	儿戏	érxì	N: a trifling matter; lit., game for children
6	責備	责备	zébèi	N/V: reproach; reprimand; rebuke; 備/备: *cf.* 22.16
	輕聲輕語	轻声轻语	qīngshēng qīngyǔ	SV: softly spoken; gently put; 輕/轻: *see* 2.1
7	猛然（地）		měngrán (de)	A: suddenly; abruptly; violently
	猛		měng	SV: fierce; fearsome
	倔強	倔强	juéqiáng; juèjiàng	SV: stubborn; unbending

第二十五景

| 1 | 訴說 | 诉说 | sùshuō | V: to tell; to recount (one's troubles) |

2	案(子)		àn(zi)	N: case (of law); 案: *cf.* 8.1
3	消息		xiāoxi	N: news; information; report; 消: *cf.* 4.6, 44.11; 息: *cf.* 17.35, 52.19
	首先		shǒuxiān	MA: first of all; in the first place; 首: *see* 33.1; *cf.* 13.12
	辭退	辞退	cítuì	V: to resign; to dismiss; to quit; 退: *cf.* 40.26
	教務	教务	jiàowù; jiàowu	N: 教書的事; 教书的事; *cf.* 17.2
4	本地		běndì	N: this place; 地 (dì): *cf.* 11.10
	地位		dìwèi	N: position; standing; status
	士紳	士绅	shìshēn	N: gentleman; gentry
	面子		miànzi	N: lit., "face": reputation; prestige
	決不		juébù	A: under no circumstances; in no way
5	精明		jīngmíng	SV: keen; sharp; astute
	代		dài	CV/V: 替; to substitute for
6	疑心		yíxīn	V: to doubt; to suspect [VO]
	誠實	诚实	chéngshí	SV: honest
	有意(地) 有意		yǒuyì (de) yǒuyì	A: intentionally; on purpose VO: to have great interest; to have a mind to
7	鎮靜	镇静	zhènjìng	SV (A): self-composed; calm; cool V: to compose or calm (oneself); 鎮/镇: *cf.* 1.2, 19.15, 41.4; 靜/静: *see* 1.2
	拖延		tuōyán	V: to delay; to put off; to drag out; to stall
	對方	对方	duìfāng	N: the other side; 方: *cf.* 4.11, 7.18, 14.2, 40.28, 40.31, 42.1
	冷淡		lěngdàn	SV: (to become) disinterested, cool, indifferent V: to treat coldly

8	而		ér	C: but: *EX 5.IV; cf.* 4.4, 9.28, 11.14, 12.42, 17.55, 42.5
10	取笑		qǔxiào	V (A): to make a joke; to poke fun [VO]; 取: *see* 40.28
12	仍舊	仍旧	réngjiù	A: as before; still
	笑話	笑话	xiàohua	V: to laugh at; to ridicule N: joke
14	繞	绕	rào	V: to go around (in a circle)
	圈		quān	N/M/V: ring; circle
16	受刺		shòucì	VO: to be stung, wounded; 受: *see* 7.44; *cf.* 1.11, 17.8; 刺: *see* 7.44
	急忙(地)		jímáng (de)	A: hurriedly; hastily
18	懇求	恳求	kěnqíu	V: (pre-pivotal) to implore; to plead; to beseech; 求: *see* 12.53

第二十六景

1	背過身去	背过身去	bèiguò shēnqù	V: to turn one's back; to turn away; 背: *see* 11.57
2	拭		shì	V: to wipe away
	一同		yìtóng	A: together; 同: *see* 55.24; *cf.* 2.3, 2.16, 7.5, 43.3
4	突破		tūpò; túpò	V/N: to break through
7	認 N1 作 N2	认 N1 作 N2	rèn N1 zuò N2	PAT: to recognize N1 as N2: *EX 5.V*
	乾女兒	干女儿	gān nǚ'ér	N: nominal daughter; "adopted" daughter; 乾/干: *cf.* 35.7, 49.2
10	根本		gēnběn	A/N: at all; simply
11	傳	传	chuán	V: to spread; to transmit; to pass on

| 13 全然（地） | | quánrán (de) | A: completely; 完全 |

第二十七景

1 等候		děnghòu	V: to wait for; to expect; 等: cf. 1.8; 候: cf. 2.1
2 眺望		tiàowàng	V: to look into the distance; 望: see 2.2; cf. 2.18, 39.5, 53.28
母女		mǔnǚ	N: 母親與女兒 母亲与女儿
3 挑		tiāo	V: to carry with a shoulder pole
柴		chái	N: firewood
8 靠		kào	V/CV: to rely on; to depend on; cf. 2.3, 45.4
9 交齊	交齐	jiāoqí	RV: paid completely; paid off; 交: cf. 9.1, 46.10
12 砍		kǎn	V: to cut; to chop
14 趕快（地）	赶快（地）	gǎnkuài (de)	A: quickly; in a hurry; 趕/赶: cf. 44.18; 快: cf. 4.15, 5.16, 19.1
17 焦慮	焦虑	jiāolǜ	SV: anxious; apprehensive; to have misgivings

第二十八景

3 彎腰	弯腰	wānyāo	VO: to bend down (lit., at the waist); to stoop
4 撲	扑	pū	V: to throw oneself on; to rush at
7 照顧	照顾	zhàogù; zhàogu	V: to take care of; to look after; 顧/顾: see 9.25

8	懷疑	怀疑	huáiyí	V/ N: doubtful; suspicious; skeptical; 懷/怀: *see* 2.5
11	性急		xìngjí	SV (A): impatient; short-tempered
	究竟		jiūjìng; jìujìng	MA: exactly; really; actually; after all; in the end: *EX 5.VI;* 究: *cf.* 55.37
12	掩飾	掩饰	yǎnshì	V: to cover up; to gloss over
	痛苦		tòngkǔ	N/SV: pain; suffering; 苦: *see* 5.8
13	不安		bù'ān	SV: uneasy; disturbed
14	呼吸		hūxī	V: lit., to exhale and inhale: to breathe; 吸: *see* 2.1
15	固執	固执	gùzhi	SV (A): stubborn; obstinate; persistent
	受累		shòulèi	VO: to be overburdened; to be inconvenienced; 受: *see* 7.44; *cf.* 1.11, 17.8
16	僅僅（地）	仅仅（地）	jǐnjǐn (de)	A: only; merely; barely (emphatic); 僅/仅: *see* 7.3
17	順路	顺路	shùnlù	SV/VO: on the way; convenient; 順/顺: *see* 7.13
22	婦女	妇女	fùnǚ	N: women
	指指戳戳		zhǐzhǐ chuōchuō	V: to make remarks or criticisms while pointing; 指: *see* 5.19
	戳		chuō	V: to jab; to poke; to pierce
	竊竊私議	窃窃私议	qièqiè sīyì	V: to exchange whispered comments; to gossip furtively
23	剩下		shèngxià	RV: to be left; to be remaining

第二十九景

| 1 | 淘氣 | 淘气 | táoqì | SV: naughty; mischievous |

5	結結 巴巴(地) 結巴	结结 巴巴(地) 结巴	jiējiē bābā (de) jiēba	A: stuttering; stammering V: to stutter; to stammer N: one who stammers
	罵	骂	mà	V: to curse; to swear; to call names; to scold
8	野爸爸		yě bàba	N: illegitimate father
9	雷擊 雷 擊	雷击 击	léijī; léijí léi jī; jí	V: to have lightning strike N: thunder (and lightning) V: to hit; to strike; to attack
	腦子	脑子	nǎozi	N: lit., brain: head
	作響	作响	zuòxiǎng	V: to break out in the sounds of; to make noise; to reverberate [VO]; 響/响: see 17.1
11	果然		guǒrán	MA: as expected; sure enough: *EX 5.III*
	湧	涌	yǒng	V: to gush; to well up; to surge
	烏	乌	wū	SV: black; dark

第三十景

1	陰沈	阴沉	yīnchén	SV: cloudy; overcast; gloomy
	細	细	xì	SV: fine; thin; exquisite; minute; meticulous
	夜幕		yèmù	N: lit., curtain of night: gathering darkness
	將要	将要	jiāngyào	AV: (used with affirmative statements indicating sometime in the future) to be going to; will; shall; 將/将: *cf.* 1.9; 要: *cf.* 12.53, 30.7
4	心思		xīnsī	N: thoughts; state of mind
6	開飯	开饭	kāifàn	V: to start serving food (in the cafeteria) [VO]

7	調皮	调皮	tiáopí	SV (A): naughty; mischievous; 調/调: cf. 1.6, 8.1, 13.6; 皮: cf. 1.7, 1.8, 4.11, 20.2, 21.22
	要挾	要挟	yāoxié	V/N: to threaten; to pressure; to coerce; 要: cf. 2.9, 12.53, 30.1
11	寂寞		jímò; jìmò	SV: lonely; cold and still
12	心事		xīnshì	N: sth. on one's mind; preoccupation with sth.; worry
15	否認 否	否认	fǒurèn fǒu	V: to deny: EX 6.III A: not (negates verb): EX 6.III
	辭職	辞职	cízhí	VO: to resign (a job)
16	冷漠		lěngmò	SV (A): cold and detached; unconcerned; indifferent
17	職務	职务	zhíwù	N: post; duties; job
	原因		yuányīn	N: cause; reason; 原: cf. 7.30
	由於	由于	yóuyú	CV/C: owing to; due to; 於/于: see 55.12; cf. 45.13
	由		yóu	CV: from; via; by; through; cf. 5.18, 43.7
18	隨口	随口	suíkǒu	CVO: to say immediately without thinking; 隨/随: see 4.16
20	狐疑		húyí	SV (A)/N: lit., suspicousness of a fox: very suspicious; full of misgivings
21	不知 不覺（地）	不知 不觉（地）	bùzhī bùjué (de)	A: without noticing; unconsciously; unaware
22	愛上	爱上	àishàng; àishang	RV: to fall in love with
23	悔不該 V	悔不该 V	huǐ bùgāi V	V: to regret V (lit., redundant expression "to regret" + "should not have" V)
25	吃吃地		jíjí de	A: (onomatopoeia) stuttering; 吃: cf. 8.7

	更加(地)	gèngjiā (de)	A: even more: *EX 6.1*
26	炸裂	zhàliè	V: to explode; to blow up/open
	迷濛	míméng	SV: misty; indistinct; hazy
28	無論 Question　无论 Question	wúlùn Question	C: no matter Question; 無/无: *see 1.9*
29	煩惱　烦恼	fánnǎo	SV/N: to have worries constantly weighing on one's mind; troubled; vexed
31	激動　激动	jīdòng	SV: excited; agitated
	頓　顿	dùn	V: to pause; 頓/顿: *cf. 21.2*
	囁嚅　嗫嚅	nièrú	V (A): to speak haltingly; to falter; to be unable to speak; to stammer
32	再三	zàisān	A: over and over again
	囑咐　嘱咐	zhǔfù; zhǔfu	V: to exhort; to tell
33	上帝	shàngdì	N: Lord on High; God
	隱瞞　隐瞒	yǐnmán	V: to hide or hold back (sth.); 隱/隐: *see 23.3*
	瞞　瞒	mán	V: to deceive; to hide the truth from
35	對於　对于	duìyú	CV: in regard to; to; for; 於/于: *see 55.12*; *cf. 45.13*
36	寬慰　宽慰	kuānwèi	N/V: comfort and consolation SV: comforted

第三十一景

1	安排	ānpái	V/N: to arrange
4	酒量	jiǔliàng	N: ability to hold one's liquor
5	往常	wǎngcháng	MA: always in the past
	騙　骗	piàn	V: to fool, to deceive

盡興	尽兴	jìnxìng	VO/SV (A): lit., to completely satisfy one's desires: to do sth. to one's heart's content; 興/兴: *cf.* 4.7, 5.2, 35.2, 55.10
8 須	须	xū	V: must; have to
9 醉		zuì	SV: drunk
莫		mò	A: (imperative) don't, 不要
使		shǐ	V: to use; to employ; to apply; *cf.* 1.9
金樽		jīnzūn	N: gold goblet

[1] *quotation from a poem by the Tang Dynasty poet* 李白 *Li Bai (701-762)*

10 眼色		yǎnsè	N: hint with the eyes; meaningful glance
一杯一杯地 一 M 一 M 地		yìbēi yìbēi de yì M yì M de	A: one cup after another A: one M after another; M by M: *EX 6.V*
禁不住		jīnbúzhù	RV (A): to not be able to refrain (from); to not be able to stop oneself; to not be able to bear it; 住: *see* 11.4
11 麻醉		mázuì	V: to anesthetize; 醉: *see* 31.9
12 毫未 VE		háowèi VE	A: 一點兒也沒有 VE; 一点儿也没有 VE; to have never VE before in the slightest to not have VE-ed at all: *EX 8.II*
未		wèi	A: not (yet)
何以		héyǐ	Q: how; why: *EX 6.IV;* 何: *see* 5.13; 以: *cf.* 5.6, 19.9, 40.30, 42.2, 42.12
解憂	解忧	jiěyōu	VO: to dispel worries
杜康		Dù Kāng	PN: (人名) allusion to wine, referring to the Zhōu 周 Dynasty wine maker.

13 [2] *quotation from a poem by* 曹操 *Cáo Cāo (AD 155-220)*

14 擔心(思) 擔心	担心(思) 担心	dānxīn(sī) dānxīn	VO: to worry SV: worried; 擔/担: *see* 5.4; *cf.* 17.35

16	藥	药	yào	N: drug; medicine
17	振奮	振奋	zhènfèn	SV: roused or invigorated; inspired; stimulated V: to rouse; to inspire; to invigorate
	勇敢		yǒnggǎn	SV: brave; courageous

第三十二景

1	錘頭	锤头	chuítóu	N: hammer
	猛力(地)		měnglì (de)	A: violently; with sudden force; 猛: *see* 24.7
	琴鍵	琴键	qínjiàn	N: keys on a musical keyboard; 琴: *see* 7.48
	奮發	奋发	fènfā	SV (A): rousing; vigorous
2	變異	变异	biànyì	N: change; alteration; variation; 變/变: *see* 7.11
3	逐漸(地)	逐渐(地)	zhújiàn (de)	A: gradually; 逐: *cf.* 37.9
	延續	延续	yánxù	V: to continue; to go on

第三十三景

1	昂首闊步	昂首阔步	ángshǒu kuòbù	V (A): to stride forward with head up; to stride proudly ahead [VOVO]; 步: *see* 4.12
	首		shǒu	N/AT/A: head; first; *cf.* 13.12
	越過	越过	yuèguò	RV: to cross; to go over
	拱橋	拱桥	gǒngqiáo	N: arched bridge
3	一把		yìbǎ	A: (in) one scoop
	揮手	挥手	huīshǒu	VO: to wave one's hand

第三十四景

1	雙方	双方	shuāngfāng	N: the two sides; both parties; 方: *cf.* 4.11, 7.18, 14.2, 40.28, 40.31, 42.1
	激烈		jīliè	SV (A): intense; fierce; heated
2	比賽	比赛	bǐsài	V/N: to compete
4	體統	体统	tǐtǒng	N: propriety; decency; decorum; 統/统: *cf.* 1.2, 1.7
5	文明		wénmíng	N/SV: civilization; culture
	表現	表现	biǎoxiàn	N/V: expression; manifestation

第三十五景

1	疲乏		pífá	SV: tired; weary
2	興奮	兴奋	xīngfèn	SV: excited; 興/兴: *cf.* 4.7, 5.2, 9.11, 9.22, 12.20, 31.5, 55.10
	激戰	激战	jīzhàn	V/N: to battle fiercely
	勝利者	胜利者	shènglì zhě	N: victor; winner
	VE 者		VE zhě	N: one who VE (nominalizer)
3	理		lǐ	V: 整理; to put in order; to arrange; *cf.* 7.39, 12.17, 12.53, 43.10
4	手巾		shǒujīn	N: lit., hand cloth: washcloth
	臉盆	脸盆	liǎnpén	N: wash basin
5	口渴		kǒukě	SV (A): thirsty
	越發（地）SV	越发（地）SV	yuèfā (de) SV	A: all the more SV; even more SV: *EX 6.VI*
7	擰乾	拧干	nǐnggān	RV: to wring dry; 乾/干: *cf.* 26.7
9	一瞬不瞬地		yíshùn búshùn de	A: unblinking

	柔嫩		róunèn	SV: tender; delicate; 嫩: *see* 1.1
	面孔		miànkǒng	N: face; 孔: *cf.* 11.17, 22.31, 46.2
10	睫毛		jiémáo	N: eyelashes
	襯	衬	chèn	V: to line; to set off
	眼珠		yǎnzhū	N: eyeball
	四周(圍)	四周(围)	sì zhōu(wéi)	L: lit., on all four sides: all around; 圍/围: *see* 9.3
	心胸		xīnxiōng	N: heart; chest
11	起伏		qǐfú	V: to rise and fall; to go up and down; 伏: *cf.* 19.12, 24.1
16	郵件	邮件	yóujiàn	N: mail
19	拆開	拆开	chāikāi	RV: to tear open
20	字樣	字样	zìyàng	N: lit., forms of characters: written or printed words
21	聚精會神	聚精会神	jùjīng huìshén	SV (A): lit., to concentrate the spirit: to do sth. with great concentration; to be absorbed [VOVO]: *EX 6.VII;* 會/会: *cf.* 15.3, 38.11, 43.10, 58.21
	討論	讨论	tǎolùn	V: to discuss

第三十六景

1	樓梯	楼梯	lóutī	N: stairs
4	認為	认为	rènwéi	V: to think; to consider; to deem; 為/为: *cf.* 2.16, 11.14, 22.12, 22.20, 23.5, 42.12

第三十七景

8	炯炯		jiǒngjiǒng	SV: (of eyes) bright and piercing
9	惡	恶	è	SV/N: evil, wicked; fierce, ferocious; *cf.* 4.9
	副		fù	M: (used for sets of things and expressions of emotions/character)
	心裁		xīncái	N: idea; conception; plan
	採	采	cǎi	V: to pick (plants, fruit)
	若		ruò	C: if; *cf.* 7.41
	驅逐	驱逐	qūzhú	V: to drive out; to expel; 逐: *cf.* 32.3
10	吾		wú	Pn: 我（們）；我（們）的 我（们）；我（们）的 (literary form)
	風化	风化	fēnghuà	N: morals and manners; 化: *cf.* 7.11
	安在		ānzài	Q: where are (literary form)
	哉		zāi	P: (phrase-final: literary form of exclamation mark)
11	蒼白	苍白	cāngbái	SV: pale; white; ashen; 白: *cf.* 9.37
	震動	震动	zhèndòng	V (A)/N: to shake; to quake; 震: *see* 7.14
	揉		róu	V: to ball up; to knead; to rub
	團	团	tuán	N/M/V: ball
	卑鄙		bēibǐ	SV: base; mean; contemptible; low
12	氣憤	气愤	qìfèn	SV (A): indignant; furious
	搶過	抢过	qiǎngguò	RV: to snatch; to grab
13	何必		hébì	Q: why; what's the point (implying that there is no need); 何: *see* 5.13
	增添		zēngtiān	V: to add to; to supplement; 添: *see* 20.17

15	徹（底）	彻（底）	chè(dǐ)	A: thoroughly; completely; to the end
16	光明正大		guāngmíng zhèngdà	SV: honest and upright; just and honorable; 光: cf. 2.16, 4.1, 4.6, 7.2, 11.34, 17.9, 21.1, 41.11
17	暗箭		ànjiàn	N: lit., hidden arrow: attack by a secret enemy
18	射		shè	V: to shoot; to fire (a weapon)
19	噙住眼淚	噙住眼泪	qínzhù yǎnlèi	RV: lit., to contain one's tears: to hold back one's tears; to be brimming with tears [VO]; 住: see 11.4
	好		hǎo	SV: close; intimate; good (of friends); cf. 4.6, 4.16, 5.18, 11.42, 53.33, 55.7, 55.43, 60.10
20	笑罵	笑骂	xiàomà	V: to deride; to ridicule; 罵/骂: see 29.5
	意志		yìzhì	N: will; determination
	堅強	坚强	jiānqiáng	SV: strong; firm V: to strengthen
21	勇氣	勇气	yǒngqì	N: courage
22	無所 VE	无所 VE	wúsuǒ VE	VO: 沒有什麼 VE; 没有什么 VE; (there is) nothing to VE: EX 8.III; 無/无: see 1.9; 所: cf. 2.16, 7.52, 19.10
	顧惜	顾惜	gùxī; gùxí	V: to value; to care for; 顧/顾: see 9.25
23	不斷（地）	不断（地）	búduàn (de)	A: unceasingly; continuously
	流言蜚語	流言蜚语	liúyán fēiyǔ; liúyán fěiyǔ	N: rumors and gossip; groundless statements; slander
	傷害	伤害	shānghài	V: to injure; to hurt; to harm; 害: cf. 7.15, 17.39

| | | | 境遇 | jìngyù | N: condition; lot; (financial) circumstances; 遇: *cf.* 11.3 |

| 25 | 殘忍 | 残忍 | cánrěn | SV: cruel; ruthless |

26	偶然（地）		ǒurán (de)	MA: by chance; accidentally; occasionally
	偶然		ǒurán	SV: fortuitous; accidental
	樹叢	树丛	shùcóng	N: grove of trees

| 28 | 決斷 | 决断 | juéduàn | V (A)/N: decisive; without hesitation |

第三十八景

| 2 | 蹲下 | | dūnxià | RV: to squat down |

| 3 | 燒 | 烧 | shāo | V: to have a fever; to burn; to cook, stew |

| 7 | 體溫表 | 体温表 | tǐwēn biǎo | N: thermometer |
| | 體溫 | 体温 | tǐwēn | N: body temperature |

| 11 | 社會 | 社会 | shèhuì | N: society; community; 會/会: *cf.* 15.3, 35.21, 43.10, 58.21 |

| | 閑話 | 闲话 | xiánhuà | N/V: gossip; casual talk |

第三十九景

| 1 | 清香園 | 清香园 | Qīngxiāng yuán | PN:（茶館名） "Garden of Pure Fragrance" |

| | 繚繞 | 缭绕 | liáorǎo; liáorào | V: to curl up; to wind around; to linger; 繞/绕: *see* 25.14 |

| | 嘈雜 | 嘈杂 | cáozá | SV: noisy; hubbub; din |

2	品茗		pǐnmíng	VO: to drink tea, with critical appreciation for its quality
	品		pǐn	V: to sample with discrimination; to appraise; to judge; *cf.* 13.4, 17.13
4	密斯脱		mìsītuō	APP: (transliteration for) "Mr."; 密: *cf.* 46.18; 脱: *cf.* 17.56
	同仁		tóngrén	N: colleague; 同: *cf.* 26.2, 55.24
5	盼望		pànwàng	V: to hope for; to look forward to; 望: *cf.* 2.2, 17.3, 27.2
6	凛然		lǐnrán	SV (A): stern; severe
12	依我看（來）	依我看（来）	yī wǒ kàn(lái)	CV Ph: in my view; as I see it; 依: *see* 20.6; 看: *cf.* 40.18, 42.3
	江湖落魄；落魄江湖		jiānghú luòpò; luòpò jiānghú	SV: poor and disheartened, wandering amongst the lakes and rivers; vagrant down on one's luck [VO] 落: *see* 1.1; *cf.* 7.51, 61.2
	喜爱	喜爱	xǐ'ài	V: to like; to love; to be fond of
	野鴨	野鸭	yěyā	N: wild duck
14	不解		bùjiě	SV (A): 不了解; uncomprehending
15	呶		náo; nào	P: "look"; "see"; "there it is!"
	比喻		bǐyù	N/V: metaphor; simile; comparison; parallel
	自鳴得意	自鸣得意	zìmíng déyì	SV (A): pleased with oneself; self-satisfied; preening [VO]
17	吸引		xīyǐn	V: to attract; to draw in; 吸: *see* 2.1

第四十景

1	試體溫	试体温	shì tǐwēn	VO: to take one's temperature
2	集中		jízhōng	V/SV: to focus on; to concentrate on

	昏迷		hūnmí	V: to be/ become unconscious, delirious, in a coma; 昏: *cf.* 56.1
	狀態	状态	zhuàngtài	N: state; condition
3	發燒	发烧	fāshāo	VO: to have a fever; 燒/烧: *see* 38.3
5	醫生	医生	yīshēng	N: doctor; 生: *cf.* 5.18, 7.50, 11.3, 19.5, 52.29
6	陳奶奶	陈奶奶	Chén Nǎinai	PN: （人名）"Granny Chen"; 陳/陈: *cf.* 4.3; 奶奶: *see* 2.8
8	察看		chákàn	V: to examine; to inspect; 看: *cf.* 40.18, 42.3
9	中醫	中医	zhōngyī	N: doctor of traditional Chinese medicine; traditional Chinese medicine
14	插言		chāyán	VO: to interrupt; lit., to insert a word (into the conversation)
17	不耐煩	不耐烦	búnàifán	SV (A): impatient [VO]
18	看病		kànbìng	VO: (of doctors) to see patients; (of patients) to see a doctor; 看: *cf.* 4.15, 4.16, 39.12, 40.8, 42.3, 48.8
19	瞥一眼		piē yìyǎn	VO: to glance at; to dart a look at
	按脈	按脉	ànmài	VO: to take one's pulse; 按: *cf.* 7.5, 55.2
21	肺炎		fèiyán	N: pneumonia
22	緊鎖眉頭	紧锁眉头	jǐnsuǒ méitóu	V: to knit the eyebrows [VO]; 緊/紧: *see* 1.10
	鎖	锁	suǒ	V/N: to lock
	故（意）作 SV		gù(yì)zuò SV	V (A): to make a show of being SV; to feign SV, to pretend to be SV [VO]: *EX 7.1*
24	驚喜	惊喜	jīngxǐ	SV (A): pleasantly surprised; 驚/惊: *see* 11.47

25	布包		bùbāo	N: cloth bag
	寒熱	寒热	hánrè	N: chills and fever
26	責問	责问	zéwèn	V (A): lit., to reproachfully question: to call sb. to account; to demand an explanation
	退燒	退烧	tuìshāo	VO: to bring the fever down; 退: cf. 17.18, 25.3, 49.16, 62.3; 燒/烧: see 38.3
27	服		fú	M: dose (of medicine) V: to take (a dose of medicine); cf. 15.17, 57.40
28	取		qǔ	V: to take; to get; to select; 拿
	開藥方	开药方	kāi yàofāng	VO: to write out a prescription; 藥/药: see 31.16; 方: cf. 4.11, 7.18, 14.2, 25.7, 34.1, 42.1
30	難以 VE	难以 VE	nányǐ VE	V: difficult to VE; hard to VE: EX 7.VI; 難/难: cf. 7.7, 7.10; 以: cf. 5.6, 7.52, 19.9, 31.12, 42.2
31	藥方單	药方单	yàofāng dān	N: prescription form; 藥/药: see 31.16; 方: cf. 4.11, 7.18, 14.2, 25.7, 34.1, 42.1; 單/单: cf. 7.7, 19.19
32	付		fù	V: to pay
	診療費	诊疗费	zhěnliáo fèi	N: lit., diagnosis and treatment fee: consultation fee
34	稍稍（地）		shāoshāo (de)	A: slightly
35	僂	偻	lóu	V: to bend; to crook (the back)
38	隱藏	隐藏	yǐncáng	V: to hide; to conceal; 隱/隐: see 23.3; 藏: see 19.12
	心酸		xīnsuān	N/SV: grief; sadness; pain
39	眼淚盈眶	眼泪盈眶	yǎnlèi yíngkuàng	V: to have eyes brimming with tears [VO]
	眼眶		yǎnkuàng	N: eye socket

第四十一景

1	勞累	劳累	láolèi	SV/V: over-worked; tired; run-down
2	疼愛	疼爱	téng'ài	V (A): to be very fond of; to love dearly
4	匆匆 忙忙(地) 匆忙		cōngcōng mángmáng (de) cōngmáng	A: hastily; hurriedly SV: in a hurry; in haste
	鎮長	镇长	zhènzhǎng	N: mayor; 鎮/镇: see 1.2; cf. 25.7, 45.3; 長/长: see 4.5; cf. 7.7, 22.21, 60.20
6	愣		lèng	V: to be taken aback; to be speechless with astonishment
	猜測	猜测	cāicè	V/N: to guess; to surmise
8	臥房	卧房	wòfáng	N: bedroom
	躺倒		tǎngdǎo	RV: to lie down; 倒: cf. 5.10, 12.15
9	擔憂	担忧	dānyōu	VO/SV (A): to be worried, anxious, apprehensive; 擔/担: see 5.4; cf. 17.35
	出事		chūshì	VO: to have sth. (bad) happen; to meet with mishap, accident
11	光(是)		guāng(shì)	A: only; merely; just; 光: cf. 2.16, 4.1, 4.6, 7.2, 11.34, 17.9, 21.1, 37.16; 是: cf. 6.2, 62.2
13	了不起		liǎobùqǐ; liǎobuqǐ	SV: extraordinary; great; impressive; lit., of such magnitude that it is beyond one's ken, or means to cope
	翻身		fānshēn	VO: to turn (the body) over; 翻: see 7.7
14	朝		cháo	CV/V: facing; towards; cf. 1.3

第四十二景

1	方		fāng	SV: square; *cf.* 4.11, 7.18, 14.2, 25.7, 34.1, 40.28, 40.31

2	如 N1, N2, ... 之類	如 N1, N2, ... 之类	rú N1, N2, ... zhīlèi	PAT: like N1, N2, ...; for example, N1, N2, ... [VO]: *EX 7.II*
	麥冬	麦冬	Màidōng	PN: (a Chinese medicine)
	半夏		Bànxià	PN: (a Chinese medicine)
	桂枝		Guìzhī	PN: (a Chinese medicine) cassia twig
	以此		yǐcǐ	CVO: lit., by means of this: in this way; thus; for this reason: *EX 7.III;* 以: *see* 5.6; *cf.* 7.52, 19.9, 31.12, 40.30, 42.12; 此: *see* 11.46
3	看護	看护	kānhù	V: to take care of; to nurse N: nurse; 看: *cf.* 4.15, 4.16, 39.12, 40.8, 40.18, 48.8
4	敷		fū	V: to apply
	濕	湿	shī	SV/V: wet; damp
	毛巾		máojīn	N: towel
5	繼而	继而	jì'ér	C: lit., continuing: then; afterwards: *EX 7.IV;* 而: *cf.* 4.4, 9.28, 11.14, 12.42, 25.8, 57.43
6	靈	灵	líng	SV: effective; efficacious; numinous
8	重新		chóngxīn	A: again; anew; 重: *cf.* 7.40, 43.5, 48.5, 53.10
9	降低		jiàngdī	RV: to lower; to reduce
10	恩德		ēndé	N: kindness; charity; benevolence; favor
	救活		jiùhuó	RV: to save (a life); to bring back to life
	母子		mǔzǐ	N: *母親與兒子；母親與孩子* *母亲与儿子；母亲与孩子*
11	性命		xìngmìng	N: life

報答	报答	bàodá	V: to repay
12 難以為情	难以为情	nányǐ wéiqíng	SV: difficult to know how to react properly; embarrassed, awkward [VO]: *EX 7.VI;* 難以／难以: *see* 40.30; 難／难: *cf.* 7.7, 7.10; 以: *cf.* 5.6, 7.52, 19.9, 31.12, 42.2; 為／为: *cf.* 11.14, 13.6, 22.12, 22.20, 36.4; 情: *cf.* 1.4, 7.41, 46.8, 52.2, 60.9
14 天色		tiānsè	N: the color of the sky, indicating the time of day or weather; 天: *cf.* 7.14, 9.39, 11.39, 12.39, 53.5
19 喃喃（地）		nánnán (de)	A: (onomatopoeia) muttering; murmuring
20 懂事		dǒngshì	VO/SV: to understand how things work in the world; sensible (said of children)
21 臉色	脸色	liǎnsè	N: complexion; (facial) expression
25 恰巧		qiàqiǎo	MA: coincidentally; luckily; fortunately
解救		jiějiù	V: to deliver; to save; to rescue
到處	到处	dàochù	L: everywhere
26 詫異	诧异	chàyì	SV: surprised; astonished
28 時常（地）	时常（地）	shícháng (de)	A: often; frequently

第四十三景

2 提醒		tíxǐng	V: to remind; to alert; to warn; 提: *cf.* 6.10, 49.17
守舊	守旧	shǒujiù	SV: lit., to defend the old: conservative [VO]; 守: *see* 55.5
3 同事		tóngshì	N/V: co-worker; colleague; 同: *cf.* 26.2, 55.24

4	執拗	执拗	zhí'ào; zhínìu	SV: stubborn; pigheaded; willful
5	緩和	缓和	huǎnhé	SV (A): mild; moderate V: to soften; to ease up; to mitigate; 緩/缓: see 11.6; 和: cf. 53.13, 55.9
	尊重		zūnzhòng	V: to respect; to esteem; 重: see 7.40; cf. 42.8
	輿論	舆论	yúlùn	N: public opinion
6	人言可畏		rényán kěwèi	SE: "What people say is worthy of deference."
	可畏		kěwèi	SV: to be worthy of commanding respect and awe; 可: cf. 2.15
	何況		hékuàng	C: let alone; much less; not to mention: EX 7.V; 何: see 5.13
	耳朵		ěrduo	N: ear
7	不管		bùguǎn	V: to not care; to not matter; cf. 12.43
	由		yóu	V: to follow; to go with; to let; cf. 2.17, 12.53, 19.16, 30.17, 57.31
	我行我素		wǒxíng wǒsù	SE: "I do what I have always done"; "I stick to my ways"; 行: cf. 1.2, 1.4, 5.4, 9.55, 19.6; 素: cf. 11.52
8	衣物		yīwù	N: clothing, stuff; articles of daily use
10	理會	理会	lǐhuì	V: to acknowledge; to take notice; to pay attention; to care; 理: see 7.39; cf. 12.17, 12.53; 會/会: cf. 35.21, 38.11

第四十四景

| 4 | 不然 | | bùrán | C: 要不然 |
| 6 | 敏感 | | mǐn'gǎn | SV (A): sensitive |

7	無辜	无辜	wúgū	SV: innocent; guiltless; blameless; 無/无: *see* 1.9
	誹謗	诽谤	fěibàng	N/V: libel; slander
8	真誠	真诚	zhēnchéng	SV: sincere, genuine
	感動	感动	gǎndòng	V/SV: to move; to touch (emotionally)
9	沈思	沉思	chénsī	V: to be deep in thought; to ponder; to meditate
10	沈吟	沉吟	chényín	V: to mutter to oneself, unable to decide
11	困難	困难	kùnnán; kùnnan	SV (A)/N: difficult; 難/难: *cf.* 7.7, 7.10
	消瘦		xiāoshòu	V: to become thin, emaciated; 消: *cf.* 25.3
12	時期	时期	shíqī	N: period (of time)
	春寒		chūnhán	N: the cold of early spring
16	約	约	yuē	N: contract; pact; agreement; *cf.* 4.5, 23.3 V: (pre-pivotal) to make an appointment or date
17	揚頭	扬头	yángtóu	VO: to lift the head (as a gesture of pride)
	果決		guǒjué	SV: strongly determined; resolute
	改變	改变	gǎibiàn	V: to change; 改: *see* 23.10; 變/变: *see* 7.11
	主意		zhǔyì	N: idea; plan; definite view; mind
18	趕走	赶走	gǎnzǒu	RV: to drive away; to expel; 趕/赶: *cf.* 27.14
	清白		qīngbái	SV (A)/N: lit., pure and white: unsullied; innocent (said of a person's character, family background); 白: *cf.* 9.37

	惹	rě	V: to invite or ask for (trouble); to provoke: *EX 7.VII*
20	連連（地）　连连（地）	liánlián (de)	A: repeatedly; again and again

第四十五景

3	周身	zhōushēn	N: 全身
	血	xiě; xuè	N: blood
	昏倒	hūndǎo	RV: to faint away; to fall down fainting; 昏: *cf.* 56.1; 倒: *cf.* 5.10, 12.15
	鎮定　镇定	zhèndìng	V: to calm; to compose (oneself) SV: calm; collected; composed; 鎮／镇: *cf.* 1.2, 19.15, 41.4
	下意識　下意识	xiàyìshí; xiàyìshì; xiàyìshi	N: subconcious
4	靠	kào	V/CV: to lean on; to lean against; *cf.* 2.3, 27.8
8	疑問　疑问	yíwèn	N: uncertainty; doubt; question
10	擁　拥	yōng	V: to gather round; to crowd; to embrace
11	側門　侧门	cèmén	N: side door
12	浮現　浮现	fúxiàn	V: to appear; to emerge
	浮	fú	V: to surface; to float
	笑容	xiàoróng	N: lit., smiling face: smile; 容: *cf.* 11.42, 60.10
13	苛政猛於虎　苛政猛于虎	Kēzhèng měngyú hǔ	SE: "Tyrannical rule is more savage than a tiger." (from the Han Dynasty classic, 禮記／礼记 [*Book of Rites*]); 猛: *see* 24.7
	SV 於　　SV 于	SV yú	PAT: more SV than (comparative construction): *EX 8.I*; 於／于: *cf.* 6.2, 7.11, 19.3, 19.24, 30.17, 30.35, 55.12

第四十六景

2	孔子		Kǒngzi	PN: Confucius; 孔: *cf.* 11.17, 22.31, 35.9
	泰山		Tàishān	PN: (地名) mountain in Shāndōng Province
3	跪		guì	V: to kneel (on both knees)
	墳墓	坟墓	fénmù	N: grave; tomb
4	躲		duǒ	V: to hide
	痛哭		tòngkū	V: to cry bitterly; to wail
	丈夫		zhàngfu	N: husband
	夫		fū	N: (literary) husband
8	情況	情况	qíngkuàng	N: circumstances; situation; 情: *cf.* 2.16, 13.5, 42.12, 53.28, 60.9
10	交涉		jiāoshè	V/N: to negotiate; 交: *cf.* 2.3, 27.9
11	毫無 N	毫无 N	háowú N	VO: 一點兒也沒有 N 一点儿也没有 N [VO]: *EX 8.II*; 無/无: *see* 1.9
	家長	家长	jiāzhǎng	N: lit., head of the family: parents, guardians; 長/长: *see* 4.5; *cf.* 7.7, 22.21, 60.20
	抗議	抗议	kàngyì	V/N: to protest
12	胡說	胡说	húshuō	V: to talk nonsense
13	通知		tōngzhī	N/V: notification; notice
	放假		fàngjià	VO: to have a holiday/ vacation; to have the day off; 放: *see* 17.36; 假: *cf.* 20.6, 53.15
14	作對	作对	zuòduì	V: to oppose; to act against [VO]
	手段		shǒuduàn	N: methods; means; 段: *cf.* 13.14, 17.28
15	驕傲	骄傲	jiāo'ào	SV (A)/N: proud; arrogant

得勝	得胜	déshèng	VO: 得到勝利 得到胜利
16 有所 VE		yǒusuǒ VE	VO (A): lit., to have sth. to VE: VE to a certain extent; to somewhat VE: *EX 8.III;* 所: *cf.* 2.16, 7.52, 19.10
醒悟		xǐngwù	V: to come to realize; lit., to wake up (to reality)
神聖	神圣	shénshèng	SV: holy; sacred
友誼	友谊	yǒuyì	N: friendship
17 顧及	顾及	gùjí	RV: to take into account; to attend to; 顧/顾: *see* 9.25
18 親密	亲密	qīnmì	SV: close; intimate; 密: *cf.* 39.4

第四十七景

1 作文		zuòwén	N/VO: composition; to write a composition

第四十八景

3 亭		tíng	N: pavilion; kiosk
5 沈重	沉重	chénzhòng	SV (A): heavy; serious; grave; 重: *see* 7.40; *cf.* 42.8
6 驚駭	惊骇	jīnghài	SV (A): frightened; panic-stricken; 驚/惊: *see* 11.47
7 喘		chuǎn	V: to gasp for breath; to pant
8 喉嚨	喉咙	hóulóng	N: throat
堵塞		dǔsāi; dǔsè	V: to block up; to stifle; 塞: *see* 22.25

眼看。。。		yǎnkàn . . .	V: to watch helplessly (as) . . . ; 看: cf. 40.18, 42.3

第四十九景

2	枯乾	枯干	kūgān	SV: dried out; 乾/干: cf. 26.7
3	隱閃	隐闪	yǐnshǎn	V: to glimmer, glint; to flash dimly; 隱/隐: see 23.3
	閃	闪	shǎn	V: to flash (light)
	滋潤	滋润	zīrùn	SV/V: moist
5	仰頭	仰头	yǎngtóu	VO: to raise the head to face up; 仰: cf. 6.4, 9.4
7	許久	许久	xǔjiǔ	SV: a long time
11	緩緩(地)	缓缓(地)	huǎnhuǎn (de)	A: slowly; 緩/缓: see 11.6
12	和婉		héwǎn	SV: gentle; mild; kind; 和: cf. 53.13, 55.9
16	運命；命運	运命；命运	yùnmìng; mìngyùn	N: fate; destiny; lot; 運/运: cf. 1.8, 9.53
	苦鬥	苦斗	kǔdòu	V: to fight bitterly; to fight no matter how difficult; 苦: see 5.8
	退讓	退让	tuìràng	V: to yield; to give in; 退: cf. 40.26; 讓/让: see 6.9; cf. 4.23, 21.19, EX 5.VII
17	提高		tígāo	RV: to raise; to heighten; to increase; to improve; 提: see 6.10; cf. 6.3, 17.15, 43.2
18	止不住		zhǐbúzhù	RV: to not be able to stop: EX 8.IV; 止: see 11.46; 住: see 11.4
22	丫頭	丫头	yātou	N: maid; servant girl
23	發怒	发怒	fā'nù	VO: to get angry, furious

27	改嫁		gǎijià	V: (of women) to remarry [VO]; 改: see 23.10
	嫁		jià	V: (of women) to marry
28	念頭	念头	niàntou	N: idea; thought
29	相當	相当	xiāngdāng	SV: suitable; appropriate; matching; 當/当: cf. 2.1, 5.2, 5.3, 11.37, 18.5, 24.2, 24.4, 52.2, 55.3, 57.23
30	驚恐	惊恐	jīngkǒng	SV: alarmed; panic-stricken; terrified; 驚/惊: see 11.47
	反應	反应	fǎnyìng	N/V: reaction; response; 應/应: cf. 6.12, 57.23
	貞節	贞节	zhēnjié	SV/N: (of women) chastity; purity; 節/节: cf. 9.12, 52.29

第五十景

1	西墜	西坠	xīzhuì	V: to drop in the west
	獨自(地)	独自(地)	dúzì (de)	A: by oneself; alone
5	胡思亂想	胡思乱想	húsī luànxiǎng	V: to let one's imagination run wild; 亂/乱: see 11.42

第五十一景

1	玻璃		bōli	N: glass
	罩		zhào	N/V: cover; (lamp) shade; hood
	煤油燈	煤油灯	méiyóu dēng	N: kerosene lamp
2	塗去	涂去	túqù	RV: to blot out; to cross out
	濕潤	湿润	shīrùn	SV: moist, wet; 濕/湿: see 42.4
	擱	搁	gē	V: to put

第五十二景

1	皎潔	皎洁	jiǎojié	SV: (of moonlight) bright and clear
	透過	透过	tòuguò	RV/CV: to pass through
	葉	叶	yè	N: leaves
	稀疏		xīshū	SV: few; sparse; scattered
	斑影		bānyǐng	N: speckled shadow
	池		chí	N: pool; pond
2	當年	当年	dāngnián	T: in those years [CVO]; 當/当: *cf.* 5.2, 5.3, 11.37, 18.5, 24.4, 49.29, 55.3, 57.23
	情景		qíngjǐng	N: scene; circumstances; 情: *cf.* 2.16, 13.5, 42.12, 53.28, 60.9
3	猶豫	犹豫	yóuyù	SV: to be hesitant, irresolute, uncertain
4	喊		hǎn	V: to shout; to cry out; to yell
14	挽留		wǎnliú	V: to persuade or urge sb. to stay; 留: *see* 18.5; *cf.* 62.1
16	諒解	谅解	liàngjiě	V: to forgive and understand
17	具有		jùyǒu	V: to have; to possess; to be provided with: *EX 8.V*; 具: *cf.* 4.3
19	必須	必须	bìxū	AV: necessarily; must; 須/须: *see* 31.8
	救濟	救济	jiùjì	V: to help in time of distress; to relieve (suffering)
	頓息	顿息	dùnxī; dùnxí	V: to pause; 頓/顿: *see* 30.31; *cf.* 21.2; 息: *cf.* 17.35, 25.3
20	妻子		qīzi	N: wife
21	遭到		zāodào	V: to suffer; to meet with; to encounter (misfortune): *EX 8.VI*
	霹靂	霹雳	pīlì	N: thunderbolt; thunderclap; lightning strike

26	面對	面对	miànduì	V: to face; to confront
27	抑制		yìzhì	V: to restrain; to control; to check
28	身影		shēnyǐng	N: (person's) silhouette, figure, form
29	節外生枝	节外生枝	jiéwài shēngzhī	V (A): lit., to grow branches outside the nodes: to have problems crop up unexpectedly; to deliberately create complications [VO]: *EX 8.VII;* 節/节: *cf.* 9.12, 49.30, 57.23; 生: *cf.* 1.3, 5.18, 7.45, 7.50, 11.3, 17.30, 40.5
	永遠	永远	yǒngyuǎn	A: always; forever

第五十三景

1	意想不到		yìxiǎng búdào	RV (A): to have sth. be completely unexpected
2	陰暗	阴暗	yīn'àn	SV: dark; gloomy
	笑容可掬		xiàoróng kějū	SV (A): all smiles; 笑容: *see* 45.12; 容: *cf.* 11.42, 60.10; 可: *cf.* 2.15
5	聊(天)		liáo(tiān)	V(O): to chat; to have a conversation; 天: *cf.* 7.14, 9.39, 11.39, 12.39, 42.14
9	比如(説)	比如(说)	bǐrú (shuō)	C: for example
	外界		wàijiè	N: outside world
10	敬重		jìngzhòng	V: to deeply respect; to revere; to honor; 重: *see* 7.40; *cf.* 42.8
13	怒火		nùhuǒ	N: lit., flames of anger: rage; fury
	附和		fùhè	V: to echo; to chime in with agreement; to repeat without conviction; 和: *cf.* 1.1, 1.6, 11.4, 43.5, 49.12
15	假如		jiǎrú	C: if; supposing; 假: *see* 20.6; *cf.* 17.32, 46.13

18	有心		yǒuxīn	VO/SV: to have one's mind set; to have the intention of; to have ambitions; to have purpose
	組織	组织	zǔzhī	V/N: to organize; to form (a group); 織/织: cf. 4.6
25	憤怒	愤怒	fènnù	SV (A): indignant; angry
28	失望		shīwàng	SV: disappointed [VO]; 望: cf. 2.2, 17.3, 27.2
	表情		biǎoqíng	N: expression; 情: cf. 1.4, 7.41, 46.8, 52.2
	尖		jiān	N: tip; point SV: sharp; pointed; piercing
29	出氣	出气	chūqì	VO: to vent anger SV: avenged; vindicated
33	沒好氣	没好气	méihǎoqì	SV (A): 很不高興; 很不高兴; sulky; grumpy [VO]; 好: cf. 5.18, 37.19, 55.43
34	哀求		āiqiú	V: (pre-pivotal) to beg pathetically; to implore; to entreat; 求: see 12.53
	請求	请求	qǐngqiú	V: (pre-pivotal) to ask; to entreat; to request; to beg; 求: see 12.53
37	侮辱		wǔrǔ	V: to insult; to humiliate

第五十四景

3	散		sàn	V (A): to scatter, to disperse
	遊	游	yóu	V: to wander about, playing; to rove; 遊/游: cf. 9.55
7	衣裳		yīshang	N: clothing
12	分手		fēnshǒu	VO: to part company; to say good-bye

回頭	回头	huítóu	MA: later [VO]; *cf.* 12.54

第五十五景

2　按期		ànqī	CVO: according to schedule; on time; 按: *cf.* 40.19
北伐		běifá	V: to attack the north PN: The Northern Expedition (1926-1928), a campaign against the northern warlords led by General Chiang Kai-shek to unite China under Republican control
不出		bùchū	CV: within; in no more than
江浙		Jiāngzhè	PN: 江蘇 　　江苏 (Jiāngsū) and 浙江 (Zhèjiāng) provinces
一帶	一带	yídài	N: area; zone; region; 帶/带: *cf.* 4.7, 9.24, 19.5, 24.4
3　江西		Jiāngxī	PN: (province name)
首當其衝	首当其冲	shǒu dāng qíchōng	N/V: the part that bears the brunt; the first to be affected [VO]; 首: *see* 33.1; *cf.* 13.12; 當/当: *cf.* 2.1, 5.2, 5.3, 11.37, 24.2, 24.4, 49.29, 52.2, 57.23
衝	冲	chōng	V: to charge; to rush; to dash; to flush
不堪		bùkān	V/SV: to not be able to withstand; to not be able to bear: *EX 9.1*
5　守		shǒu	V: to guard; to defend
難保	难保	nánbǎo	SV: difficult to protect, preserve; 難/难: *cf.* 7.7, 7.10
7　正好		zhènghǎo	SV/A: just right; perfect; opportune; 好: *cf.* 5.18, 37.19, 55.43
8　發表	发表	fābiǎo	V: to express; to issue; to deliver; to publish
高論	高论	gāolùn	N: grand statement; brilliant views

9	應和	应和	yìnghè	V: to respond in agreement; to echo; 應/应: *cf.* 57.23; 和: *cf.* 1.1, 1.6, 11.4, 43.5, 49.12
10	政府		zhèngfǔ	N: government
	興師	兴师	xīngshī	VO: to send an army; to dispatch troops; 興/兴: *cf.* 4.7, 5.2, 9.11, 9.22, 12.20, 31.5, 35.2; 師/师: *cf.* 4.1, 9.45, 12.24, 17.8
11	加入		jiārù	RV: to join in; 入: *see* 4.14
	滴		dī	M: drop V: to drip
12	融於 於	融于 于	róngyú yú	V: to dissolve in; to blend in P: (preposition) in, of, at, on: *EX 9.II;* 於/于: *cf.* 45.13
13	唐		Táng	PN: (姓)
	死		sǐ	A: to the death; resolutely; no matter what; at all costs; *cf.* 2.14, 57.43, 62.13
15	幫	帮	bāng	M: gang; group; band
	軍閥	军阀	jūnfá	N: warlord
	腐敗	腐败	fǔbài	SV: corrupt; lit., rotten
	得人心		dé rénxīn	SV/VO: to win favor with the people; to be popular
16	樁	桩	zhuāng	M: (for affairs or matters)
20	從此	从此	cóngcǐ	CVO/MA: lit., from this point on: thereupon; 此: *see* 11.46
	豈	岂	qǐ	Q: (literary interrogative used in rhetorical questions) "How could it possibly be that . . . ?"
22	一齊	一齐	yìqí	A: simultaneously; in unison; all together

24	同		tóng	CV: with; 同: cf. 2.3, 2.16, 7.5, 39.4, 43.3
31	未來	未来	wèilái	T: the future; lit., time to come; 未: see 31.12
32	不悦		búyuè	SV: displeased
34	失敗	失败	shībài	SV/N: to lose; to be defeated; to fail
37	聚集		jùjí	V: to gather; to collect
	疑團	疑团	yítuán	N: a mass of suspicions; 團:/团: see 37.11
	推究		tuījiū; tuījiù	V: to examine; to study; 推: see 7.13; 究: cf. 11.43, 28.11
	奇聞	奇闻	qíwén	N: sth. unheard of; strange news
41	嘴唇		zuǐchún	N: lip
	打顫	打颤	dǎchàn; dǎzhàn	V: to shake; to tremble; to quiver [VO]
43	好 VE		hǎo VE	AV: the better to VE; to make it possible to VE; cf. 4.6, 4.16, 5.18, 11.42, 37.19, 53.33, 55.7, 60.10
44	清醒		qīngxǐng	SV: to regain one's head; to become clear-headed
49	等不及		děngbùjí	RV: to not be able to wait; cf. 等: 1.8
	一道		yídào	A: lit., (by) a single route: together; 道: cf. 2.11, 7.7
	逕直(地)	径直(地)	jìngzhí (de)	A: directly; straight for
50	片刻		piànkè	N: a while
	蚊帳	蚊帐	wénzhàng	N: mosquito netting

第五十六景

1	黄昏		huánghūn	N: dusk; 昏: cf. 1.9, 40.2, 45.3
	飄蕩	飘荡	piāodàng	V: to drift
3	惟恐。。。		wéikǒng . . .	V: lit., to be afraid of nothing but . . . : for fear that . . . : EX 9.III
	驚動	惊动	jīngdòng	V: to alarm; to disturb; to startle; 驚/惊: see 11.47
4	惆悵	惆怅	chóuchàng	N/SV: melancholy; disconsolateness; extreme dejection
7	撫（摸）	抚（摸）	fǔ(mō)	V: to stroke gently
	出遠門	出远门	chū yuǎnmén	VO: to go far from home
	出門	出门	chūmén	VO: to go out; to leave home

第五十七景

1	佈置	布置	bùzhì	V/N: to arrange
2	斟		zhēn	V: to pour
3	明明		míngmíng	A: obviously; clearly
	欲		yù	V/N: 要; to desire; to want
5	舒暢	舒畅	shūchàng	SV: to have one's mind at ease; to be free of worry
13	謙讓	谦让	qiānràng	V: to modestly decline; 讓/让: see 6.9; cf. 4.23, 21.19, EX 5.VII
14	招呼		zhāohu	V: to take care of; cf. 22.21
16	較量	较量	jiàoliàng	V: to compare strengths; to have a contest
18	對手	对手	duìshǒu	N: equal; match; suitable opponent

23	N1 作 N2 論	N1 作 N2 论	N1 zuò N2 lùn	PAT: to consider N1 as N2; to speak of N1 as N2: *EX 9.IV*
	應當	应当	yīngdāng	AV: 應該; 应该; 應/应: *cf.* 6.12, 17.24, 18.9, 49.30, 55.9; 當/当: *cf.* 2.1, 5.2, 5.3, 11.37, 18.5, 24.2, 24.4, 49.29, 52.2, 55.3
	節婦	节妇	jiéfù	N: a woman who dies in defense of her honor or chastity; a woman who steadfastly remains a widow; 節/节: *cf.* 9.12, 52.29
24	正派		zhèngpài	SV: upright; honest; decent; 派: *cf.* 5.20
	逼		bī	V: to force; to compel; to drive
26	殉		xùn	V: lit., to be buried with the dead: to sacrifice one's life for
31	由此可見	由此可见	yóucǐ kějiàn	C: lit., from this, we can see that: this shows that; thus it's clear that [CV Ph]; 由: *see* 30.17; *cf.* 5.18, 43.7; 此: *see* 11.46; 可: *cf.* 2.15
34	恩人		ēnrén	N: benefactor
35	敬你一杯		jìngnǐ yìbēi	SE: (toast) "I drink a cup to you!" Lit., [let me] honor you with a glass [VO]
	男女老幼		nánnǚ lǎoyòu	N: (lit.) men and women, young and old: everyone
36	自我		zìwǒ	Pn: self N: ego
	譏諷	嘲讽	cháofěng; cháofèng	V: to sneer at; to ridicule; to taunt
	展覽	展览	zhǎnlǎn	V/N: to exhibit; to display
38	打岔		dǎchà	VO: to interrupt; to cut in
40	煞費苦心	煞费苦心	shàfèi kǔxīn	SV (A): taking great pains; painstaking [VO]: *EX 9.VII*; 苦: *see* 5.8

令		lìng	V: (causative) to cause one to; to make one do sth.; 令: cf. 7.5
佩服		pèifu	V: to admire; 服: cf. 15.17, 57.40
41 料想		liàoxiǎng	V: to think of; to anticipate
42 激怒		jī'nù	N: rage V: to enrage
沈痛	沉痛	chéntòng	SV (A): deeply bitter
43 反而		fǎn'ér	C: but instead; but on the contrary: EX 9.V; 而: see 25.8; cf. 4.4, 9.28, 11.14, 17.55, 42.5
害死		hàisǐ	RV: lit., to harm someone to death: to murder; to cause great trouble (to sb.); 害: cf. 7.15, 17.39; 死: see 2.14; cf. 55.13
冷言冷語	冷言冷语	lěngyán lěngyǔ	V/N: to make sarcastic remarks
居然		jūrán	MA: unexpectedly; to one's pleasant surprise (typically used for unexpected positive events): EX 9.VI; 居: cf. 2.12
44 喝彩		hècǎi	VO: to acclaim; to cheer; to applaud
46 膽怯	胆怯	dǎnqiè	SV (A): timid; cowardly
47 小人		xiǎorén	N: base, mean person; person of vile character
灑	洒	sǎ	V: to spill

第五十八景

3 惡夢	恶梦	èmèng	N: nightmare; 惡: see 37.9; cf. 4.9
4 勸慰	劝慰	quànwèi	V: to console; to soothe; 勸/劝: see 24.2

5	握住		wòzhù	RV: to clasp; to hold tight (of hands); 住: see 11.4
6	嬌羞	娇羞	jiāoxiū	SV (A): shy; modest and retiring (of women)
21	會意	会意	huìyì	VO (A): to understand; to know; to comprehend; 會/会: cf. 35.21, 38.11
23	有關	有关	yǒuguān	CV: 關於 关于
26	摔斷	摔断	shuāiduàn	RV: to break in a fall
29	悲憤	悲愤	bēifèn	SV/N: grief-stricken and indignant

第六十景

1	就		jiù	CV: by; near; cf. 2.9, 7.21, 9.4
	閱讀	阅读	yuèdú	V: to read; 閱/阅: see 13.1; cf. 7.45
4	夜宵		yèxiāo	N: refreshments late at night; midnight snack
9	深情		shēnqíng	SV (A)/N: to have deep feelings, love, concern; 深: see 1.7; 情: cf. 1.4, 7.41, 46.8, 52.2
10	好容易		hǎo róngyì	A: 好不容易: see 11.42; 好: cf. 5.18, 37.19, 55.43; 容: cf. 2.4, 45.12, 53.2
11	蒙在鼓裏	蒙在鼓里	méngzài gǔlǐ	V: to be kept in the dark; lit., to be kept in the drum
12	全部		quánbù	N/A: whole; all; total
	委託	委托	wěituō	V: (pre-pivotal) to entrust; to leave to; 委: cf. 11.43
16	堅決	坚决	jiānjué	SV (A): firm; resolute; determined

18	三五		sānwǔ	Nu: lit., 3-5: several
19	堅持	坚持	jiānchí	V: to persist; to stick to; to insist
20	意味		yìwèi	N/V: meaning; significance; implication
	深長	深长	shēncháng	SV: profound; deep; 深: *see* 1.7; 長/长: *cf.* 4.5, 17.5, 41.4, 46.11

第六十一景

1	碼頭	码头	mǎtou	N: wharf; dock; pier
	輕便	轻便	qīngbiàn	SV: light; portable; convenient; easy to use; 輕/轻: *see* 2.1
2	村落		cūnluò	N: village; hamlet; 落: *cf.* 1.1, 7.51, 19.23, 39.12
	乳白色		rǔbáisè	N: lit., milky white color: creamy white; 白: *cf.* 9.37
	薄		báo; bó	SV: lit., thin; light; weak
3	翠綠	翠绿	cuìlǜ	N: lit., jade green: emerald green

第六十二景

1	留下		liúxià	RV: to have left (sth. for sb.); 留: *cf.* 14.1, 18.5, 52.14
2	是非		shìfēi	N: right and wrong; truth and falsehood; gossip; scandal; 是: *cf.* 5.10, 6.2, 7.21, 7.33, 9.5, 17.13, 22.12, 41.11
	漩渦	漩涡	xuánwō	N: whirlpool
3	溺死		nìsǐ	RV: to drown to death; 死: *see* 2.14; *cf.* 55.13

退學	退学	tuìxué	VO: to withdraw from school; 退: cf. 40.26
鐵棒	铁棒	tiěbàng	N: iron club
4 暈旋	晕旋	yūnxuán; yùnxuán	SV: dizzy; spinning; 暈/晕: cf. 19.34
終止	终止	zhōngzhǐ	V: to stop; to end; 止: see 11.46
道路		dàolù	N: road; way; 道: cf. 2.11, 7.7
5 投身		tóushēn	V: to throw oneself into; to plunge oneself into [VO]; 投: see 8.9
洪流		hóngliú	N: mighty current; powerful flow
7 堅信	坚信	jiānxìn	V: to believe firmly; 信: cf. 9.56
9 劇終	剧终	jùzhōng	SE: lit., end of the play: "The End"; "Curtain" (used for theatrical works)

練習

liànxí

Exercises

练习

練習一：第一景至第五景

一。閱讀測驗

　　　一至二景

1. 《早春二月》大概發生在陽曆甚麼時候？那時候天氣怎麼樣？梅花和柳樹怎麼樣？

2. 船在哪兒行駛？船上坐着些甚麼樣的人？那些人談論着甚麼？

3. 船上的那位青年甚麼樣？為甚麼在人羣中顯得不調和呢？

4. 那位青年為甚麼要走出艙去？

5. 在那位青年人眼中，船舷的欄杆處坐着的青年婦人快樂嗎？她身旁有幾個小孩？

6. 老奶奶與青年婦人是甚麼關係？

7. 小女孩的父親離家到甚麼地方去了？是怎麼死的？

8. 為甚麼那位青年很注意那位青年婦人？

9. 為甚麼那位婦人呆呆地看着懷中的孩子？

10. 女孩子有多麼喜歡橘子？

　　　四至五景

1. 陶家的房子甚麼式樣？

2. 陶嵐是誰？她正在廳堂中做甚麼？

练习一：第一景至第五景

一。阅读测验

一至二景

1. 《早春二月》大概发生在阳历什么时候？那时候天气怎么样？梅花和柳树怎么样？

2. 船在哪儿行驶？船上坐着些什么样的人？那些人谈论着什么？

3. 船上的那位青年什么样？为什么在人群中显得不调和呢？

4. 那位青年为什么要走出舱去？

5. 在那位青年人眼中，船舷的栏杆处坐着的青年妇人快乐吗？她身旁有几个小孩？

6. 老奶奶与青年妇人是什么关系？

7. 小女孩的父亲离家到什么地方去了？是怎么死的？

8. 为什么那位青年很注意那位青年妇人？

9. 为什么那位妇人呆呆地看着怀中的孩子？

10. 女孩子有多么喜欢橘子？

四至五景

1. 陶家的房子什么式样？

2. 陶岚是谁？她正在厅堂中做什么？

3. 那兩位教師叫甚麼名字？陶嵐歡迎他們來嗎？你怎麼看得出來？

4. 方謀為甚麼暗自好笑？

5. 陶嵐的母親甚麼樣？

6. 說說芙蓉鎮市街上的情形。

7. 阿榮是誰？他的工作是甚麼？

8. 陶校長甚麼樣？他認為芙蓉鎮怎麼樣？

9. 蕭澗秋為甚麼打算在芙蓉鎮多住幾年？

10. 鎮上的人都好奇地注視蕭澗秋，陶校長怎麼解釋？

二。語法練習

I. 其中： of them; in them; there; of which; in which

Locative phrase: makes reference to antecedent, which may be singular or plural

PATTERN: (clause) S 在其中 VE

　　　　　(clause) 其中(有)。。。

例

1.4　　統艙裏擠滿了人，

Steerage was jam-packed with people.

　　　　一個賣瓜子的也擠在其中叫賣。

A melon seed vendor was also squeezed in among them hawking [his wares].

　　　　其中擠在那裏叫賣的(有)一個賣瓜子的。

Squeezed in among them hawking [his wares] was a melon seed vendor.

1.　船票分為頭等，二等，三等，統艙。二等票在其中賣得最多。

Boat tickets are divided into first, second, third, and steerage classes, of which second class sells the most.

2.　賣瓜子的一共有五個。其中(有)一個叫賣聲特別大。

There are a total of five people selling melon seeds. One of them has an especially loud chant.

3. 那两位教师叫什么名字？陶岚欢迎他们来吗？你怎么看得出来？

4. 方谋为什么暗自好笑？

5. 陶岚的母亲什么样？

6. 说说芙蓉镇市街上的情形。

7. 阿荣是谁？他的工作是什么？

8. 陶校长什么样？他认为芙蓉镇怎么样？

9. 萧涧秋为什么打算在芙蓉镇多住几年？

10. 镇上的人都好奇地注视萧涧秋，陶校长怎么解释？

二。语法练习

I. 其中：of them; in them; there; of which; in which

Locative phrase: makes reference to antecedent, which may be singular or plural

PATTERN: (clause) S 在其中 VE

　　　　　 (clause) 其中（有）。。。

例
1.4　　统舱里挤满了人，
　　　 Steerage was jam-packed with people.

　　　　　 一个卖瓜子的也挤在其中叫卖。
　　　　　 A melon seed vendor was also squeezed in among them hawking [his wares].

　　　　　 其中挤在那里叫卖的（有）一个卖瓜子的。
　　　　　 Squeezed in among them hawking [his wares] was a melon seed vendor.

1.　　船票分为头等，二等，三等，统舱。二等票在其中卖得最多。
　　　 Boat tickets are divided into first, second, third, and steerage classes, of which second class sells the most.

2.　　卖瓜子的一共有五个。其中（有）一个叫卖声特别大。
　　　 There are a total of five people selling melon seeds. One of them has an especially loud chant.

完成 (use the grammar pattern to complete the following sentences):

1. 。。。其中很多字我都不認識。

2. 小鎮上有很多鋪子。。。

II. 為 N（所）V: to be V-ed by N

wéi   Passive voice construction

例

2.16   為同情心所驅駛，那位青年的目光已經落到這位婦人身上了。
Spurred on by his sense of sympathy, the young person's gaze had already fallen on the figure of this married woman.

1.   當鋪大多不為窮人所喜。
Most pawnshops are not liked by poor people.

2.   船艙為客商所擠滿。
The ship's hold was packed full with businessmen.

變換 (rewrite the following sentences in the grammar pattern):

1. 人們議論着陌生人的衣着。

2. 日光曬黑了廊簷。

III. 似： to seem; to appear; to look as if

Functions by itself as a verb, or in a modifying phrase

PATTERN:

pronounced shì:	（好）像 N 似的/地	"like an N"
	N 似的/地	
	（好）像 VE 似的/地	"appearing as if to VE"
	VE 似的/地	
pronounced sì:	似 VE 地	"appearing as if to VE"

完成 *(use the grammar pattern to complete the following sentences):*

1. 。。。其中很多字我都不认识。

2. 小镇上有很多铺子。。。

II. 为 N（所）V: to be V-ed by N

wéi　　　　　　　*Passive voice construction*

例

2.16　为同情心所驱驶，那位青年的目光已经落到这位妇人身上了。
Spurred on by his sense of sympathy, the young person's gaze had already fallen on the figure of this married woman.

1.　当铺大多不为穷人所喜。
Most pawnshops are not liked by poor people.

2.　船舱为客商所挤满。
The ship's hold was packed full with businessmen.

变换 *(rewrite the following sentences in the grammar pattern):*

1. 人们议论着陌生人的衣着。

2. 日光晒黑了廊檐。

III. 似: to seem; to appear; to look as if

Functions by itself as a verb, or in a modifying phrase

PATTERN:
pronounced shì:　　　（好）像 N 似的／地　　　"like an N"

　　　　　　　　　　　　N 似的／地

　　　　　　　　　　（好）像 VE 似的／地　　　"appearing as if to VE"

　　　　　　　　　　　　VE 似的／地

pronounced sì:　　　　似 VE 地　　　　　　　"appearing as if to VE"

例

4.6 　她像無聊似地消磨着自己的時光。
　　　Looking bored, she [continued to] fritter away her time.

4.16 　方謀暗自好笑，卻又安慰似地說：「。。。」
　　　Fang Mou laughed to himself, but also said in a comforting-like way, " . . ."

5.23 　陶校長似解釋地說：「。。。」
　　　Headmaster Tao said as if to explain, " . . ."

1. 　他好像心不在焉似地望着窗外。
　　Seeming preoccupied, he looked out the window.

2. 　小女孩穿着長裙，（像）老太婆似的。
　　Wearing a long skirt, the little girl looks like an old woman.

3. 　小女孩老太婆似地穿着長裙。
　　The little girl wears a long skirt in the way of an old woman.

4. 　他似安慰地回答道：「別着急。我們總有辦法的。」
　　He replied in a comforting-like way, "Don't be anxious. We can always find a way."

5. 　他的臉頰很紅，（好像）剛跑回來似的。
　　His cheeks were very red —(they looked) as if he had just run back.

參考 (cf.)

7.44 　蕭澗秋似受到諷刺一般（一樣/似的）。
　　　Xiao Jianqiu looked as if he had been mocked.

12.1 　蕭澗秋有如一隻鶴在空中飛翔一樣（一般/似的）。
　　　Xiao Jianqiu seemed like a crane gliding around in the air.

12.30 　蕭澗秋自供（一）般地說：「。。。」
　　　Xiao Jianqiu said as if confessing: " . . ."

變換

1. 他說：「您好。」彬彬有禮。

2. 文嫂凝視着河水給人一種絕望的樣子。

例

4.6　她像无聊似地消磨着自己的时光。
Looking bored, she [continued to] fritter away her time.

4.16　方谋暗自好笑，却又安慰似地说：「。。。」
Fang Mou laughed to himself, but also said in a comforting-like way, " . . ."

5.23　陶校长似解释地说：「。。。」
Headmaster Tao said as if to explain, " . . ."

1.　他好像心不在焉似地望着窗外。
Seeming preoccupied, he looked out the window.

2.　小女孩穿着长裙，（像）老太婆似的。
Wearing a long skirt, the little girl looks like an old woman.

3.　小女孩老太婆似地穿着长裙。
The little girl wears a long skirt in the way of an old woman.

4.　他似安慰地回答道：「别着急。我们总有办法的。」
He replied in a comforting-like way, "Don't be anxious. We can always find a way."

5.　他的脸颊很红，（好像）刚跑回来似的。
His cheeks were very red —(they looked) as if he had just run back.

参考 (cf.)

7.44　萧涧秋似受到讽刺一般（一样/似的）。
Xiao Jianqiu looked as if he had been mocked.

12.1　萧涧秋有如一只鹤在空中飞翔一样（一般/似的）。
Xiao Jianqiu seemed like a crane gliding around in the air.

12.30　萧涧秋自供（一）般地说：「。。。」
Xiao jianqiu said as if confessing: " . . ."

变换

1. 他说：「您好。」彬彬有礼。

2. 文嫂凝视着河水给人一种绝望的样子。

IV. 卻：　yet; however; nevertheless

Adverb: appears before the verb

PATTERN: S VE1（可是/但是）卻 VE2　　　　*Links two predicates for one subject*

　　　　　S1 VE1（可是/但是）S2 卻 VE2　　*Links two clauses with two different subjects*

例

4.16　方謀暗自好笑，卻又安慰似地說：「。。。」

　　　方謀暗自好笑，但他卻又安慰似地說：「。。。」

　　　方謀暗自好笑，但卻安慰似地說：「。。。」

　　　Fang Mou laughed to himself, but nevertheless said in a comforting-like way, " . . ."

5.18　有的人看了看也就算了。有的人卻指點着他，與別人議論：「欸，這是誰呀？」

　　　Some people took a look and then let it pass. However, [there were also] some people who, pointing at him, would talk about him with others: "Hey, who is that?"

1.　　他雖是我的鄰居，卻沒跟他說過話。

　　　Even though he is my neighbor, nevertheless, I have never spoken to him.

2.　　那小店鋪雖比不上大公司，可是賣的東西卻有些特別。

　　　Even though that small store cannot compare to a big company, the things for sale there nevertheless are somewhat unusual.

完成

1. 鎮上的人都認識陶校長，。。。

2. 。。。，可是陶校長卻很得意。

V. 無可奈何：　powerless, helpless; to not be able to do anything

Verb-object construction: may stand alone as a predicate or function as a modifier

例

4.15　方謀無可奈何地看了錢正興一眼。

　　　Powerless to do anything, Fang Mou glanced at Qian Zhengxing.

IV. 却: yet; however; nevertheless

Adverb: appears before the verb

PATTERN: S VE1（可是/但是）却 VE2　　　*Links two predicates for one subject*

　　　　　　S1 VE1（可是/但是）S2 却 VE2　　*Links two clauses with two different subjects*

例

4.16　方谋暗自好笑，却又安慰似地说：「。。。」

方谋暗自好笑，但他却又安慰似地说：「。。。」

方谋暗自好笑，但却安慰似地说：「。。。」

Fang Mou laughed to himself, but nevertheless said in a comforting-like way, " . . ."

5.18　有的人看了看也就算了。有的人却指点着他，与别人议论：「欸，这是谁呀？」

Some people took a look and then let it pass. However, [there were also] some people who, pointing at him, would talk about him with others: "Hey, who is that?"

1.　他虽是我的邻居，却没跟他说过话。

Even though he is my neighbor, nevertheless, I have never spoken to him.

2.　那小店铺虽比不上大公司，可是卖的东西却有些特别。

Even though that small store cannot compare to a big company, the things for sale there nevertheless are somewhat unusual.

完成

1.镇上的人都认识陶校长，。。。。

2.。。。，可是陶校长却很得意。

V. 无可奈何：powerless, helpless; to not be able to do anything

Verb-object construction: may stand alone as a predicate or function as a modifier

例

4.15　方谋无可奈何地看了钱正兴一眼。

Powerless to do anything, Fang Mou glanced at Qian Zhengxing.

1. 錢先生看着陶小姐走向內房不願意跟他説話，很是無可奈何，只好走向一把椅子坐下。
   Upon seeing that Miss Tao, unwilling to speak with him, was heading for the inside of the house, Mr. Qian felt very helpless and could only walk to a chair and sit down.

2. 老太太看着没人幫助的孤兒寡婦，無可奈何地歎了一口氣。
   Seeing that there was no one to help the orphan and widow, the old lady sighed, helpless to do anything.

解釋

1. 無可奈何花落去。

2. 他甚麽辦法都没有，唯有無可奈何的奈何了。

VI. 與：跟

PATTERN: N1 與 N2   N1 and N2   *Conjunction*

           N1 與 N2 V   N1 V with N2   *Coverb*

例

1.4 他們在談論着天氣與菩薩。
   They are talking about the weather and bodhisattvas.

5.19 有的人卻指點着他，與別人議論。
   Some people however, pointing at him, talked [about him] with others.

1. 老奶奶與孫女一起坐在船頭。
   The old granny and her granddaughter sat together at the bow of the boat.

2. 老奶奶與女孩子作朋友。
   The old granny makes friends with the girl.

解釋 (explain the following sentences):

1. 父親與兒子都在船上。

2. 父親與兒子談話。

1. 钱先生看着陶小姐走向内房不愿意跟他说话，很是无可奈何，只好走向一把椅子坐下。

   Upon seeing that Miss Tao, unwilling to speak with him, was heading for the inside of the house, Mr. Qian felt very helpless and could only walk to a chair and sit down.

2. 老太太看着没人帮助的孤儿寡妇，无可奈何地叹了一口气。

   Seeing that there was no one to help the orphan and widow, the old lady sighed, helpless to do anything.

解释

1. 无可奈何花落去。

2. 他什么办法都没有，唯有无可奈何的奈何了。

VI. 与：跟

PATTERN: N1 与 N2	N1 and N2	*Conjunction*
N1 与 N2 V	N1 V with N2	*Coverb*

例

1.4 他们在谈论着天气与菩萨。

They are talking about the weather and bodhisattvas.

5.19 有的人却指点着他，与别人议论。

Some people however, pointing at him, talked [about him] with others.

1. 老奶奶与孙女一起坐在船头。

The old granny and her granddaughter sat together at the bow of the boat.

2. 老奶奶与女孩子作朋友。

The old granny makes friends with the girl.

解释 *(explain the following sentences):*

1. 父亲与儿子都在船上。

2. 父亲与儿子谈话。

VII. 心不在焉： inattentive; preoccupied

Stative verb clause: stands alone as a predicate or functions as a modifier

PATTERN: S 心不在焉。

　　　　 S 心不在焉地 VE

例

4.17　錢正興心不在焉地勉強笑了一下。
　　　 Preoccupied, Qian Zhengxing forced a smile.

1.　　他並不是聽不懂英文，他(是)心不在焉。
　　　 It's not that he doesn't understand English; [it's that] he's preoccupied.

2.　　欸，我在問你呢！你怎麼那麼心不在焉地坐在那裏，呆呆地一句話也不說？
　　　 Hey, I'm asking you [a question]! How can you sit there so preoccupied, woodenly not saying a single thing?

回答

1. 他為甚麼心不在焉呢？

2. 你怎麼知道他心不在焉呢？

三。生詞練習

填空一 *(fill in the blanks)*

為；將；引起；向；破舊；卻；其中；寬敞；似；似乎；使；幾乎；要；唯有；隨即；異常；顯得；珍惜；至

1. 自紐約（　　）芝加哥有多少英里？

2. 蕭澗秋（　　）同情心所驅駛，自然地去幫助有困難的人。

3. 人人都向蕭澗秋注視，（　　）他很不好意思。

4. 他下了課，（　　）向圖書館走去，並沒有跟同學說甚麼話。

VII. 心不在焉： inattentive; preoccupied

Stative verb clause: stands alone as a predicate or functions as a modifier

PATTERN: S 心不在焉。

S 心不在焉地 VE

例

4.17   钱正兴心不在焉地勉强笑了一下。

Preoccupied, Qian Zhengxing forced a smile.

1.   他并不是听不懂英文，他（是）心不在焉。

It's not that he doesn't understand English; [it's that] he's preoccupied.

2.   欸，我在问你呢！你怎么那么心不在焉地坐在那里，呆呆地一句话也不说？

Hey, I'm asking you [a question]! How can you sit there so preoccupied, woodenly not saying a single thing?

回答

1. 他为什么心不在焉呢？

2. 你怎么知道他心不在焉呢？

三。生词练习

填空一 *(fill in the blanks)*

为；将；引起；向；破旧；却；其中；宽敞；似；似乎；使；几乎；要；唯有；随即；异常；显得；珍惜；至

1. 自纽约（   ）芝加哥有多少英里？

2. 萧涧秋（   ）同情心所驱驶，自然地去帮助有困难的人。

3. 人人都向萧涧秋注视，（   ）他很不好意思。

4. 他下了课，（   ）向图书馆走去，并没有跟同学说甚么话。

5. 那胖子是個買賣橘子的客商，你提到今年橘子的行情，當然會（　）他的興趣。

6. 錢正興樣子看起來有些扭捏，但他的同事態度（　）很自然。

7. 今天是週末，同學們都出去玩兒去了。（　）小民一人在家。

8. 那飛機飛（　）藍天白雲，一會兒就看不見了。

9. 飛機場上的服務員正忙着（　）托運標籤分給旅客。

10. 大城市使我厭倦了，這小鎮倒像是世外桃源（　）的，讓人覺得平安。

11. 校役是甚麼事都得會做的。（　）擔行李就擔行李，做飯時候就到廚房去。

12. 她在房中走來走去，又總是抬頭看看鐘，（　）有些着急。

13. 怎麼你看起來那麼面熟？我（　）在甚麼地方見過你。哦，對了。你去年是不是也到西湖去開會了？

14. 多年不見，你長得那麼高了，樣子完全變了。我（　）不認識你了。

15. 梅花有幾種不同的顏色，（　）有一種我不喜歡。

16. 這是一所老式的房子。房中的陳設也非常（　）。

17. 那個庭院中有花有樹。跟擠滿了客商的大街比起來顯得（　）幽靜。

18. 我覺得地方太狹小了。我們把那張大桌子搬出去吧。使屋子裏（　）一些。

19. 很多人都知道時間一去不回，卻還是忘了（　）時間。

5. 那胖子是个买卖橘子的客商，你提到今年橘子的行情，当然会（　　）他的兴趣。

6. 钱正兴样子看起来有些扭捏，但他的同事态度（　　）很自然。

7. 今天是周末，同学们都出去玩儿去了。（　　）小民一人在家。

8. 那飞机飞（　　）蓝天白云，一会儿就看不见了。

9. 飞机场上的服务员正忙着（　　）托运标签分给旅客。

10. 大城市使我厌倦了，这小镇倒像是世外桃源（　　）的，让人觉得平安。

11. 校役是什么事都得会做的。（　　）担行李就担行李，做饭时候就到厨房去。

12. 她在房中走来走去，又总是抬头看看钟，（　　）有些着急。

13. 怎么你看起来那么面熟？我（　　）在什么地方见过你。哦，对了。你去年是不是也到西湖去开会了？

14. 多年不见，你长得那么高了，样子完全变了。我（　　）不认识你了。

15. 梅花有几种不同的颜色，（　　）有一种我不喜欢。

16. 这是一所老式的房子。房中的陈设也非常（　　）。

17. 那个庭院中有花有树。跟挤满了客商的大街比起来显得（　　）幽静。

18. 我觉得地方太狭小了。我们把那张大桌子搬出去吧。使屋子里（　　）一些。

19. 很多人都知道时间一去不回，却还是忘了（　　）时间。

填空二

無聊；氣悶；輕鬆；探索；悲哀；微微；世外桃源；約；心不在焉；無可奈何；
　足足；消磨；不時地；勉強；扭捏；厭倦；模樣；興隆；呆呆地；不自在

1. 我念中文念了（　　）三年了，一天也不少。

2. 世界上真有一個甚麼問題都沒有的、人人都快樂的（　　）嗎？

3. 他凝視着窗外，（　　）坐在那裏，好像在想着甚麼事情。

4. 他在圖書館見了我，只（　　）點了點頭就又去看書了。我們沒機會多説話。

5. 生活在世界上甚麼是人最不幸，最（　　）的事呢？回答是：很小的時候父母
　就死了；中年的時候丈夫或妻子死了；老年的時候兒女死了。

6. 每天一個人只是吃了睡，睡了吃，真是沒有意思，太（　　）了。

7. 屋子裏窗戶都關着，空氣不新鮮，使人覺得非常（　　）。

8. 考試完了，一點也不緊張了，感覺很（　　）。

9. 上個週末老張跟朋友們去酒館兒（　　）了一個晚上。

10. 女孩子大聲地唱着歌，態度非常自然，一點兒沒有（　　）的樣子。

11. 統艙裏太氣悶了，那位青年（　　）坐了一會兒，實在忍受不了，就到船頭上
　去了。

12. 他這兩天上課總是看着窗外，不知老師同學們在講些甚麼，顯然是（　　）。

13. 女朋友生了病，他（　　）問她要不要喝橘子水，還是回房間去休息一下。

14. 他對每天九點上班，五點下班的工作實在是（　　）了，所以想回學校去再
　念點書。

15. 生，老，病，死，人人都得經過，是（　　）的事。

16. 小方買那汽車用去（　　）兩萬塊錢。你問到底一共是兩萬幾千幾百幾，他
　自己也説不清。

17. 他是做買賣的，當然希望生意（　　），賺很多錢。

填空二

无聊；气闷；轻松；探索；悲哀；微微；世外桃源；约；心不在焉；无可奈何；
足足；消磨；不时地；勉强；扭捏；厌倦；模样；兴隆；呆呆地；不自在

1. 我念中文念了（　　）三年了，一天也不少。

2. 世界上真有一个什么问题都没有的、人人都快乐的（　　）吗？

3. 他凝视着窗外，（　　）坐在那里，好像在想着什么事情。

4. 他在图书馆见了我，只（　　）点了点头就又去看书了。我们没机会多说话。

5. 生活在世界上什么是人最不幸，最（　　）的事呢？回答是：很小的时候父母
   就死了；中年的时候丈夫或妻子死了；老年的时候儿女死了。

6. 每天一个人只是吃了睡，睡了吃，真是没有意思，太（　　）了。

7. 屋子里窗户都关着，空气不新鲜，使人觉得非常（　　）。

8. 考试完了，一点也不紧张了，感觉很（　　）。

9. 上个周末老张跟朋友们去酒馆儿（　　）了一个晚上。

10. 女孩子大声地唱着歌，态度非常自然，一点儿没有（　　）的样子。

11. 统舱里太气闷了，那位青年（　　）坐了一会儿，实在忍受不了，就到船头上
    去了。

12. 他这两天上课总是看着窗外，不知老师同学们在讲些什么，显然是（　　）。

13. 女朋友生了病，他（　　）问她要不要喝橘子水，还是回房间去休息一下。

14. 他对每天九点上班，五点下班的工作实在是（　　）了，所以想回学校去再
    念点书。

15. 生，老，病，死，人人都得经过，是（　　）的事。

16. 小方买那汽车用去（　　）两万块钱。你问到底一共是两万几千几百几，他
    自己也说不清。

17. 他是做买卖的，当然希望生意（　　），赚很多钱。

18. 他雖然明白朋友對他說那些話完全是好意，但是還是覺得很（　　）。

19. 小張對甚麼都有興趣，都要研究。他說連一片花瓣都值得（　　）。

20. 你說的張先生是甚麼（　　）啊？是不是高高瘦瘦的，穿長袍的那位啊？

四。說話練習

　　　　用括號 (parentheses) 中的詞介紹
　　　　下列人物的年齡、身材、外表、衣着、想法等等：

1. 青年，即蕭澗秋（風塵；身穿。。。；足下。。。）

2. 寡婦，即文嫂（年齡；身穿。。。；凝視；瞧；酸痛；絕望）

3. 女孩（橘子；癡癡地；玩弄）

4. 方謀（年齡；身穿。。。；老臉皮）

5. 陶嵐（年齡；美貌；厭惡；消磨；無聊）

6. 錢正興（紈絝子弟；彬彬有禮；扭捏；心不在焉）

7. 陶慕侃（年齡；渾厚；身材）

　　　　　討論 (discuss)：

介紹一個你所認識的人。

五。作文 (Composition)

　　第三景《渡頭》的畫面上有些甚麼？要告訴我們甚麼？

18. 他虽然明白朋友对他说那些话完全是好意，但是还是觉得很（　　）。

19. 小张对什么都有兴趣，都要研究。他说连一片花瓣都值得（　　）。

20. 你说的张先生是什么（　　）啊？是不是高高瘦瘦的，穿长袍的那位啊？

四。说话练习

用括号 (parentheses) 中的词介绍
下列人物的年龄、身材、外表、衣着、想法等等。

1. 青年，即萧涧秋（风尘；身穿。。。；足下。。。）
2. 寡妇，即文嫂（年龄；身穿。。。；凝视；瞧；酸痛；绝望）
3. 女孩（橘子；痴痴地；玩弄）
4. 方谋（年龄；身穿。。。；老脸皮）
5. 陶岚（年龄；美貌；厌恶；消磨；无聊）
6. 钱正兴（纨袴子弟；彬彬有礼；扭捏；心不在焉）
7. 陶慕侃（年龄；浑厚；身材）

讨论 (discuss)：
介绍一个你所认识的人。

五。作文 (Composition)

第三景《渡头》的画面上有些什么？要告诉我们什么？

練習二：第六景至第十景

一。閱讀測驗

六至八景

1. 陶校長怎麼向錢正興、方謀兩位介紹蕭澗秋？兩位又怎麼回答？

2. 方謀怎麼自我介紹？

3. 陶校長吩咐阿榮甚麼？

4. 錢正興和蕭澗秋對自然現象與人間的關係有甚麼不同的看法？

5. 方謀說近幾年有甚麼災難？

6. 陶嵐為甚麼想跟蕭澗秋請教？

7. 陶校長說他妹妹的脾氣怎麼樣？陶嵐怎麼解釋自己的脾氣？

8. 錢正興為甚麼走出房去？

9. 陶媽媽在廚房裏做甚麼？

10. 陶媽媽為甚麼認為蕭澗秋會吃不來那些菜？錢正興為甚麼不同意？

九景

1. 方謀說信仰怎麼重要？他有甚麼信仰？

2. 錢正興為甚麼不能完全同意方謀的說法？

3. 蕭澗秋為甚麼不信仰一種主義？

4. 陶嵐對那些喜歡談信仰的人有甚麼看法？

练习二：第六景至第十景

一。阅读测验

六至八景

1. 陶校长怎么向钱正兴、方谋两位介绍萧涧秋？两位又怎么回答？

2. 方谋怎么自我介绍？

3. 陶校长吩咐阿荣什么？

4. 钱正兴和萧涧秋对自然现象与人间的关系有什么不同的看法？

5. 方谋说近几年有什么灾难？

6. 陶岚为什么想跟萧涧秋请教？

7. 陶校长说他妹妹的脾气怎么样？陶岚怎么解释自己的脾气？

8. 钱正兴为什么走出房去？

9. 陶妈妈在厨房里做什么？

10. 陶妈妈为什么认为萧涧秋会吃不来那些菜？钱正兴为什么不同意？

九景

1. 方谋说信仰怎么重要？他有什么信仰？

2. 钱正兴为什么不能完全同意方谋的说法？

3. 萧涧秋为什么不信仰一种主义？

4. 陶岚对那些喜欢谈信仰的人有什么看法？

5. 蕭澗秋怎麼認識李志豪先生？

6. 在陶校長口中李先生是個甚麼樣的人？

7. 李志豪和蕭澗秋在學校時參加了甚麼運動？

8. 方謀、錢正興、陶慕侃、蕭澗秋、陶嵐對李志豪和他的家小的態度怎麼不同？

二。語法練習

I. 以 N V: to V with N; to use N to V
(V= 作答；表示；解釋；招待；歡迎；請教）
Coverb construction marking the object: precedes the main verb
cf. EX 2.II, 7.VI

例

7.3   蕭澗秋僅以微笑作答。
Xiao Jianqiu merely replied with a smile.

1.   他以玩笑的口吻解釋。
He used a joking tone to explain.
He explained in a joking tone.

2.   校長以茶與點心招待教師們。
The principal extended his hospitality to the teachers by [serving] tea and cakes.

變換

1. 為了表示不同意，他搖搖頭。

2. 他向蕭先生請教一個信仰的問題。

5. 萧涧秋怎么认识李志豪先生？

6. 在陶校长口中李先生是个什么样的人？

7. 李志豪和萧涧秋在学校时参加了什么运动？

8. 方谋、钱正兴、陶慕侃、萧涧秋、陶岚对李志豪和他的家小的态度怎么不同？

二。语法练习

I. 以 N V: to V with N; to use N to V
（V=作答；表示；解释；招待；欢迎；请教）
Coverb construction marking the object: precedes the main verb
cf. EX 2.II, 7.VI

例

7.3　萧涧秋仅以微笑作答。
Xiao Jianqiu merely replied with a smile.

1.　他以玩笑的口吻解释。
He used a joking tone to explain.
He explained in a joking tone.

2.　校长以茶与点心招待教师们。
The principal extended his hospitality to the teachers by [serving] tea and cakes.

变换

1. 为了表示不同意，他摇摇头。

2. 他向萧先生请教一个信仰的问题。

II. 以： "with"

Post-verbal construction marking the direct object

cf. EX 2.I, 7.VI

PATTERN: 給 X (indirect object) 以 Y (direct object)   "to give Y to X"

回 [X (indirect object)] 以 Y (direct object)   "to reply [to X] with Y"

例

5.6   他的面貌給人以渾厚的印象。
His appearance gives people the impression of being simple and honest.

5.25   蕭澗秋回〔他〕以淡淡的一笑。
Xiao Jianqiu responded (to him) with a weak smile.

1.   那所房子給人以幽靜的感覺。
That house gives people a feeling of peace and seclusion.

2.   一聽說來了個陌生人，大家不由得回以好奇的目光。
When everyone heard that a stranger had arrived, they could only respond with curious stares.

變換

1. 朋友送他一枝梅花，他送朋友淡墨山水一幅。

2. 朝香的人要菩薩保護，菩薩總是微笑地回答。

III. 至於 X： as for X

Coverb-object construction at the beginning of a sentence that introduces

a new, often contrasting, topic X to the discussion

cf. 於: EX 4.III, 8.I, 9.II

例

7.11   天氣的變化是自然的現象。至於人間的災難。。。
Changes in the weather are natural phenomena. As for human disasters . . .

1.   現在重要的是向前看。至於以前的不幸，人們大多已經忘記，不必再談了。
The important thing now is to look ahead. As for past misfortunes, most people have already forgotten them; there is no need to speak of them any further.

II. 以："with"

Post-verbal construction marking the direct object

cf. *EX 2.I, 7.VI*

PATTERN: 给 X (indirect object) 以 Y (direct object)　　　　"to give Y to X"

　　　　　　回 [X (indirect object)] 以 Y (direct object)　　"to reply [to X] with Y"

例

5.6　他的面貌给人以浑厚的印象。

His appearance gives people the impression of being simple and honest.

5.25　萧涧秋回〔他〕以淡淡的一笑。

Xiao Jianqiu responded (to him) with a weak smile.

1.　那所房子给人以幽静的感觉。

That house gives people a feeling of peace and seclusion.

2.　一听说来了个陌生人，大家不由得回以好奇的目光。

When everyone heard that a stranger had arrived, they could only respond with curious stares.

变换

1. 朋友送他一枝梅花，他送朋友淡墨山水一幅。

2. 朝香的人要菩萨保护，菩萨总是微笑地回答。

III. 至于 X： as for X

Coverb-object construction at the beginning of a sentence that introduces

a new, often contrasting, topic X to the discussion

cf. 于： *EX 4.III, 8.I, 9.II*

例

7.11　天气的变化是自然的现象。至于人间的灾难。。。

Changes in the weather are natural phenomena. As for human disasters ...

1.　现在重要的是向前看。至于以前的不幸，人们大多已经忘记，不必再谈了。

The important thing now is to look ahead. As for past misfortunes, most people have already forgotten them; there is no need to speak of them any further.

2.　蕭澗秋跑遍了大半個中國，旅行過很多地方。至於閱歷，恐怕不如陶校長。

Xiao Jianqiu has traveled all over the greater half of China, visiting many places. [But] as for experience, perhaps, he doesn't have as much as Principal Tao.

完成

1. 。。。，至於我是沒有問題的。

2. 說到人情世故他並不懂。。。

IV. 。。。就是了：... and that's it; that's all there is to it; just

Sentence-final particle

例

7.21　我有甚麼好介紹的？以後我們認識就是了。

What is there about me to introduce? We'll get to know each other later, that's all.

1.　怎麼？他生氣了嗎？你寫一封信解釋一下就是了。

What, he got mad? Just write a letter of apology; that's all there is to it.

2.　皇后說，「他們餓得沒有米吃了嗎？吃點兒點心就是了。」

The empress said, "They're starving with no rice to eat? They could just eat some cakes."

完成

1. 。。。我不告訴他就是了。

2. 你不必做甚麼山珍海味招待客人，。。。

2.　萧涧秋跑遍了大半个中国，旅行过很多地方。至于阅历，恐怕不如陶校长。

Xiao Jianqiu has traveled all over the greater half of China, visiting many places. [But] as for experience, perhaps, he doesn't have as much as Principal Tao.

完成

1.。。。，至于我是没有问题的。

2. 说到人情世故他并不懂。。。

IV. 。。。就是了：... and that's it; that's all there is to it; just

Sentence-final particle

例
7.21　我有什么好介绍的？以后我们认识就是了。

What is there about me to introduce? We'll get to know each other later, that's all.

1.　怎么？他生气了吗？你写一封信解释一下就是了。

What, he got mad? Just write a letter of apology; that's all there is to it.

2.　皇后说，「他们饿得没有米吃了吗？吃点儿点心就是了。」

The empress said, "They're starving with no rice to eat? They could just eat some cakes."

完成

1.。。。我不告诉他就是了。

2. 你不必做什么山珍海味招待客人，。。。

V. 不過/僅是/只是。。。罷了：　nothing more than . . . and that's all;
only . . . and nothing more

Adverbial construction

cf. 僅：*EX 3.V*

例

7.41　我不過是不懂人情世故罷了。
我僅是不懂人情世故罷了。
我只是不懂人情世故罷了。
It's only that I don't understand the ways of the world and nothing more.

1.　他不過考取了大學罷了。至於將來的前途還說不定呢。
He did nothing more than get into college. As for his future, it's still hard to say.

2.　學生們遊行僅是表示反對罷了。並不是要鬧革命。
The demonstrations merely express students' opposition; they don't really want to stir up revolution.

完成

1. 他不過去過的地方多一點兒罷了。哪裏。。。

2. 。。。並不要你給他買房子。

VI. 凡是 specified N 都 。。。 ： all those N that fit the specification . . .

例

9.5　凡是想救國的青年都應該信仰三民主義。
All young people who want to save China should believe in the Three Principles of the People.

1.　凡是在座的人都舉起酒杯一飲而盡。
All those present raised their wine cups and emptied them in a single gulp.

2.　那時候凡是有志氣的青年都要到廣州去。
At that time, all the young people with ambition wanted to go to Guangzhou.

V. 不过/仅是/只是 。。。罢了：　nothing more than . . . and that's all;
　　　　　　　　　　　　　　　　　only . . . and nothing more

Adverbial construction

cf. 仅：*EX 3.V*

例

7.41　我不过是不懂人情世故罢了。
　　　我仅是不懂人情世故罢了。
　　　我只是不懂人情世故罢了。
　　　It's only that I don't understand the ways of the world and nothing more.

1.　他不过考取了大学罢了。至于将来的前途还说不定呢。
　　He did nothing more than get into college. As for his future, it's still hard to say.

2.　学生们游行仅是表示反对罢了。并不是要闹革命。
　　The demonstrations merely express students' opposition; they don't really want to stir up revolution.

完成

1. 他不过去过的地方多一点儿罢了。哪里 。。。

2. 。。。并不要你给他买房子。

VI. 凡是 specified N 都 。。。：　all those N that fit the specification . . .

例

9.5　凡是想救国的青年都应该信仰三民主义。
　　All young people who want to save China should believe in the Three Principles of the People.

1.　凡是在座的人都举起酒杯一饮而尽。
　　All those present raised their wine cups and emptied them in a single gulp.

2.　那时候凡是有志气的青年都要到广州去。
　　At that time, all the young people with ambition wanted to go to Guangzhou.

變換

1. 誰有新思想誰就想出國去。

2. 不論甚麼鋪子賣日本貨，他們都要去搜查。

VII. 旁若無人： lit., as if no one else were there: as if no one else mattered; completely self-assured

Stative verb phrase: stands alone as a predicate or functions as a modifier

例

7.41　陶嵐繼續旁若無人地說：「。。。」
Tao Lan continued talking as if no else were there, " . . ."

1.　　為甚麼她的態度像皇后似的，那麼旁若無人？
Why does she have an attitude like an empress, so self-assured?

2.　　他一個人在人羣中走着，旁若無人似地誰也不理。
He walked along by himself in the midst of the crowd, ignoring everyone as if they didn't matter.

回答

1. 為甚麼你覺得他旁若無人呢？

2. 什麼情形會使一個人旁若無人呢？

三。生詞練習

填空一

東奔西跑；非；呈現；負擔；以；至於；嘛；其實；就是了；冷落；抱歉；領；
難道；凡；待；白；敝；一般；變化；閱歷

1. 她（　）茶和瓜子來招待客人。

2. 這一種奇怪的病，到現在還不知道是甚麼原因引起的，正（　）我們去研究。

变换

1. 谁有新思想谁就想出国去。

2. 不论什么铺子卖日本货，他们都要去搜查。

VII. 旁若无人： lit., as if no one else were there: as if no one else mattered; completely self-assured
Stative verb phrase: stands alone as a predicate or functions as a modifier

例

7.41   陶岚继续旁若无人地说：「。。。」
Tao Lan continued talking as if no else were there, " . . ."

1.   为什么她的态度像皇后似的，那么旁若无人？
Why does she have an attitude like an empress, so self-assured?

2.   他一个人在人群中走着，旁若无人似地谁也不理。
He walked along by himself in the midst of the crowd, ignoring everyone as if they didn't matter.

回答

1. 为什么你觉得他旁若无人呢？

2. 什么情形会使一个人旁若无人呢？

三。生词练习

填空一

东奔西跑；非；呈现；负担；以；至于；嘛；其实；就是了；冷落；抱歉；领；
难道；凡；待；白；敝；一般；变化；阅历

1. 她（   ）茶和瓜子来招待客人。

2. 这一种奇怪的病，到现在还不知道是什么原因引起的，正（   ）我们去研
究。

3. 今晚我還得開兩個小時的汽車呢，不能陪您多喝酒，真（　　）。

4. 他辦事很有經驗，這件事（　　）得他去辦不成。

5. 「您貴姓？」「（　　）姓張。」

6. 你說甚麼？他考取了？他用功了那麼久，總算時間沒有（　　）費。

7. 那時候，（　　）是信三民主義的人都是革命黨。

8. 李先生跑過很多地方，又有很多人生經驗。可以說（　　）豐富。

9. 他是最好的主人，對每一位客人都熱情招待，不會讓人受到（　　）的。

10. （　　）他真的離開這個世界了嗎？我不信。上星期他還給我打過電話，只說最近有點不舒服。

11. 昨夜下了一場大雪。今早出門一看，眼前（　　）出一片銀色世界。

12. 雖然他只是我的同學，我卻看他似老師（　　），甚麼都要向他請教。

13. 他們兩人看起來很像兄弟，（　　）他們並不是兄弟。

14. 你不願意我去，我不去（　　）。你為甚麼還不高興呢？

15. 我的事情已經解決了，（　　）你的問題，只好明天再說吧！

16. 平常他的意見是很多的。可是提起這件事情（　　），他可沒說甚麼。

17. 他的公司在西邊，工廠在東邊，又不時地到外國去談生意，（　　），非常地忙。

18. 你們都跟我來，我（　　）你們去。

19. 去年他回老家去看父母。老家汽車多了，房子也多了。人人都穿得很漂亮。（　　）很大。

20. 他上有父母，下有兒女，全家的生活都要靠他，（　　）很重。

3. 今晚我还得开两个小时的汽车呢，不能陪您多喝酒，真（　　）。

4. 他办事很有经验，这件事（　　）得他去办不成。

5. 您贵姓？」「（　　）姓张。」

6. 你说什么？他考取了？他用功了那么久，总算时间没有（　　）费。

7. 那时候，（　　）是信三民主义的人都是革命党。

8. 李先生跑过很多地方，又有很多人生经验。可以说（　　）丰富。

9. 他是最好的主人，对每一位客人都热情招待，不会让人受到（　　）的。

10. （　　）他真的离开这个世界了吗？我不信。上星期他还给我打过电话，只说最近有点不舒服。

11. 昨夜下了一场大雪。今早出门一看，眼前（　　）出一片银色世界。

12. 虽然他只是我的同学，我却看他似老师（　　），什么都要向他请教。

13. 他们两人看起来很像兄弟，（　　）他们并不是兄弟。

14. 你不愿意我去，我不去（　　）。你为什么还不高兴呢？

15. 我的事情已经解决了，（　　）你的问题，只好明天再说吧！

16. 平常他的意见是很多的。可是提起这件事情（　　），他可没说什么。

17. 他的公司在西边，工厂在东边，又不时地到外国去谈生意，（　　），非常地忙。

18. 你们都跟我来，我（　　）你们去。

19. 去年他回老家去看父母。老家汽车多了，房子也多了。人人都穿得很漂亮。（　　）很大。

20. 他上有父母，下有儿女，全家的生活都要靠他，（　　）很重。

填空二

罷了；吃不來；感觸；原諒；順水推舟；沈寂；竭力；一飲而盡；高談闊論；
不祥之兆；示意；程度；興致勃勃；人情世故；光臨；熱氣騰騰；生疏；按；
旁若無人；各色各樣

1. 他對看電影最有興趣了，一提起電影來，他就高興起來，（　　）地說個沒完。

2. 這個人天真得像小孩子一樣，不懂人與人之間的關係，（　　）一點都不知道。

3. 他覺得自己是天下第一重要的人，說話、做事老是（　　），愛怎麼就怎麼，完全不管別人怎麼想。

4. （　　）陽曆來說，十一月還是秋天呢。

5. 對不起，請（　　），我不是故意要你生氣。我不知道是他先打你，你才打他的。

6. 提起老朋友病得厲害，一時大家都感到無話可說，空氣（　　）了下來。

7. 你連豆腐都（　　），還說自己愛吃中國飯！

8. 謝謝你到我家來。我們非常歡迎你的（　　）。

9. 他的中文已經學到了很深的（　　）了。寫一封簡單的信會有甚麼問題呢？

10. 聽到李先生的死，蕭澗秋（　　）很深。

11. 那家百貨公司賣（　　）的東西，甚麼都買得到。

12. 在那個又冷又餓的晚上，我們見了這（　　）的火鍋，立刻覺得暖和起來。

13. 老錢一聽經理要去紐約，就立刻（　　）地說他也要去紐約，可以開車送經理去。

14. 他在外面跑了半天，一回家就將一大杯橘子水（　　）。

15. 聽說，狗忽然在夜裏哭叫對它的主人是（　　）。也許那家人將有不幸的事發生。

填空二

罢了；吃不来；感触；原谅；顺水推舟；沉寂；竭力；一饮而尽；高谈阔论；
不祥之兆；示意；程度；兴致勃勃；人情世故；光临；热气腾腾；生疏；按；
旁若无人；各色各样

1. 他对看电影最有兴趣了，一提起电影来，他就高兴起来，（　　）地说个没完。

2. 这个人天真得像小孩子一样，不懂人与人之间的关系，（　　）一点都不知道。

3. 他觉得自己是天下第一重要的人，说话、做事老是（　　），爱怎么就怎么，完全不管别人怎么想。

4. （　　）阳历来说，十一月还是秋天呢。

5. 对不起，请（　　），我不是故意要你生气。我不知道是他先打你，你才打他的。

6. 提起老朋友病得厉害，一时大家都感到无话可说，空气（　　）了下来。

7. 你连豆腐都（　　），还说自己爱吃中国饭！

8. 谢谢你到我家来。我们非常欢迎你的（　　）。

9. 他的中文已经学到了很深的（　　）了。写一封简单的信会有什么问题呢？

10. 听到李先生的死，萧涧秋（　　）很深。

11. 那家百货公司卖（　　）的东西，什么都买得到。

12. 在那个又冷又饿的晚上，我们见了这（　　）的火锅，立刻觉得暖和起来。

13. 老钱一听经理要去纽约，就立刻（　　）地说他也要去纽约，可以开车送经理去。

14. 他在外面跑了半天，一回家就将一大杯橘子水（　　）。

15. 听说，狗忽然在夜里哭叫对它的主人是（　　）。也许那家人将有不幸的事发生。

16. 幾位先生都對國家大事有興趣，一見面就（　　）起來，越說聲音越大，個個都以為自己最有道理。

17. 一個夏天沒念中文，很多字都不認識了，變得（　　）了。

18. 他手指着房門上「不準抽煙」的牌子，（　　）想抽煙的人走出房去。

19. 他不過隨便說說（　　）。誰又會真的相信？

20. 他（　　）要把那件工作作好，可是時間不夠，不能完成。

四。說話練習

   用括號中的詞來說：

1. 陶嵐給人的印象。（大方；活潑；神態；嬌養；柔媚）
2. 李志豪這個人。（演講；家小；有志氣；前途；陣亡）
3. 在廚房裏做飯做菜的活動。（切菜；烹調；打雜；山珍海味）

   討論：

談一個朋友的不幸。

五。作文

  描畫 (describe) 第十景：《陶嵐在蕭澗秋的房間裏》

16. 几位先生都对国家大事有兴趣，一见面就（　　）起来，越说声音越大，个个都以为自己最有道理。

17. 一个夏天没念中文，很多字都不认识了，变得（　　）了。

18. 他手指着房门上「不准抽烟」的牌子，（　　）想抽烟的人走出房去。

19. 他不过随便说说（　　）。谁又会真的相信？

20. 他（　　）要把那件工作作好，可是时间不够，不能完成。

四。说话练习

用括号中的词来说：

1. 陶岚给人的印象。（大方；活泼；神态；娇养；柔媚）

2. 李志豪这个人。（演讲；家小；有志气；前途；阵亡）

3. 在厨房里做饭做菜的活动。（切菜；烹调；打杂；山珍海味）

讨论：

谈一个朋友的不幸。

五。作文

描画 *(describe)* 第十景：《陶岚在萧涧秋的房间里》

練習三：第十一景至第十五景

一。閱讀測驗

十一至十二景

1. 蕭澗秋到了小屋前就立刻敲門進去了嗎？

2. 文嫂看見有人到她家來，她歡迎嗎？

3. 蕭澗秋說他為甚麼到她家來？

4. 文嫂的孩子在哪兒？為甚麼？

5. 文嫂以後的生活可以靠親戚和田地嗎？

6. 文嫂說她為甚麼要活下去？

7. 蕭澗秋用甚麼話來安慰文嫂活下去？

8. 蕭澗秋說他以後打算負擔一點兒這兩個孩子的責任是甚麼意思？為甚麼呢？

9. 蕭澗秋想給文嫂鈔票；她怎麼想？

10. 我們怎麼知道蕭澗秋離開文嫂家時很愉快？

11. 陶嵐看見蕭澗秋，說了些甚麼話？

12. 蕭澗秋看見陶嵐，說了甚麼客氣話？

13. 蕭澗秋以為陶嵐要看哪方面的書？

14. 陶嵐以前想過要學些甚麼？她真有興趣嗎？

15. 陶嵐怎麼知道蕭澗秋去了西村？

练习三：第十一景至第十五景

一。阅读测验

十一至十二景

1. 萧涧秋到了小屋前就立刻敲门进去了吗？

2. 文嫂看见有人到她家来，她欢迎吗？

3. 萧涧秋说他为什么到她家来？

4. 文嫂的孩子在哪儿？为什么？

5. 文嫂以后的生活可以靠亲戚和田地吗？

6. 文嫂说她为什么要活下去？

7. 萧涧秋用什么话来安慰文嫂活下去？

8. 萧涧秋说他以后打算负担一点儿这两个孩子的责任是什么意思？为什么呢？

9. 萧涧秋想给文嫂钞票；她怎么想？

10. 我们怎么知道萧涧秋离开文嫂家时很愉快？

11. 陶岚看见萧涧秋，说了些什么话？

12. 萧涧秋看见陶岚，说了什么客气话？

13. 萧涧秋以为陶岚要看哪方面的书？

14. 陶岚以前想过要学些什么？她真有兴趣吗？

15. 陶岚怎么知道萧涧秋去了西村？

16. 蕭澗秋對陶嵐的印象如何？

17. 陶嵐對自己的情形怎麼不滿意？

18. 陶嵐來找蕭澗秋的目的是甚麼？

十三至十五景

1. 蕭澗秋寫的樂譜叫甚麼名字？

2. 陶嵐聽了蕭澗秋彈奏的曲調時，有甚麼感覺？

3. 描畫一下夏天西湖的夜晚。

4. 陶嵐那時看見的青年是誰？陶嵐以為那位青年將要做甚麼？

5. 蕭澗秋說那時候有兩個女學生在做甚麼？

6. 那時候蕭澗秋為甚麼徬徨？

7. 蕭澗秋怎麼克服了他的徬徨？

二。語法練習

    I. 為 X 而 VE: because of X, VE; for the sake of X, VE

     wèi   *Coverb construction in which X, the reason or purpose,*
                           may be either a noun or verbal expression

        cf. 而： *EX 2.VI, 3.V, 5.IV, 7.IV, 9.V*

例

11.14 她衣單，全身為寒冷而顫抖。
      She wore only a single layer of clothing; her whole body was shivering because she was so cold.

1.   小孩子為看到陌生人而受驚。
      Because the child saw a stranger, he became frightened.

2.   他並不是為了好看而穿皮袍。
      He did not really wear a leather jacket just to look good.

16. 萧涧秋对陶岚的印象如何？

17. 陶岚对自己的情形怎么不满意？

18. 陶岚来找萧涧秋的目的是什么？

十三至十五景

1. 萧涧秋写的乐谱叫什么名字？

2. 陶岚听了萧涧秋弹奏的曲调时，有什么感觉？

3. 描画一下夏天西湖的夜晚。

4. 陶岚那时看见的青年是谁？陶岚以为那位青年将要做什么？

5. 萧涧秋说那时候有两个女学生在做什么？

6. 那时候萧涧秋为什么彷徨？

7. 萧涧秋怎么克服了他的彷徨？

二。语法练习

    I. 为 X 而 VE: because of X, VE; for the sake of X, VE

    wèi   *Coverb construction in which X, the reason or purpose,*
                              may be either a noun or verbal expression

    cf. 而: *EX 2.VI, 3.V, 5.IV, 7.IV, 9.V*

例
11.14　她衣单，全身为寒冷而颤抖。
    She wore only a single layer of clothing; her whole body was shivering because she was so cold.

1.   小孩子为看到陌生人而受惊。
    Because the child saw a stranger, he became frightened.

2.   他并不是为了好看而穿皮袍。
    He did not really wear a leather jacket just to look good.

完成

1. 學生們為天氣和暖。。。。

2. 。。。。而流淚。

II. 不禁 VE： cannot help VE-ing; cannot refrain from VE-ing

Verb construction

例

11.40   文嫂不禁哭出聲來。
Wen Sao could not help crying out loud.

1.   聽了孩子天真的問話，他不禁微笑起來。
When he heard the child's innocent question, he couldn't refrain from smiling.

2.   人們說起中國的災難來，就不禁嘆氣。
When people start talking about China's disasters, they can't help but sigh.

完成

1. 方謀看見錢正興僵窘的樣子。。。

2. 。。。，不禁高興得跳了起來。

完成

1. 学生们为天气和暖。。。

2. 。。。而流泪。

II. 不禁 VE： cannot help VE-ing; cannot refrain from VE-ing

Verb construction

例

11.40　文嫂不禁哭出声来。

Wen Sao could not help crying out loud.

1.　　听了孩子天真的问话，他不禁微笑起来。

When he heard the child's innocent question, he couldn't refrain from smiling.

2.　　人们说起中国的灾难来，就不禁叹气。

When people start talking about China's disasters, they can't help but sigh.

完成

1. 方谋看见钱正兴僵窘的样子。。。

2. 。。。，不禁高兴得跳了起来。

III. 終究：eventually; in the end

Adverbial construction that contrasts with preceding statements

PATTERN:（雖然。。。，可是/但是）S 終究。。。
（不論。。。，）S 終究。。。

例

11.42 （雖然現在生活很苦，可是/但是）
(Although life is very hard now,)

（不論現在生活怎麼苦，）
(No matter how hard life is now,)

我相信好人終究不會受委曲的。
I have faith that good people will not be wronged in the end.

1. （雖然很多人都想鈔票不是好東西，可是）鈔票終究是生活中非有不可的。
(Even though many people think that money is not a good thing,) in the end, money is [something] that everyone needs.

2. 黑是黑，白是白，（不論怎麼弄，）你終究不能把白的說成黑的。
Black is black, and white is white. (No matter how you talk about it,) in the end, you cannot turn white into black.

完成

1. 。。。人終究是要活下去的。

2. 不論他怎麼努力學數學，。。。

IV. 一手 V: V with a single movement of the hand; V with ease; V quickly
一腳 V: V with a single movement of the foot

Adverbial construction

例

12.4 蕭潤秋一手推門進去。。。。
Xiao Jianqiu opened the door with a single push [of the hand] and went in. . . .

III. 终究： eventually; in the end

Adverbial construction that contrasts with preceding statements

PATTERN: （虽然。。。，可是/但是）S 终究。。。
　　　　　（不论。。。，）S 终究。。。

例
11.42　（虽然现在生活很苦，可是/但是）
　　　　(Although life is very hard now,)

　　　（不论现在生活怎么苦，）
　　　　(No matter how hard life is now,)

　　　　　我相信好人终究不会受委曲的。
　　　　　I have faith that good people will not be wronged in the end.

1.　（虽然很多人都想钞票不是好东西，可是）钞票终究是生活中非有不可的。
　　(Even though many people think that money is not a good thing,) in the end, money is [something] that everyone needs.

2.　黑是黑，白是白，（不论怎么弄，）你终究不能把白的说成黑的。
　　Black is black, and white is white. (No matter how you talk about it,) in the end, you cannot turn white into black.

　　　完成

1.。。。人终究是要活下去的。

2. 不论他怎么努力学数学，。。。

IV. 一手 V: V with a single movement of the hand; V with ease; V quickly

　　一脚 V: V with a single movement of the foot

Adverbial construction

例
12.4　萧涧秋一手推门进去。。。。
　　Xiao Jianqiu opened the door with a single push [of the hand] and went in. . . .

1.   當土匪跑向他的時候，他一手就把土匪推倒了。
When the bandit ran at him, he pushed the bandit down with ease.

2.   他酒喝多了。晚上回家時，一腳踢開房門就倒在地板上了。
He had too much to drink. When he got home, he opened the door with one kick of the foot and then fell to the floor.

解釋

1. 我向他要求幫助，他一口答應了。

2. 在下飛機的人羣中他一眼就找到了他的哥哥。

V. 僅： only

Adverb

cf. *EX 2.V*

PATTERN: 不僅 X（而已），而且 Y   not only X, but also Y
　　　　　僅。。。而已   only . . . and that's all.
　　　　cf. 而： *EX 2.VI, 3.I, 5.IV, 7.IV, 9.V*

例

12.42 她不僅是美麗，而〔且〕又是那麼聰慧。
It was not only that she was beautiful, but also that she was so very intelligent.

9.28   蕭澗秋僅舉杯呷了一口示意而已。
Xiao Jianqiu only made a gesture of raising his cup and sipping a little.

1.   錢正興對陶媽媽不僅非常關心，而且彬彬有禮。
Qian Zhengxing treats Tao Mama not only with much concern, but also in a refined and courteous manner.

2.   他不僅沒吃過山珍海味（而已），（而且）好像連豬都沒有見過。
Not only has he never eaten delicacies from land and sea, it seems that he's never even seen pork before.

3.   我們不僅是要幫助孤兒寡婦現在的生活，（而且）還要為孩子的前途打算。
We not only need to help the widow and orphans with their present life, but also need to make plans for the children's future.

1.　当土匪跑向他的时候，他一手就把土匪推倒了。

When the bandit ran at him, he pushed the bandit down with ease.

2.　他酒喝多了。晚上回家时，一脚踢开房门就倒在地板上了。

He had too much to drink. When he got home, he opened the door with one kick of the foot and then fell to the floor.

解释

1.我向他要求帮助，他一口答应了。

2. 在下飞机的人群中他一眼就找到了他的哥哥。

V. 仅：only

Adverb

cf. *EX 2.V*

PATTERN: 不仅 X（而已），而且 Y　　　　not only X, but also Y

仅。。。而已　　　　　　　　　only . . . and that's all.

cf. 而：*EX 2.VI, 3.I, 5.IV, 7.IV, 9.V*

例

12.42　她不仅是美丽，而〔且〕又是那么聪慧。

It was not only that she was beautiful, but also that she was so very intelligent.

9.28　萧涧秋仅举杯呷了一口示意而已。

Xiao Jianqiu only made a gesture of raising his cup and sipping a little.

1.　钱正兴对陶妈妈不仅非常关心，而且彬彬有礼。

Qian Zhengxing treats Tao Mama not only with much concern, but also in a refined and courteous manner.

2.　他不仅没吃过山珍海味（而已），（而且）好像连猪都没有见过。

Not only has he never eaten delicacies from land and sea, it seems that he's never even seen pork before.

3.　我们不仅是要帮助孤儿寡妇现在的生活，（而且）还要为孩子的前途打算。

We not only need to help the widow and orphans with their present life, but also need to make plans for the children's future.

4. 他僅喝了一杯酒而已，怎麼就能好像忘了一切似的？

He only drank one glass and that was all; how can he act as if he's forgotten everything?

5. 其實並不是人人都愛吃狗肉，僅是幾個地方有吃狗肉的習慣而已。

Actually, not everyone likes to eat dog meat; it is only in a few places that people have the custom of eating dog meat.

完成

1. 我們不僅應該同情不幸的人，。。。。

2. 。。。。並没有別的意思。

VI. 而： and

Conjunction

cf. *EX 2.VI, 3.I, 3.V, 5.IV, 7.IV, 9.V*

PATTERN: SV1 而 SV2   SV1 and SV2

       clause 1, 而 clause 2   clause 1, and clause 2

例

4.3 廳堂裏陳設着舊式的紅木家具。。。。顯得寬敞而幽静。

The main hall was furnished with old-style redwood furniture. . . . It looked spacious, quiet and secluded.

1. 女孩子眼秀而頰紅。

The girl has pretty eyes and red cheeks.

2. 那時候，中國日子不好過，甘肅鬧地震而河南鬧土匪。

At that time life was not easy in China —Gansu suffered from earthquakes while He'nan had trouble with banditry.

變換

1. 橘子又新鮮又便宜。

2. 空氣清新，景色又美麗。

4. 他仅喝了一杯酒而已，怎么就能好像忘了一切似的？

He only drank one glass and that was all; how can he act as if he's forgotten everything?

5. 其实并不是人人都爱吃狗肉，仅是几个地方有吃狗肉的习惯而已。

Actually, not everyone likes to eat dog meat; it is only in a few places that people have the custom of eating dog meat.

完成

1. 我们不仅应该同情不幸的人，。。。。

2. 。。。并没有别的意思。

VI. 而： and

Conjunction

cf. *EX 2.VI, 3.I, 3.V, 5.IV, 7.IV, 9.V*

PATTERN: SV1 而 SV2　　　　SV1 and SV2

　　　　　clause 1, 而 clause 2　　clause 1, and clause 2

例

4.3 厅堂里陈设着旧式的红木家具。。。。显得宽敞而幽静。

The main hall was furnished with old-style redwood furniture. . . . It looked spacious, quiet and secluded.

1. 女孩子眼秀而颊红。

The girl has pretty eyes and red cheeks.

2. 那时候，中国日子不好过，甘肃闹地震而河南闹土匪。

At that time life was not easy in China —Gansu suffered from earthquakes while He'nan had trouble with banditry.

变换

1. 橘子又新鲜又便宜。

2. 空气清新，景色又美丽。

VII. 手足無措： lit., not to know what to do with one's hands and feet: at a loss what to do; flustered

Stative verb clause: stands alone as a predicate or functions as a modifier

例

11.12 文嫂〔見蕭澗秋來看她的孩子〕一時手足無措。
　　　 Wen Sao (seeing that Xiao Jianqiu had come to see her children) was momentarily flustered.

1. 他的房間亂得不像樣子，母親忽然說要來，把他急得手足無措。
His room was such an unpardonable mess that when his mother suddenly said that she was going to come visit, it completely threw him off.

2. 陶嵐看見錢正興來了，就立刻走出廳堂，叫錢正興手足無措地僵窘在那裏。
When Tao Lan saw that Qian Zhengxing had arrived, she immediately left him there in the main hall, making him flustered and embarrassed.

　　　　回答

1. 甚麼情況會使人手足無措？

2. 手足無措是甚麼樣子？

三。生詞練習

填空一

傍徨；僅是；不成其為；多餘；簡短；感情衝動；而且；介意；偏；好不容易；
感染；終究；説不上；立即；補充；緩一緩；寒冷；不料

1. 欸，別那麼（　　）好不好？怎麼一生氣就要打人，一高興就要請人吃飯呢？

2. 他不僅覺得芙蓉鎮是桃花源，（　　）更以為在芙蓉鎮教書是最有意義的。

3. 他已經明白了，你還要說了又說，說得太多了，說（　　）的話是沒有必要的。

4. 父親自己是醫生，想要兒子也念醫科，兒子卻（　　）不學。

VII. 手足无措： lit., not to know what to do with one's hands and feet: at a loss what to do; flustered

Stative verb clause: stands alone as a predicate or functions as a modifier

例

11.12　文嫂〔见萧涧秋来看她的孩子〕一时手足无措。
Wen Sao (seeing that Xiao Jianqiu had come to see her children) was momentarily flustered.

1.　他的房间乱得不像样子，母亲忽然说要来，把他急得手足无措。
His room was such an unpardonable mess that when his mother suddenly said that she was going to come visit, it completely threw him off.

2.　陶岚看见钱正兴来了，就立刻走出厅堂，叫钱正兴手足无措地僵窘在那里。
When Tao Lan saw that Qian Zhengxing had arrived, she immediately left him there in the main hall, making him flustered and embarrassed.

回答

1. 什么情况会使人手足无措？

2. 手足无措是什么样子？

三。生词练习

填空一

彷徨；仅是；不成其为；多余；简短；感情冲动；而且；介意；偏；好不容易；
感染；终究；说不上；立即；补充；缓一缓；寒冷；不料

1. 欸，别那么（　　）好不好？怎么一生气就要打人，一高兴就要请人吃饭呢？

2. 他不仅觉得芙蓉镇是桃花源，（　　）更以为在芙蓉镇教书是最有意义的。

3. 他已经明白了，你还要说了又说，说得太多了，说（　　）的话是没有必要的。

4. 父亲自己是医生，想要儿子也念医科，儿子却（　　）不学。

5. 他本來想世界上沒有人會記得他的生日的。（　　）他一開門，就聽見很多人說「生日快樂！」真是想不到的事。

6. 「你寫的字好漂亮啊！」「哪裏？我寫的不像樣子。簡直（　　）字。」

7. 那年冬天，最（　　）了。溫度低到零下二十度。

8. 她一聽見蕭澗秋彈這首曲子，（　　）想起了那個夏夜西湖的夜晚。

9. 親戚（　　）是親戚，雖然你說他們冷落了你，最後幫助你的還是親戚。

10. 文嫂覺得采蓮上學的事一時還（　　）；因為生活還成問題，孩子的教育就更不必說了。

11. 這（　　）他的意見而已，聽不聽完全要看你怎麼想了。

12. 鋼琴又大又重，我一個人（　　）才放好位置。我不能再搬了。

13. 每過一個時候人們就會問「我們走哪條路？」彷彿人們總是（　　）在十字路口上。

14. 據說牛也愛聽音樂。如果牛受到音樂的（　　），牛奶就會增多。

15. 你最近太忙太累了。我看你（　　）吧！晚點作完也不要緊吧。

16. 他平常不多說話，非說話不可的時候，也說得非常（　　）。

17. 你剛才說的我完全同意，另外我再提兩點意見（　　）一下。

18. 請不要生氣，不要（　　）。他不是故意的，是說着玩兒的。

5. 他本来想世界上没有人会记得他的生日的。（　　）他一开门，就听见很多人说「生日快乐！」真是想不到的事。

6. 「你写的字好漂亮啊！」「哪里？我写的不像样子。简直（　　）字。」

7. 那年冬天，最（　　）了。温度低到零下二十度。

8. 她一听见萧涧秋弹这首曲子，（　　）想起了那个夏夜西湖的夜晚。

9. 亲戚（　　）是亲戚，虽然你说他们冷落了你，最后帮助你的还是亲戚。

10. 文嫂觉得采莲上学的事一时还（　　）；因为生活还成问题，孩子的教育就更不必说了。

11. 这（　　）他的意见而已，听不听完全要看你怎么想了。

12. 钢琴又大又重，我一个人（　　）才放好位置。我不能再搬了。

13. 每过一个时候人们就会问「我们走哪条路？」仿佛人们总是（　　）在十字路口上。

14. 据说牛也爱听音乐。如果牛受到音乐的（　　），牛奶就会增多。

15. 你最近太忙太累了。我看你（　　）吧！晚点作完也不要紧吧。

16. 他平常不多说话，非说话不可的时候，也说得非常（　　）。

17. 你刚才说的我完全同意，另外我再提两点意见（　　）一下。

18. 请不要生气，不要（　　）。他不是故意的，是说着玩儿的。

填空二

來得及；誤會；認真；慌亂；受委曲；見外；躊躇；冒昧；手足無措；感興趣；
監視；不禁；見笑；天無絕人之路；顫抖；暴露；感激；胡亂

1. 請別客氣，我們是一家人，送這麼點小東西你還不肯收，太（　　）了。

2. 「這是你畫的畫兒嗎？真好。」「哪裏，哪裏。我（　　）畫的。」

3. 請不要（　　）我的意思，我說的是他，不是她。

4. 那所房子裏有人被殺了。所以警察（　　）着所有進出房子的人。

5. 這件事應不應該幫助朋友去做，很難決定。他（　　）了很久才同意了。

6. 對不起，（　　）問您一個問題。您認識一位名叫李志豪的嗎？

7. 做事可不能太隨便。一定要（　　）。

8. 我的那篇作文是寫着玩兒的。你看了可別（　　）啊！

9. 他的個人主義的思想不知不覺地從談話中（　　）出來。

10. 你是應該去住大旅館的，現在卻住在這不像樣子的小破房子，使你（　　），
真太對不起你了。

11. 希望總是有的，一定不要去自殺。要知道（　　）啊！

12. 考試的時候不要怕，不能（　　）。要不然連會的題目也不會作了。

13. 你在我最沒辦法的時候幫助我，真使我心中（　　）。多謝，多謝。

14. 他的手（　　）得厲害，連筆也拿不住。

15. 他說他不喜歡演講，那麼多人都看着他，使他很不好意思，使他（　　）。

16. 兩個老朋友在一塊兒喝酒喝多了，話也（　　）多起來了。甚麼不好意思的
事都說了出來。

17. 要坐飛機一定要在飛機起飛前一小時到飛機塲才（　　），要不然時間不
夠。

18. 我對法律不（　　），我們不談這個好嗎？

填空二

来得及；误会；认真；慌乱；受委曲；见外；踌躇；冒昧；手足无措；感兴趣；
监视；不禁；见笑；天无绝人之路；颤抖；暴露；感激；胡乱

1. 请别客气，我们是一家人，送这么点小东西你还不肯收，太（　　）了。

2. 「这是你画的画儿吗？真好。」「哪里，哪里。我（　　）画的。」

3. 请不要（　　）我的意思，我说的是他，不是她。

4. 那所房子里有人被杀了。所以警察（　　）着所有进出房子的人。

5. 这件事应不应该帮助朋友去做，很难决定。他（　　）了很久才同意了。

6. 对不起，（　　）问您一个问题。您认识一位名叫李志豪的吗？

7. 做事可不能太随便。一定要（　　）。

8. 我的那篇作文是写着玩儿的。你看了可别（　　）啊！

9. 他的个人主义的思想不知不觉地从谈话中（　　）出来。

10. 你是应该去住大旅馆的，现在却住在这不像样子的小破房子，使你（　　），真太对不起你了。

11. 希望总是有的，一定不要去自杀。要知道（　　）啊！

12. 考试的时候不要怕，不能（　　）。要不然连会的题目也不会作了。

13. 你在我最没办法的时候帮助我，真使我心中（　　）。多谢，多谢。

14. 他的手（　　）得厉害，连笔也拿不住。

15. 他说他不喜欢演讲，那么多人都看着他，使他很不好意思，使他（　　）。

16. 两个老朋友在一块儿喝酒喝多了，话也（　　）多起来了。什么不好意思的事都说了出来。

17. 要坐飞机一定要在飞机起飞前一小时到飞机场才（　　），要不然时间不够。

18. 我对法律不（　　），我们不谈这个好吗？

四。説話練習

　　　　用括號中的詞來説：

1. 蕭澗秋非常愉悦。（有如；飛翔；貪戀；顧盼；跳躍）

2. 律師的責任。（打官司；寫狀紙；出庭；辯護）

　　　　討論：

當一個人感覺徬徨時會做些甚麼？

五。作文

　　在陶嵐眼中，蕭澗秋與她周圍認識的人有甚麼不同？

四。说话练习

　　　　用括号中的词来说：

1. 萧涧秋非常愉悦。（有如；飞翔；贪恋；顾盼；跳跃）

2. 律师的责任。（打官司；写状纸；出庭；辩护）

　　　　讨论：

当一个人感觉彷徨时会做些什么？

五。作文

　　在陶岚眼中，萧涧秋与她周围认识的人有什么不同？

練習四：第十六景至第二十二景

一。閱讀測驗

十六至十九景

1. 當老師快要走進教室時學生們都做甚麼？

2. 陶校長怎麼向學生介紹蕭澗秋？

3. 蕭澗秋在點名的同時也可以達到甚麼目的？

4. 遲到的學生叫甚麼名字？他為甚麼滿頭大汗？他回答老師的問題了嗎？

5. 錢正興怎麼孝敬陶媽媽？錢正興聽說陶嵐不在家時感覺怎麼樣？

6. 蕭澗秋打球的時候，在陶嵐看起來，蕭澗秋顯得有些甚麼不同？

7. 芙蓉鎮給蕭澗秋甚麼感覺？陶嵐覺得蕭澗秋的感覺對不對？

8. 蕭澗秋為甚麼說他自己像一隻孤雁？

9. 陶嵐為甚麼要借一本關於教育的書？

10. 說說陶慕侃對她妹妹的脾氣完全沒有辦法。

二十至二十二景

1. 文嫂一家人對蕭澗秋的態度怎麼樣？

2. 文嫂所說的「有家」是甚麼意思？

3. 蕭澗秋在文嫂家所談的是甚麼事情？

4. 采蓮上學那天早晨的天氣跟風景怎麼樣？

练习四：第十六景至第二十二景

一。阅读测验

十六至十九景

1. 当老师快要走进教室时学生们都做什么？

2. 陶校长怎么向学生介绍萧涧秋？

3. 萧涧秋在点名的同时也可以达到什么目的？

4. 迟到的学生叫什么名字？他为什么满头大汗？他回答老师的问题了吗？

5. 钱正兴怎么孝敬陶妈妈？钱正兴听说陶岚不在家时感觉怎么样？

6. 萧涧秋打球的时候，在陶岚看起来，萧涧秋显得有些什么不同？

7. 芙蓉镇给萧涧秋什么感觉？陶岚觉得萧涧秋的感觉对不对？

8. 萧涧秋为什么说他自己像一只孤雁？

9. 陶岚为什么要借一本关于教育的书？

10. 说说陶慕侃对她妹妹的脾气完全没有办法。

二十至二十二景

1. 文嫂一家人对萧涧秋的态度怎么样？

2. 文嫂所说的「有家」是什么意思？

3. 萧涧秋在文嫂家所谈的是什么事情？

4. 采莲上学那天早晨的天气跟风景怎么样？

5. 文嫂送采蓮上學，對采蓮說甚麼？

6. 采蓮離開媽媽時變得要哭，蕭澗秋對文嫂說甚麼？又怎麼哄采蓮？

7. 陶嵐、錢正興和方謀在教務室各做甚麼事？

8. 陶嵐沒有吃早飯，錢正興怎麼幫忙？

9. 陶校長為甚麼勸妹妹吃糖？最後錢正興的糖被誰拿去了？

10. 方謀將采蓮比作孔雀是甚麼意思？

二。語法練習

I. 好 VE: to like to VE

hào　　Verb construction

例

17.3　學生們都好奇地向窗外張望。
The students looked outside the window, full of curiosity.

1.　他很好問，甚麼事都要問清楚。
He really loves to ask questions; he asks about everything [until he is] clear.

2.　胖子都好打盹兒嗎？
Do all fat people love to take naps?

解釋

1. 他簡直像豬似的，好吃得很。

2. 他好好說故事啊！一說就說個沒完。

5. 文嫂送采莲上学，对采莲说什么？

6. 采莲离开妈妈时变得要哭，萧涧秋对文嫂说什么？又怎么哄采莲？

7. 陶岚、钱正兴和方谋在教务室各做什么事？

8. 陶岚没有吃早饭，钱正兴怎么帮忙？

9. 陶校长为什么劝妹妹吃糖？最后钱正兴的糖被谁拿去了？

10. 方谋将采莲比作孔雀是什么意思？

二。语法练习

I. 好 VE: to like to VE

hào   Verb construction

例

17.3　学生们都好奇地向窗外张望。
The students looked outside the window, full of curiosity.

1.　他很好问，什么事都要问清楚。
He really loves to ask questions; he asks about everything [until he is] clear.

2.　胖子都好打盹儿吗？
Do all fat people love to take naps?

解释

1. 他简直像猪似的，好吃得很。

2. 他好好说故事啊！一说就说个没完。

II. 待 V: waiting to be V-ed; about to V

例

8.1 案板上放着各色各樣正待烹調的菜餚。
On the cutting board there were all kinds of [ingredients of] dishes just about to be cooked.

19.5 兩人並肩在含苞待放的桃李中穿行。
Shoulder to shoulder, the two crossed through a grove of peach and pear trees about to bloom.

1. 點過名的學生都走了。現在只有待點名的學生留在這裏。
All the students whose names have been called have gone; the only ones left now are those waiting to be called.

2. 有很多問題待解釋。
There are many questions awaiting explanation.

解釋

1. 待續

2. 待完成的作品

III. 甚至(於)﹕ even (to the point of)

Conjunction

cf. 於﹕ *EX 2.III, 8.I, 9.II*

PATTERN: S predicate 1, 甚至(於) predicate 2

        S 不但／不僅 predicate 1, 甚至(於)(都) predicate 2

        S predicate l, predicate 2, 甚至(於)(都) predicate 3

        S1 predicate, (S2 predicate,) 甚至(於) S3 也／都 predicate

例

19.3 蕭澗秋突然年輕了許多，甚至露出幾分天真的笑容。
蕭澗秋不但突然年輕了許多，甚至都露出幾分天真的笑容。
Xiao Jianqiu suddenly looked a lot younger, even smiling somewhat innocently.

II. 待 V: waiting to be V-ed; about to V

例

8.1   案板上放着各色各样正待烹调的菜肴。
On the cutting board there were all kinds of [ingredients of] dishes just about to be cooked.

19.5   两人并肩在含苞待放的桃李中穿行。
Shoulder to shoulder, the two crossed through a grove of peach and pear trees about to bloom.

1.   点过名的学生都走了。现在只有待点名的学生留在这里。
All the students whose names have been called have gone; the only ones left now are those waiting to be called.

2.   有很多问题待解释。
There are many questions awaiting explanation.

解释

1. 待续

2. 待完成的作品

III. 甚至 (于)： even (to the point of)

Conjunction

cf. 于: *EX 2.III, 8.I, 9.II*

PATTERN: S predicate 1, 甚至 (于) predicate 2

　　　S 不但/不仅 predicate 1, 甚至 (于) (都) predicate 2

　　　S predicate l, predicate 2, 甚至 (于) (都) predicate 3

　　　S1 predicate, (S2 predicate,) 甚至 (于) S3 也/都 predicate

例

19.3   萧涧秋突然年轻了许多，甚至露出几分天真的笑容。
萧涧秋不但突然年轻了许多，甚至都露出几分天真的笑容。
Xiao Jianqiu suddenly looked a lot younger, even smiling somewhat innocently.

1.　　他洗了衣服，收拾了屋子，
He washed the clothes, cleaned up his room,

甚至（都）做好了晚飯。
甚至晚飯都做好了。
and even made dinner.

2.　　看見陌生人來了，
When he saw the stranger coming,

他不僅手足無措，甚至於都説不出話來了。
他不僅手足無措，甚至於話也説不出來了。
he not only was at a loss what to do, he couldn't even speak.
he was flustered to the point where he couldn't even speak.

3.　　那天大家都圍着桌子吃火鍋，甚至陶嵐也吃了一點兒。
That day, everyone sat around the hot pot at the table eating; even Tao Lan had some.

完成

1. 。。。，甚至哭了起來。

2. 那天孩子們一個遲到的也没有，林月仙、段王海、甚至。。。

IV.　連 V1 帶 V2 地：V1-ing together with V2-ing　　*Adverbial phrase*
　　　連 N1 帶 N2 都：both N1 and N2　　　　　　　*Noun phrase*

例
19.5　　蕭澗秋連跑帶跳地到了陶嵐的面前。
Xiao Jianqiu went running and skipping up to Tao Lan.

1.　　他連吃帶喝地一下子把一大碗麵都吃完了。
Eating and drinking, in an instant he finished off a big bowl of noodles.

2.　　他連湯帶麵一下子都吃了。
Both the noodles and soup —in an instant he ate it all.

變換

1. 他又哭又笑地説：「叫我怎麼謝你才好呢？」

2. 他買了橘子，也買了蘋果。

1.　　他洗了衣服，收拾了屋子，
　　　　He washed the clothes, cleaned up his room,

　　　　　　　甚至(都)做好了晚饭。
　　　　　　　甚至晚饭都做好了。
　　　　　　　and even made dinner.

2.　　看见陌生人来了，
　　　　When he saw the stranger coming,

　　　　　　　他不仅手足无措，甚至于都说不出话来了。
　　　　　　　他不仅手足无措，甚至于话也说不出来了。
　　　　　　　he not only was at a loss what to do, he couldn't even speak.
　　　　　　　he was flustered to the point where he couldn't even speak.

3.　　那天大家都围着桌子吃火锅，甚至陶岚也吃了一点儿。
　　　　That day, everyone sat around the hot pot at the table eating; even Tao Lan had some.

完成

1.。。。，甚至哭了起来。

2.那天孩子们一个迟到的也没有，林月仙、段王海、甚至。。。

IV. 连 V1 带 V2 地：V1-ing together with V2-ing　　　*Adverbial phrase*
　　连 N1 带 N2 都：both N1 and N2　　　　　　　　　*Noun phrase*

例

19.5　萧涧秋连跑带跳地到了陶岚的面前。
　　　Xiao Jianqiu went running and skipping up to Tao Lan.

1.　　他连吃带喝地一下子把一大碗面都吃完了。
　　　　Eating and drinking, in an instant he finished off a big bowl of noodles.

2.　　他连汤带面一下子都吃了。
　　　　Both the noodles and soup —in an instant he ate it all.

变换

1.他又哭又笑地说：「叫我怎么谢你才好呢？」

2.他买了橘子，也买了蘋果。

V. 拿 N 没辦法：　　　　cannot do anything about N

拿 N 無可奈何：　　　　cannot do anything about N

拿 N1 當 N2:　　　　　to consider N1 as N2

Coverb construction with 拿

PATTERN: 拿 N VE

例

19.33　他不要我教書，我倒偏要教。哥哥拿我也没辦法。

[Now] he doesn't want me to teach, but I just insist on teaching. My brother can't do anything about me.

1.　　方謀拿酒當水喝。

Fang Mou drinks wine as if it were water.

2.　　我解釋了半天可是他還不明白。真是拿他無可奈何！

I explained it and explained it but he still didn't get it. I really am at my wits' end about him!

變換

1. 孩子不肯學習，父母也無可奈何。

2. 陶嵐認為蕭澗秋是自由的大雁，蕭澗秋卻認為自己只是孤雁。

VI. 不成其為 N: not good enough to be a N; not qualified to be a N

Verb-object construction

例

13.5　「那是我在三年以前，一時感情衝動，胡亂寫的。不成其為甚麼曲調。」

"I haphazardly threw that together three years ago when I was momentarily overwhelmed with emotion. It doesn't really count as any kind of melody."

22.2　〔錢正興〕嘴裏哼着不成（其為）曲調的歌曲。

Qian Zhengxing hummed a tune that did not qualify as a melody.

1.　　我的所謂中文學校只有我母親一個人教我中文。不成其為學校。

My so-called Chinese school consisted only of my mother teaching me Chinese —it didn't count as a [real] school.

V. 拿 N 没办法：　　　　　cannot do anything about N

拿 N 无可奈何：　　　　cannot do anything about N

拿 N1 当 N2:　　　　　　to consider N1 as N2

Coverb construction with 拿

PATTERN: 拿 N VE

例

19.33 他不要我教书，我倒偏要教。哥哥拿我也没办法。

[Now] he doesn't want me to teach, but I just insist on teaching. My brother can't do anything about me.

1. 方谋拿酒当水喝。

Fang Mou drinks wine as if it were water.

2. 我解释了半天可是他还不明白。真是拿他无可奈何！

I explained it and explained it but he still didn't get it. I really am at my wits' end about him!

变换

1. 孩子不肯学习，父母也无可奈何。

2. 陶岚认为萧涧秋是自由的大雁，萧涧秋却认为自己只是孤雁。

VI. 不成其为 N: not good enough to be a N; not qualified to be a N

Verb-object construction

例

13.5 「那是我在三年以前，一时感情冲动，胡乱写的。不成其为什么曲调。」

"I haphazardly threw that together three years ago when I was momentarily overwhelmed with emotion. It doesn't really count as any kind of melody."

22.2 〔钱正兴〕嘴里哼着不成（其为）曲调的歌曲。

Qian Zhengxing hummed a tune that did not qualify as a melody.

1. 我的所谓中文学校只有我母亲一个人教我中文。不成其为学校。

My so-called Chinese school consisted only of my mother teaching me Chinese —it didn't count as a [real] school.

2.   他那封信僅表示他受了委屈而已，不成其為狀紙。
That letter of his merely expresses that he was wronged; it is not enough to constitute a lawsuit.

完成

1. 。。。簡直不成其為書房。

2. 半歲的孩子可以發出很多聲音，但他的聲音。。。

VII. 廢寢忘食： to go without sleep and forget to eat

Verb-object phrase: stands alone as a predicate or functions as a modifier

例

22.16 密斯陶備課心切，已經到了廢寢忘食的程度了。
Miss Tao is preparing for class with all her heart; she's already reached the point of going without sleep and forgetting to eat.

1.   他熱心地教書，簡直廢寢忘食了。
He teaches school [so] enthusiastically that he actually goes without sleep and forgets to eat.

2.   他廢寢忘食地練習彈鋼琴。
He practices playing the piano, going without food and sleep.

回答

1. 甚麼事可以叫你作到廢寢忘食的程度？

2. 你怎麼知道那人正在廢寢忘食地工作？

2.　　他那封信仅表示他受了委屈而已，不成其为状纸。

That letter of his merely expresses that he was wronged; it is not enough to constitute a lawsuit.

完成

1. 。。。简直不成其为书房。

2. 半岁的孩子可以发出很多声音，但他的声音。。。。

VII. 废寝忘食：to go without sleep and forget to eat

Verb-object phrase: stands alone as a predicate or functions as a modifier

例

22.16　　密斯陶备课心切，已经到了废寝忘食的程度了。

Miss Tao is preparing for class with all her heart; she's already reached the point of going without sleep and forgetting to eat.

1.　　他热心地教书，简直废寝忘食了。

He teaches school [so] enthusiastically that he actually goes without sleep and forgets to eat.

2.　　他废寝忘食地练习弹钢琴。

He practices playing the piano, going without food and sleep.

回答

1. 什么事可以叫你作到废寝忘食的程度？

2. 你怎么知道那人正在废寝忘食地工作？

三。生詞練習

填空一

既然；孝敬；甚至；尷尬；除此以外；氣息；不敢當；稱得起；不盡然；溫柔；
之間；殷勤；一一；支持；擔任；幸福；考慮；推卻

1. 錢正興送禮物給陶媽媽，想要把錢陶兩家（　　）的關係拉近些。

2. 父親離家時，將家事（　　）對孩子説清楚了才放心走了。

3. 一般人以為中文是很難學好的。其實（　　）。你看，現在中文説得很好的美國人不是很多嗎？所以這種説法不一定對。

4. 他學語言有自己的方法，學得比一般人都快；（　　）念中文一年級的時候，他就已經會查字典看報了。

5. 我要送他兩瓶酒，卻為他的妻子所（　　）。她不讓他多喝酒。

6. 芙蓉鎮雖然離上海南京很遠，卻也有些都市的（　　）。

7. 你説這裏只有天氣你不喜歡，難道（　　），甚麼都好嗎？

8. 這個問題他想了又想，（　　）了很久，才叫我這麼作的。

9. 他文科理科方面的知識都很豐富，可以（　　）學問淵博了。

10. 你（　　）認為教育是有意義的，那麼你為甚麼不念教育呢？

11. 我今天請朋友出去一塊兒吃午飯，吃完了卻發現沒有帶錢，當時真（　　）極了。

12. 中國人總以為人人都要（　　）父母，聽他們的話，給他們買禮物，做一切使他們高興的事。

13. 律師所（　　）的工作是寫狀紙，辯訴。

14. 百貨商店的服務員對客人態度非常（　　）有禮貌。

15. 那女孩子雖然不特別好看，但是説話的聲音很輕很好聽，態度很（　　），讓人喜歡。

三。生词练习

填空一

既然；孝敬；甚至；尴尬；除此以外；气息；不敢当；称得起；不尽然；温柔；
　　之间；殷勤；一一；支持；担任；幸福；考虑；推却

1. 钱正兴送礼物给陶妈妈，想要把钱陶两家（　　）的关系拉近些。

2. 父亲离家时，将家事（　　）对孩子说清楚了才放心走了。

3. 一般人以为中文是很难学好的。其实（　　）。你看，现在中文说得很好的美国人不是很多吗？所以这种说法不一定对。

4. 他学语言有自己的方法，学得比一般人都快；（　　）念中文一年级的时候，他就已经会查字典看报了。

5. 我要送他两瓶酒，却为他的妻子所（　　）。她不让他多喝酒。

6. 芙蓉镇虽然离上海南京很远，却也有些都市的（　　）。

7. 你说这里只有天气你不喜欢，难道（　　），什么都好吗？

8. 这个问题他想了又想，（　　）了很久，才叫我这么作的。

9. 他文科理科方面的知识都很丰富，可以（　　）学问渊博了。

10. 你（　　）认为教育是有意义的，那么你为什么不念教育呢？

11. 我今天请朋友出去一块儿吃午饭，吃完了却发现没有带钱，当时真（　　）极了。

12. 中国人总以为人人都要（　　）父母，听他们的话，给他们买礼物，做一切使他们高兴的事。

13. 律师所（　　）的工作是写状纸，辩诉。

14. 百货商店的服务员对客人态度非常（　　）有礼貌。

15. 那女孩子虽然不特别好看，但是说话的声音很轻很好听，态度很（　　），让人喜欢。

16. 一位小説家説（　　）的家庭家家都一樣，但不快樂的家庭卻各有各的麻煩。

17. 他三天三夜没睡覺，今天終於（　　）不下去，不能繼續工作了。

18. 我不過只比你們大幾歲，就被你們叫作奶奶，實在（　　）。

填空二

稍微；孤單；品學並茂；活躍；心神不寧；連跑帶跳；含苞待放；廢寢忘食；
問長問短；稱讚；精緻；心切；羨慕；休養；截住；愛護；拿；張望

1. 他這兩天飯吃不下，覺睡不好，跟他説話他也聽不見，總是非常慌亂不平靜的樣子。為甚麼他（　　）呢？

2. 如果他對一件事情有興趣，他就會甚麼都不管，（　　）地去做。

3. 他人又好，又有學問。真是個（　　）的好老師。

4. 你看，一羣天真的小孩子（　　）地過來了。小孩子是不會一步一步地慢慢地走着來的。

5. 去年十二月二十四日，他開了十二小時的車回家，一會兒也没有休息。那是因為他回家（　　）啊。

6. 春天來了，天氣很暖和，園子裏的花都（　　）了呢，不久以後就會開了。

7. 他從小失去了母親，很（　　）有母親的人。

8. 他對烹調非常有興趣，做出來的點心和菜都非常（　　），普通飯館兒的粗魚笨肉簡直不能比。

9. 他出了醫院以後，還不能上班，還得繼續（　　）一個時期。

10. 那一羣十幾歲的孩子，白天不上學，晚上很晚才回家，大人們都管不了他們，簡直（　　）他們没辦法。

11. 老太太見上大學的孫子回來了，忍不住東一句，西一句地（　　）。

12. 他在大學參加了很多活動，是個很（　　）的人。

16. 一位小说家说（　　）的家庭家家都一样，但不快乐的家庭却各有各的麻烦。

17. 他三天三夜没睡觉，今天终于（　　）不下去，不能继续工作了。

18. 我不过只比你们大几岁，就被你们叫作奶奶，实在（　　）。

填空二

稍微；孤单；品学并茂；活跃；心神不宁；连跑带跳；含苞待放；废寝忘食；问长问短；称赞；精致；心切；羡慕；休养；截住；爱护；拿；张望

1. 他这两天饭吃不下，觉睡不好，跟他说话他也听不见，总是非常慌乱不平静的样子。为什么他（　　）呢？

2. 如果他对一件事情有兴趣，他就会什么都不管，（　　）地去做。

3. 他人又好，又有学问。真是个（　　）的好老师。

4. 你看，一群天真的小孩子（　　）地过来了。小孩子是不会一步一步地慢慢地走着来的。

5. 去年十二月二十四日，他开了十二小时的车回家，一会儿也没有休息。那是因为他回家（　　）啊。

6. 春天来了，天气很暖和，园子里的花都（　　）了呢，不久以后就会开了。

7. 他从小失去了母亲，很（　　）有母亲的人。

8. 他对烹调非常有兴趣，做出来的点心和菜都非常（　　），普通饭馆儿的粗鱼笨肉简直不能比。

9. 他出了医院以后，还不能上班，还得继续（　　）一个时期。

10. 那一群十几岁的孩子，白天不上学，晚上很晚才回家，大人们都管不了他们，简直（　　）他们没办法。

11. 老太太见上大学的孙子回来了，忍不住东一句，西一句地（　　）。

12. 他在大学参加了很多活动，是个很（　　）的人。

13. 一般人都喜歡人家（　　）而不願意被批評。其實不好聽的話常是有用的話。

14. 在這離家很遠的地方，沒有親戚也沒有朋友，只是一個人走來走去的，感覺十分（　　）。

15. 你不要隨便打你的狗，應該（　　）動物。

16. 最近經常有人在家附近徘徊（　　），他這樣東看西看的，不知道有什麼目的。

17. 「喂，您找李先生聽電話嗎？請（　　）等一等，他馬上就來。」

18. 他開車開得太快，被警察（　　）了。

四。說話練習

　　　用括號中的詞來說：

1. 介紹一位新老師。（學問；品學並茂；見識廣闊；求教）
2. 將學生上課開始的一般情形說一說。（點名；號令）
3. 中國人送禮物跟接納禮物時說的客氣話。（孝敬；小意思；不敢當；見外）

　　　討論：

1. 蕭澗秋為甚麼在芙蓉鎮感覺非常愉快？
2. 方謀將采蓮比作孔雀，為甚麼陶嵐聽了就要走出去？

五。作文

　　描畫第十六景《學校大門前的攤子》。

13. 一般人都喜欢人家（　　）而不愿意被批评。其实不好听的话常是有用的话。

14. 在这离家很远的地方，没有亲戚也没有朋友，只是一个人走来走去的，感觉十分（　　）。

15. 你不要随便打你的狗，应该（　　）动物。

16. 最近经常有人在家附近徘徊（　　），他这样东看西看的，不知道有什么目的。

17.「喂，您找李先生听电话吗？请（　　）等一等，他马上就来。」

18. 他开车开得太快，被警察（　　）了。

四。说话练习

　　　用括号中的词来说：

1. 介绍一位新老师。（学问；品学并茂；见识广阔；求教）

2. 将学生上课开始的一般情形说一说。（点名；号令）

3. 中国人送礼物跟接纳礼物时说的客气话。（孝敬；小意思；不敢当；见外）

　　　讨论：

1. 萧涧秋为什么在芙蓉镇感觉非常愉快？

2. 方谋将采莲比作孔雀，为什么陶岚听了就要走出去？

五。作文

　　描画第十六景《学校大门前的摊子》。

練習五：第二十三景至第二十九景

一。閱讀測驗

二十三至二十六景

1. 蕭澗秋到了陶家為甚麼不先跟陶家的人見面就自己彈起鋼琴來？

2. 當初陶嵐提出的結婚條件是甚麼？

3. 錢正興所提的結婚條件陶嵐為甚麼不同意呢？

4. 陶媽媽怎麼責備陶嵐？

5. 陶校長認為如果陶家不同意這婚事，會有甚麼結果？

6. 蕭澗秋提出甚麼辦法幫助陶校長解決問題？

7. 陶校長要蕭澗秋幫忙勸陶嵐，蕭澗秋覺得怎麼樣？

8. 陶嵐聽說蕭澗秋要進來了，就做了些甚麼？

9. 陶嵐問蕭澗秋甚麼問題？

10. 芙蓉鎮流傳着的消息含有甚麼意思？

二十七至二十九景

1. 王福生每天早上上課以前做甚麼？

2. 王福生家裏的生活都靠王福生嗎？

3. 蕭澗秋為甚麼到西村去？

4. 蕭澗秋跨進文嫂家的門時，文嫂母女倆正在做甚麼？

练习五：第二十三景至第二十九景

一。阅读测验

二十三至二十六景

1. 萧涧秋到了陶家为什么不先跟陶家的人见面就自己弹起钢琴来？

2. 当初陶岚提出的结婚条件是什么？

3. 钱正兴所提的结婚条件陶岚为什么不同意呢？

4. 陶妈妈怎么责备陶岚？

5. 陶校长认为如果陶家不同意这婚事，会有什么结果？

6. 萧涧秋提出什么办法帮助陶校长解决问题？

7. 陶校长要萧涧秋帮忙劝陶岚，萧涧秋觉得怎么样？

8. 陶岚听说萧涧秋要进来了，就做了些什么？

9. 陶岚问萧涧秋什么问题？

10. 芙蓉镇流传着的消息含有什么意思？

二十七至二十九景

1. 王福生每天早上上课以前做什么？

2. 王福生家里的生活都靠王福生吗？

3. 萧涧秋为什么到西村去？

4. 萧涧秋跨进文嫂家的门时，文嫂母女俩正在做什么？

5. 文嫂對蕭澗秋説她不要采蓮上學的第一個理由是甚麼？

6. 文嫂對蕭澗秋説她不要采蓮上學的第二個理由是甚麼？

7. 蕭澗秋説接送采蓮上學對他有甚麼好處？

8. 最後，蕭澗秋提出甚麼辦法送采蓮上學？

9. 采蓮説她媽媽為甚麼哭了？

10. 「天邊湧起了烏雲」含有甚麼意思？

二。語法練習

I. 不便 VE: inappropriate, unsuitable to VE

Verb construction

(note: refers only to inconvenience to others, not oneself)

例

23.2　他以為主人在吃晚飯，不便前去打擾。
He thought that the owners [of the house] were having dinner, so it would be inappropriate to go and disturb them.

1.　這是他個人的事，我們不便問長問短。
This is his private affair; it would be inappropriate for us to ask him all the details.

2.　我們跟他並不熟，不便去懇求他。
We don't really know him that well; it would be unsuitable for us to plead with him.

完成

1. 。。。實在不便給他打電話。

2. 他正在準備考試，。。。

5. 文嫂对萧涧秋说她不要采莲上学的第一个理由是什么？

6. 文嫂对萧涧秋说她不要采莲上学的第二个理由是什么？

7. 萧涧秋说接送采莲上学对他有什么好处？

8. 最后，萧涧秋提出什么办法送采莲上学？

9. 采莲说她妈妈为什么哭了？

10.「天边涌起了乌云」含有什么意思？

二。语法练习

I. 不便 VE: inappropriate, unsuitable to VE

Verb construction

(note: refers only to inconvenience to others, not oneself)

例

23.2　他以为主人在吃晚饭，不便前去打扰。

He thought that the owners [of the house] were having dinner, so it would be inappropriate to go and disturb them.

1.　这是他个人的事，我们不便问长问短。

This is his private affair; it would be inappropriate for us to ask him all the details.

2.　我们跟他并不熟，不便去恳求他。

We don't really know him that well; it would be unsuitable for us to plead with him.

完成

1.。。。实在不便给他打电话。

2.他正在准备考试，。。。

II. 曾經 V（過）：　to have V-ed before　　　　　　　*Past-tense: affirmative construction*

　　不曾 V 過：　　　沒有 V 過；to have never V-ed before　*Past-tense: negative construction*

　　未曾 V 過：　　　沒有 V 過；to have never V-ed before　*Past-tense: negative construction*

例

23.7　她自己曾經隨便說過。
　　　She has informally said so herself before.

1.　　他不曾去過南方和暖的地方。
　　　他未曾去過南方和暖的地方。
　　　He has never been to the warm areas of the south.

2.　　他以前曾經覺得婚姻是終身大事，現在卻說那不過是兒戲罷了。
　　　Before, he believed that marriage was the great event of one's life; yet now he says that it is nothing more than a trifling matter.

回答

1. 他怎麼那麼有學問？

2. 他怎麼那麼沒學問？

III.　竟（然）：　　unexpectedly; surprisingly

　　　果然：　　　　as expected; sure enough

Movable adverb

例

9.50　「誰知前途剛有希望，竟在去年十月，攻打惠州的時候，陣亡了！」
　　　"Who knew that just when he began to have hope for his future, that he would be unexpectedly killed in action last year in the tenth month in the attack against Huizhou!"

23.10　不過條件稍修改一下。。。。我母親竟答應了。
　　　But [he] changed the conditions a little. . . . My mother surprisingly agreed.

29.11　果然天邊湧起了烏雲。
　　　Sure enough, black clouds billowed forth from the sky's edge.

1.　　我早就告訴你這條件不成，現在你看，果然要修改了吧！
　　　I told you long ago that your conditions would not work. Now look, sure enough, you have to change them, don't you!

II. 曾经 V（过）：　　to have V-ed before　　　　　　*Past-tense: affirmative construction*

　　不曾 V 过：　　　没有 V 过；to have never V-ed before　　*Past-tense: negative construction*

　　未曾 V 过：　　　没有 V 过；to have never V-ed before　　*Past-tense: negative construction*

例

23.7　她自己曾经随便说过。

She has informally said so herself before.

1.　他不曾去过南方和暖的地方。

　　他未曾去过南方和暖的地方。

He has never been to the warm areas of the south.

2.　他以前曾经觉得婚姻是终身大事，现在却说那不过是儿戏罢了。

Before, he believed that marriage was the great event of one's life; yet now he says that it is nothing more than a trifling matter.

回答

1. 他怎么那么有学问？

2. 他怎么那么没学问？

III. 竟（然）：　　unexpectedly; surprisingly

　　果然：　　　　as expected; sure enough

Movable adverb

例

9.50　「谁知前途刚有希望，竟在去年十月，攻打惠州的时候，阵亡了！」

"Who knew that just when he began to have hope for his future, that he would be unexpectedly killed in action last year in the tenth month in the attack against Huizhou!"

23.10　不过条件稍修改一下。。。。我母亲竟答应了。

But [he] changed the conditions a little. . . . My mother surprisingly agreed.

29.11　果然天边涌起了乌云。

Sure enough, black clouds billowed forth from the sky's edge.

1.　我早就告诉你这条件不成，现在你看，果然要修改了吧！

I told you long ago that your conditions would not work. Now look, sure enough, you have to change them, don't you!

2.　我曾經告訴你不要過河，過河很危險，現在果然出事了。

I told you before not to cross the river, that crossing the river was dangerous. Sure enough, something has happened now.

3.　我曾經告訴你不要過河，你竟不聽我的話，現在出事了吧。

I told you before not to cross the river, but surprisingly, you wouldn't listen to me, and now something has happened, hasn't it.

4.　我早就告訴你這條件不成，你竟然不肯聽。

I told you long ago that your conditions would not work, and surprisingly, you wouldn't listen.

完成

1. 。。。，果然答應了。

2. 。。。，竟然答應了。

IV-A. 而

Conjunction connecting two verbal expressions in which

the process of the first expression (VE1) results in the second (VE2)

cf. 而 : *EX 3.I, 3.V, 5.IV, 7.IV, 9.V*

PATTERN: VE1 而 VE2　　　　VE1-ing, VE2; VE1 and VE2

　　　　一V1 而 V2　　　　V1-ing resulting in V2　　　*4-character pattern*

例

23.2　蕭澗秋輕輕地推門而入。

Gently pushing the door open, Xiao Jianqiu went in.

9.28　方謀、錢正興都隨着陶校長一飲而盡。

Both Fang Mou and Qian Zhengxing, following Principal Tao, drank [their wine], completely finishing it.　　　　　　　　(= completely finished their wine all in one gulp.)

1.　別人都不同意他的想法，他就一怒而去，以後再也不提這個問題了。

No one agreed with his views. So getting angry, he left (= left in anger). After that he never associated with them again.

2.　小張站在屋外凝神而聽，知道屋中有人在彈奏《月光曲》。

Xiao Zhang stood outside the room listening with fixed attention. He knew that someone in the room was playing the *Moonlight Sonata*.

2. 我曾经告诉你不要过河，过河很危险，现在果然出事了。

I told you before not to cross the river, that crossing the river was dangerous. Sure enough, something has happened now.

3. 我曾经告诉你不要过河，你竟不听我的话，现在出事了吧。

I told you before not to cross the river, but surprisingly, you wouldn't listen to me, and now something has happened, hasn't it.

4. 我早就告诉你这条件不成，你竟然不肯听。

I told you long ago that your conditions would not work, and surprisingly, you wouldn't listen.

完成

1. ○。○。○。○，果然答应了。

2. ○。○。○。○，竟然答应了。

IV-A. 而

Conjunction connecting two verbal expressions in which

the process of the first expression (VE1) results in the second (VE2)

cf. 而：*EX 3.I, 3.V, 5.IV, 7.IV, 9.V*

PATTERN: VE1 而 VE2   VE1-ing, VE2; VE1 and VE2

一 V1 而 V2   V1-ing resulting in V2   *4-character pattern*

例

23.2 萧涧秋轻轻地推门而入。

Gently pushing the door open, Xiao Jianqiu went in.

9.28 方谋、钱正兴都随着陶校长一饮而尽。

Both Fang Mou and Qian Zhengxing, following Principal Tao, drank [their wine], completely finishing it.   (= completely finished their wine all in one gulp.)

1. 别人都不同意他的想法，他就一怒而去，以后再也不提这个问题了。

No one agreed with his views. So getting angry, he left (= left in anger). After that he never associated with them again.

2. 小张站在屋外凝神而听，知道屋中有人在弹奏《月光曲》。

Xiao Zhang stood outside the room listening with fixed attention. He knew that someone in the room was playing the *Moonlight Sonata*.

解釋

1. 兩人把過去不愉快的事說清楚以後，就一笑而罷，又變成好朋友了。

2. 當老師點名的時候，學生一個個的應聲而起。

3. 他的衣著那麼漂亮，一望而知是個紈絝子弟。

IV-B. 而：but

Conjunction

cf. *EX 2.VI, 3.I, 3.V, 7.IV, 9.V*

PATTERN: SV1 而 SV2   SV1 but SV2

      clause 1, 而 clause 2   clause 1, but clause 2

例

25.8   我代她拖延，而妹妹偏不拖延！

I [am willing to] stall for her, but my little sister just refuses to stall!

1.   那位青年說話的態度彬彬有禮而脾氣倔強固執。

That young person speaks in a refined and courteous manner but is extremely stubborn in temperament.

2.   母親答應了而父親不同意。

My mother said yes, but my father would not agree.

完成

1. 橘子新鮮。。。

2. 。。。而我卻覺得不對。

V. 認 N1 作 N2: to recognize N1 as N2

Coverb construction: delimits relationships of identity

例

26.7   你要認采蓮作乾女兒了嗎？

Are you going to recognize Cailian as your adopted daughter?

解释

1. 两人把过去不愉快的事说清楚以后，就一笑而罢，又变成好朋友了。

2. 当老师点名的时候，学生一个个的应声而起。

3. 他的衣着那么漂亮，一望而知是个纨袴子弟。

IV-B. 而：but

Conjunction

cf. EX 2.VI, 3.I, 3.V, 7.IV, 9.V

PATTERN: SV1 而 SV2   SV1 but SV2

      clause 1, 而 clause 2   clause 1, but clause 2

例

25.8   我代她拖延，而妹妹偏不拖延！

        I [am willing to] stall for her, but my little sister just refuses to stall!

1.   那位青年说话的态度彬彬有礼而脾气倔强固执。

        That young person speaks in a refined and courteous manner but is extremely stubborn in temperament.

2.   母亲答应了而父亲不同意。

        My mother said yes, but my father would not agree.

完成

1. 橘子新鲜。。。。

2. 。。。而我却觉得不对。

V. 认 N1 作 N2: to recognize N1 as N2

Coverb construction: delimits relationships of identity

例

26.7   你要认采莲作干女儿了吗？

        Are you going to recognize Cailian as your adopted daughter?

1. 既然那隻小狗老隨着你，認你作主人，你當然應該給他些吃的。
   Since that little dog always follows you around, and takes you for his master, of course you should feed him something.

2. 他竟然認賊 *(zéi)* 作父，出賣了自己的父母。
   To everyone's astonishment, he [only] recognizes that blackguard as his father, [thus] betraying his own parents.

變換

1. 她對貓，狗好像對自己的孩子一般。

2. 他是土匪，誰能把土匪當親戚呢？

VI. 究竟： exactly; really; actually; after all; in the end
Adverb of emphasis

PATTERN: 本來。。。，現在。。。，究竟。。。
先。。。，後來。。。，究竟。。。
跟。。。比較，究竟。。。
雖然。。。，可是。。。，究竟。。。

例

28.11 〔文嫂本來同意采蓮去上學的，現在又要她照顧阿寶，所以蕭澗秋問：〕
「這究竟是怎麼回事啊？」
[Wen Sao had originally agreed to have Cailian go to school, but now she wants her daughter to take care of Abao. This is why Xiao Jianqiu asks,] "What is this really about?"

1. 他先說要學哲學，後來又說要學數學，究竟要學甚麼？
   First he said that he wanted to study philosophy, then he said he wanted to study math. What does he really want to study?

2. 跟鄉鎮上的人比較起來，他究竟見識廣闊，學問淵博。所以陶校長請他來教書了。
   Compared to the people in the village, he really is vast in knowledge and profound in learning. That's why Principal Tao has invited him to come and teach here.

1. 既然那只小狗老随着你，认你作主人，你当然应该给他些吃的。

   Since that little dog always follows you around, and takes you for his master, of course you should feed him something.

2. 他竟然认贼 (zéi) 作父，出卖了自己的父母。

   To everyone's astonishment, he [only] recognizes that blackguard as his father, [thus] betraying his own parents.

变换

1. 她对猫，狗好像对自己的孩子一般。

2. 他是土匪，谁能把土匪当亲戚呢？

VI. 究竟：exactly; really; actually; after all; in the end

Adverb of emphasis

PATTERN: 本来。。。，现在。。。，究竟。。。

先。。。，后来。。。，究竟。。。

跟。。。比较，究竟。。。

虽然。。。，可是。。。，究竟。。。

例

28.11 〔文嫂本来同意采莲去上学的，现在又要她照顾阿宝，所以萧涧秋问：〕「这究竟是怎么回事啊？」

[Wen Sao had originally agreed to have Cailian go to school, but now she wants her daughter to take care of Abao. This is why Xiao Jianqiu asks,] "What is this really about?"

1. 他先说要学哲学，后来又说要学数学，究竟要学什么？

   First he said that he wanted to study philosophy, then he said he wanted to study math. What does he really want to study?

2. 跟乡镇上的人比较起来，他究竟见识广阔，学问渊博。所以陶校长请他来教书了。

   Compared to the people in the village, he really is vast in knowledge and profound in learning. That's why Principal Tao has invited him to come and teach here.

3.　采蓮雖然不願意離開媽媽去上學，可是聽説學校裏很好玩就不哭了。孩子究竟是孩子，很容易哄。

Although Cailian did not want to leave her mother to go to school, when she heard that school was so much fun, she stopped crying. Children are children after all, easily humored.

完成

1. 雖然他本來不願意辦這件事，拖延了很久。。。

2. 。。。究竟掩飾不了她的痛苦。

3. 跟男孩子比較，女孩究竟。。。

VII. 叫/讓

Causative construction vs. Passive construction

PATTERN: 叫/讓 N VE　　　　　to have N VE; to cause N to VE

causative: usually expresses agency

vs.　　叫/讓 N（給）VE　　　to be VE-ed by N

passive: used typically to express adversity

例

14.12　你看你，叫人家笑話我們了。

Look at [what] you [did], you're causing people to laugh at us.　　*(causative)*

vs.　你看你，叫人家（給）笑話了。

Look at [what] you [did! As a result], We're being laughed at by people.　　*(passive)*

25.12　〔陶媽媽〕見了蕭澗秋仍舊很客氣。

When [Tao Mama] met Xiao Jianqiu, she was as always very polite.

「蕭先生，讓你笑話了。」

"Mr. Xiao, [what we've done] has made you laugh at us."　　*(causative)*

vs.　"Mr. Xiao, [because of what we've done] we're being laughed at by you."　　*(passive)*

These examples show a convergence of causative and passive constructions: although grammatically causative, they also express a passive sense of adversity, that something is happening against the will of the speaker in each case.

3.　　采莲虽然不愿意离开妈妈去上学，可是听说学校里很好玩就不哭了。孩子究竟是孩子，很容易哄。

Although Cailian did not want to leave her mother to go to school, when she heard that school was so much fun, she stopped crying. Children are children after all, easily humored.

完成

1. 虽然他本来不愿意办这件事，拖延了很久。。。。

2. 。。。究竟掩饰不了她的痛苦。

3. 跟男孩子比较，女孩究竟。。。

VII. 叫/让

Causative construction vs. Passive construction

PATTERN:　叫/让 N VE　　　　　to have N VE; to cause N to VE

causative: usually expresses agency

vs.　　叫/让 N（给）VE　　　to be VE-ed by N

passive: used typically to express adversity

例

14.12　你看你，叫人家笑话我们了。

Look at [what] you [did], you're causing people to laugh at us.　　(causative)

vs.　你看你，叫人家（给）笑话了。

Look at [what] you [did! As a result], We're being laughed at by people.　　(passive)

25.12　〔陶妈妈〕见了萧涧秋仍旧很客气。

When [Tao Mama] met Xiao Jianqiu, she was as always very polite.

「萧先生，让你笑话了。」

"Mr. Xiao, [what we've done] has made you laugh at us."　　(causative)

vs.　　"Mr. Xiao, [because of what we've done] we're being laughed at by you."　　(passive)

These examples show a convergence of causative and passive constructions: although grammatically causative, they also express a passive sense of adversity, that something is happening against the will of the speaker in each case.

1.　他走出屋子來，讓文嫂關上了門。
　　He came out of the room and asked Wen Sao to close the door.　　　*(causative)*

vs.　他想進屋子去，卻讓文嫂（給）關上了門。
　　He came out of the room but had the door closed on him by Wen Sao.　　*(passive)*

2.　母親要他早點回來，叫他吃完了點心就回家。
　　His mother wants him to come home early, so she tells him to come home as soon as he finished
　　selling the cakes.　　　*(causative)*

vs.　母親本來是要請人來喝茶、吃點心的。可是現在叫孩子（給）吃完了。沒
　　有東西招待客人了。
　　The mother had wanted to invite people over for tea and cakes. But they were all eaten by her
　　children, so now there's nothing left to serve the guests.　　*(passive)*

　　　　完成

1.。。。那幾本書叫孩子放回原處了。

2.。。。那幾本書叫孩子給放回原處了。

三。生詞練習

　　　　　填空一

不便；決不；為難；果然；當初；隱約；任性；懷疑；認；究竟；曾經；招呼；
　　　　　叫；修改；當真；焦慮；受累；招呼

1. 他長得像中國人，說話像美國人，（　　）是中國人還是美國人？實在搞不清
　楚。

2. 他又把條件修改過了。我們（　　）能同意。我們怎麼能完全依他的條件辦
　事？

3. 父親很生氣地對女兒說：「如果你再這麼晚才回家，你就不必回來了，我
　也不（　　）你作我女兒了。」

4. 你猜的真對，你說他今天會來，（　　）他就來了。

5. 我認為這文章寫得不錯，稍微（　　）一下，將多餘的一段拿掉就可以了。

1.　他走出屋子来，让文嫂关上了门。
　　He came out of the room and asked Wen Sao to close the door.　　*(causative)*

vs.　他想进屋子去，却让文嫂(给)关上了门。
　　He came out of the room but had the door closed on him by Wen Sao.　　*(passive)*

2.　母亲要他早点回来，叫他吃完了点心就回家。
　　His mother wants him to come home early, so she tells him to come home as soon as he finished selling the cakes.　　*(causative)*

vs.　母亲本来是要请人来喝茶、吃点心的。可是现在叫孩子(给)吃完了。没有东西招待客人了。
　　The mother had wanted to invite people over for tea and cakes. But they were all eaten by her children, so now there's nothing left to serve the guests.　　*(passive)*

完成

1. 。。。那几本书叫孩子放回原处了。
2. 。。。那几本书叫孩子给放回原处了。

三。生词练习

填空一

不便；决不；为难；果然；当初；隐约；任性；怀疑；认；究竟；曾经；招呼；
叫；修改；当真；焦虑；受累；招呼

1. 他长得像中国人，说话像美国人，（　　）是中国人还是美国人？实在搞不清楚。

2. 他又把条件修改过了。我们（　　）能同意。我们怎么能完全依他的条件办事？

3. 父亲很生气地对女儿说：「如果你再这么晚才回家，你就不必回来了，我也不（　　）你作我女儿了。」

4. 你猜的真对，你说他今天会来，（　　）他就来了。

5. 我认为这文章写得不错，稍微（　　）一下，将多余的一段拿掉就可以了。

6. 我不過跟他見了一次面而已，（　　）自己一個人到他家去請他幫忙，你陪我去好嗎？

7. 你不給她錢買米買菜，卻又怪她不做飯給你吃，這不是使她（　　）嗎？

8. 上海那地方他是去過的。他以前（　　）在那兒工作過一個時候。

9. 他走到陶媽媽跟前，向陶媽媽（　　）：「伯母，您好。」

10. 那學生這幾天上課總是遲到，上課心不在焉，使人（　　）他有甚麼特別的問題。

11. 聽說因為天氣不好，飛機不能飛到，接飛機的人都在飛機場（　　）地等着。

12. （　　）你說要出國，現在你要留在國內。是甚麼使你完全改變了呢？

13. 其實他是讓你的，如果他（　　）跟你比起來，你的功夫是比不過他的。

14. 他遠遠地看見在花樹之間（　　）有個甚麼東西在動，就跑過去想看個清楚。

15. 錢先生太（　　）了，一生氣就辭退了工作。

16. 你今天為我的事跑了一天，讓你（　　）了。請喝點兒茶。過兩天我一定要重重謝你。

17. 提起此人，會（　　）他父母吃不下飯。

填空二

終身大事；懇求；兒戲；指指戳戳；竊竊私議；結結巴巴；竟；責備；拖延；照顧；突破；不安；打擾；精明；掩飾；莫名其妙；眺望

1. 他覺得自己並沒有做錯甚麼，沒甚麼可羞愧的；別人在他背後（　　）地說閒話，他並不介意。

2. 因為太性急了，他說話總是（　　）地，不夠流利。

3. 他本來正在高高興興地說着話，忽然就大哭起來，叫人（　　）。

6. 我不过跟他见了一次面而已，（　　）自己一个人到他家去请他帮忙，你陪我去好吗？

7. 你不给她钱买米买菜，却又怪她不做饭给你吃，这不是使她（　　）吗？

8. 上海那地方他是去过的。他以前（　　）在那儿工作过一个时候。

9. 他走到陶妈妈跟前，向陶妈妈（　　）：「伯母，您好。」

10. 那学生这几天上课总是迟到，上课心不在焉，使人（　　）他有什么特别的问题。

11. 听说因为天气不好，飞机不能飞到，接飞机的人都在飞机场（　　）地等着。

12. （　　）你说要出国，现在你要留在国内。是什么使你完全改变了呢？

13. 其实他是让你的，如果他（　　）跟你比起来，你的功夫是比不过他的。

14. 他远远地看见在花树之间（　　）有个什么东西在动，就跑过去想看个清楚。

15. 钱先生太（　　）了，一生气就辞退了工作。

16. 你今天为我的事跑了一天，让你（　　）了。请喝点儿茶。过两天我一定要重重谢你。

17. 提起此人，会（　　）他父母吃不下饭。

填空二

终身大事；恳求；儿戏；指指戳戳；窃窃私议；结结巴巴；竟；责备；拖延；
照顾；突破；不安；打扰；精明；掩饰；莫名其妙；眺望

1. 他觉得自己并没有做错什么，没什么可羞愧的；别人在他背后（　　）地说闲话，他并不介意。

2. 因为太性急了，他说话总是（　　）地，不够流利。

3. 他本来正在高高兴兴地说着话，忽然就大哭起来，叫人（　　）。

4. 按中國人的老看法，結婚對女孩子是決定了就很難改變的事，十分重要，所以叫作（　　）。

5. 這是大家的錯，請別罵他，請別怪他。只（　　）他一個人是不對的。

6. 母親對女兒說：「你一個人到遠地去上學，要學會自己（　　）自己啊！」

7. 他並不想（　　）自己的弱點，所以很明白地說了出來。

8. 他的新辦法有如天邊一聲雷響，（　　）了僵局。

9. 陶嵐和蕭澗秋一起打籃球，小鎮上的人都在背後（　　）。

10. 他十分（　　）。以前做小生意時就很賺錢，後來開當鋪當然更有錢了。

11. 今天的事情最好今天作完，不要（　　）到明天。明天又是新的一天，有明天的事情。

12. 晚上十二點鐘怎麼好意思給人打電話呢？別去（　　）別人了吧！

13. 我們學校當初聘你教三年哲學的課，你是同意的。現在你怎麼可以突然離開呢？這可不能當（　　）啊！

14. 他向遠處（　　），看見一羣大雁從北邊飛來。

15. 他向朋友（　　），請朋友千萬別把這事說出去。

16. 朋友送他一件小禮物，他非要立刻回送一件不可。他說要不然心裏（　　）。

17. 錢正興以為只要有錢、衣着漂亮，就會使人喜歡，他（　　）不知陶嵐最討厭的就是紈袴子弟了。

4. 按中国人的老看法，结婚对女孩子是决定了就很难改变的事，十分重要，所以叫作（　）。

5. 这是大家的错，请别骂他，请别怪他。只（　）他一个人是不对的。

6. 母亲对女儿说：「你一个人到远地去上学，要学会自己（　）自己啊！」

7. 他并不想（　）自己的弱点，所以很明白地说了出来。

8. 他的新办法有如天边一声雷响，（　）了僵局。

9. 陶岚和萧涧秋一起打篮球，小镇上的人都在背后（　）。

10. 他十分（　）。以前做小生意时就很赚钱，后来开当铺当然更有钱了。

11. 今天的事情最好今天作完，不要（　）到明天。明天又是新的一天，有明天的事情。

12. 晚上十二点钟怎么好意思给人打电话呢？别去（　）别人了吧！

13. 我们学校当初聘你教三年哲学的课，你是同意的。现在你怎么可以突然离开呢？这可不能当（　）啊！

14. 他向远处（　），看见一群大雁从北边飞来。

15. 他向朋友（　），请朋友千万别把这事说出去。

16. 朋友送他一件小礼物，他非要立刻回送一件不可。他说要不然心里（　）。

17. 钱正兴以为只要有钱、衣着漂亮，就会使人喜欢，他（　）不知陶岚最讨厌的就是纨袴子弟了。

四。說話練習

用你的瞭解來說：

1. 王福生的早晨。
2. 芙蓉鎮上的人談着關於文嫂的事。

討論：

陶嵐應該同意跟錢正興結婚嗎？

五。作文

描畫第二十九景：《暴風雨就要來了》。

四。说话练习

　　　　用你的了解来说：

1. 王福生的早晨。

2. 芙蓉镇上的人谈着关于文嫂的事。

　　　　讨论：

陶岚应该同意跟钱正兴结婚吗？

五。作文

　　描画第二十九景：《暴风雨就要来了》。

練習六：第三十景至第三十八景

一。閱讀測驗

三十至三十四景

1. 誰派陶嵐來請蕭澗秋吃飯？陶嵐怎麼讓蕭澗秋不能不去她家吃飯？

2. 錢正興給陶校長的信上說他為甚麼要辭職？

3. 過路的人看見蕭澗秋、陶嵐兩人走過，心中可能狐疑着甚麼？

4. 錢正興的信上說陶嵐為甚麼愛上了蕭澗秋？

5. 陶嵐說她為甚麼把不該告訴蕭澗秋的話都說了出來？

6. 那晚上吃飯喝酒的時候蕭澗秋有些甚麼異樣？

7. 陶校長對蕭澗秋的異樣說甚麼？

8. 陶嵐向蕭澗秋做眼色示意甚麼？蕭澗秋說他為甚麼喝酒？

9. 蕭澗秋彈鋼琴，又去接采蓮上學，這些事都告訴我們甚麼？

10. 教師們竊竊私議着甚麼？

三十五至三十八景

1. 蕭澗秋和陶嵐打完了籃球，感覺如何？

2. 打完籃球之後，蕭澗秋怎麼招待陶嵐？

3. 蕭澗秋接到的郵件是甚麼？

4. 蕭澗秋一進門在地上拾起一封信，那信是誰寫給誰的？

练习六：第三十景至第三十八景

一。阅读测验

三十至三十四景

1. 谁派陶岚来请萧涧秋吃饭？陶岚怎么让萧涧秋不能不去她家吃饭？

2. 钱正兴给陶校长的信上说他为什么要辞职？

3. 过路的人看见萧涧秋、陶岚两人走过，心中可能狐疑着什么？

4. 钱正兴的信上说陶岚为什么爱上了萧涧秋？

5. 陶岚说她为什么把不该告诉萧涧秋的话都说了出来？

6. 那晚上吃饭喝酒的时候萧涧秋有些什么异样？

7. 陶校长对萧涧秋的异样说什么？

8. 陶岚向萧涧秋做眼色示意什么？萧涧秋说他为什么喝酒？

9. 萧涧秋弹钢琴，又去接采莲上学，这些事都告诉我们什么？

10. 教师们窃窃私议着什么？

三十五至三十八景

1. 萧涧秋和陶岚打完了篮球，感觉如何？

2. 打完篮球之后，萧涧秋怎么招待陶岚？

3. 萧涧秋接到的邮件是什么？

4. 萧涧秋一进门在地上拾起一封信，那信是谁写给谁的？

5. 信上寫的是關於甚麼？

6. 陶嵐是不是很勇敢的人？她看了那封信就決定要怎麼辦？

7. 蕭澗秋對這事的態度怎麼樣？

8. 蕭澗秋最擔憂的事是甚麼？

9. 采蓮告訴蕭澗秋她家裏發生了甚麼事？

10. 蕭澗秋為甚麼不想去看阿寶？

二。語法練習

I. N1（比 N2）更加（地）SV: N1 is even more SV (than N2)

Comparative construction

cf. 越發: *EX 6.VI*

例

30.24 陶嵐説到每個「愛」字。。。已經吃吃地説不出來，這時她更加臉紅地低着頭。

Whenever Tao Lan got to the word "love," . . . she would already be stuttering, unable to get it out. At this point, she lowered her head, her face even redder [than before].

1. 這孩子從小就很調皮，現在長到七，八歲，比從前更加地調皮了。

From infancy this child has always been very mischievous. Now at seven or eight, he's even more mischievous than before.

2. 他很興奮而他的朋友比他更加興奮。

He's very excited, but his friend is even more excited than he is.

完成

1. 他的態度很冷漠。。。

2. 。。。他現在比以前更加煩惱。

5. 信上写的是关于什么？

6. 陶岚是不是很勇敢的人？她看了那封信就决定要怎么办？

7. 萧涧秋对这事的态度怎么样？

8. 萧涧秋最担忧的事是什么？

9. 采莲告诉萧涧秋她家里发生了什么事？

10. 萧涧秋为什么不想去看阿宝？

二。语法练习

I. N1（比 N2）更加（地）SV: N1 is even more SV (than N2)

Comparative construction

cf. 越发: *EX 6.VI*

例

30.24　陶岚说到每个「爱」字。。。已经吃吃地说不出来，这时她更加脸红地低着头。

Whenever Tao Lan got to the word "love," . . . she would already be stuttering, unable to get it out. At this point, she lowered her head, her face even redder [than before].

1.　这孩子从小就很调皮，现在长到七，八岁，比从前更加地调皮了。

From infancy this child has always been very mischievous. Now at seven or eight, he's even more mischievous than before.

2.　他很兴奋而他的朋友比他更加兴奋。

He's very excited, but his friend is even more excited than he is.

完成

1. 他的态度很冷漠。。。

2. 。。。他现在比以前更加烦恼。

II. 簡直： simply; just; practically (emphatic)

Adverb

PATTERN: 簡直 VE (modified by adverb or verbal complement)

簡直是 VE (modified by adverb or verbal complement)

簡直地 VE (modified by adverb or verbal complement)

簡直(好)像。。。

例

34.4　〔男女在一起打籃球，〕簡直是不成體統。

[Men and women playing basketball together— it] simply does not constitute [any kind of] decency.

7.33　她這樣滔滔地説着，簡直好像房間内是她一個人佔領着似的。

She spoke so ebulliently, practically as if she were the only person there.

1.　他簡直(是)快要哭了。

He's practically about to cry.

2.　他頭低着，簡直像在打盹兒一般。

With his head lowered, he looks just as if he has nodded off.

3.　他穿着灰鼠長袍，

Wearing that long squirrel-fur gown,

　　　簡直(地)都熱得出汗了，還是不肯換下來。

　　　he is just so hot he's sweating, but he still refuses to change.

　　　熱得簡直都出汗了，還是不肯換下來。

　　　he is so hot he's practically sweating, but he still refuses to change.

完成

1. 他這幾年東奔西跑，簡直。。。

2. 。。。他簡直想要永遠離開那裏。

II. 简直： simply; just; practically (emphatic)

Adverb

PATTERN: 简直 VE (modified by adverb or verbal complement)

简直是 VE (modified by adverb or verbal complement)

简直地 VE (modified by adverb or verbal complement)

简直(好)像。。。

例

34.4 〔男女在一起打篮球，〕简直是不成体统。

[Men and women playing basketball together— it] simply does not constitute [any kind of] decency.

7.33 她这样滔滔地说着，简直好像房间内是她一个人占领着似的。

She spoke so ebulliently, practically as if she were the only person there.

1. 他简直(是)快要哭了。

He's practically about to cry.

2. 他头低着，简直像在打盹儿一般。

With his head lowered, he looks just as if he has nodded off.

3. 他穿着灰鼠长袍，

Wearing that long squirrel-fur gown,

简直(地)都热得出汗了，还是不肯换下来。

he is just so hot he's sweating, but he still refuses to change.

热得简直都出汗了，还是不肯换下来。

he is so hot he's practically sweating, but he still refuses to change.

完成

1. 他这几年东奔西跑，简直。。。

2. 。。。他简直想要永远离开那里。

III. 否： not

Adverb that negates the verb

PATTERN: 否 VE   not to VE

       VE 否？   VE or not?

例

30.15   蕭澗秋否認着。

Xiao Jianqiu kept denying [it].

1.   她是否將終身大事視為兒戲？

Is it true or not that she considers the great event in her life to be a trifling matter?

2.   家中一切平安否？

Is everything well at home?

3.   否定之否定是否肯定？

Is the negation of a negation affirmation?

變換

1. 他說這種說法不是那位教授發明的。

2. 身體疲乏不疲乏？

IV. 何？ What?

Question word

PATTERN: 何 N？   what N?

       如何。。。？   怎麼。。。？ How . . . ?

       。。。如何？   。。。怎麼樣？ How about . . . ? What . . . ?

       何以。。。？   How . . . ? Why . . . ?

例

5.13   陶校長又問：「澗秋，這個芙蓉鎮，你印象如何？」

Continuing, Principal Tao asked, "How is your impression of this Hibiscus Town?"

III. 否： not

Adverb that negates the verb

PATTERN: 否 VE　　　　　　not to VE

　　　　 VE 否？　　　　　 VE or not?

例

30.15　萧涧秋否认着。

Xiao Jianqiu kept denying [it].

1.　她是否将终身大事视为儿戏？

Is it true or not that she considers the great event in her life to be a trifling matter?

2.　家中一切平安否？

Is everything well at home?

3.　否定之否定是否肯定？

Is the negation of a negation affirmation?

变换

1. 他说这种说法不是那位教授发明的。

2. 身体疲乏不疲乏？

IV. 何？ What?

Question word

PATTERN: 何 N?　　　　　　what N?

　　　　 如何。。。？　　　怎么。。。？ How . . .?

　　　　 。。。如何？　　　。。。怎么样？ How about . . .? What . . .?

　　　　 何以。。。？　　　How . . .? Why . . .?

例

5.13　陶校长又问：「涧秋，这个芙蓉镇，你印象如何？」

Continuing, Principal Tao asked, "How is your impression of this Hibiscus Town?"

30.28 我求你，無論如何不要煩惱。
I beg you, no matter what, don't be troubled.

31.12 何以解憂？惟有杜康。
How does one dispel worries? There is only Du Kang [wine].

1. 何人不忙？
Who is not busy?

2. 事情發生在何時何地？
Where and when did this happen?

3. 我們如何驅逐敵人？
How do we drive out the enemy?

4. 到我家喝兩杯，如何？
How about coming over to my house and having some wine?

5. 他們將如何增添工作機會？
How are they going to add to their employment opportunities?

6. 人們何以認為男的女的在一起打籃球不成體統呢？
Why do people consider co-ed basketball to be indecent?
How can people consider co-ed basketball to be indecent?

變換

1. 酒為甚麼能麻醉人呢？

2. 今晚去看一場籃球，怎麼樣？

3. 他怎麼能得勝呢？

4. 請問那件事是甚麼人甚麼時候甚麼地方所作？

V. 一M一M地：	M by M; one M after another	*Adverb used in a time sequence*
一一：	one by one	*Adverb used in a spatial sequence*

例

31.10 蕭澗秋卻一杯一杯地喝。
Yet Xiao Jianqiu drank cup after cup.

30.28　我求你，无论如何不要烦恼。
I beg you, no matter what, don't be troubled.

31.12　何以解忧？惟有杜康。
How does one dispel worries? There is only Du Kang [wine].

1.　何人不忙？
Who is not busy?

2.　事情发生在何时何地？
Where and when did this happen?

3.　我们如何驱逐敌人？
How do we drive out the enemy?

4.　到我家喝两杯，如何？
How about coming over to my house and having some wine?

5.　他们将如何增添工作机会？
How are they going to add to their employment opportunities?

6.　人们何以认为男的女的在一起打篮球不成体统呢？
Why do people consider co-ed basketball to be indecent?
How can people consider co-ed basketball to be indecent?

变换

1. 酒为什么能麻醉人呢？

2. 今晚去看一场篮球，怎么样？

3. 他怎么能得胜呢？

4. 请问那件事是什么人什么时候什么地方所作？

V.　一 M 一 M 地：　M by M; one M after another　*Adverb used in a time sequence*

　　一一：　　　　　one by one　　　　　*Adverb used in a spatial sequence*

例

31.10　萧涧秋却一杯一杯地喝。
Yet Xiao Jianqiu drank cup after cup.

22.21　采蓮一一喚着陶校長、方老師。。。。
One by one Cailian greeted Principal Tao, Teacher Fang. . . .

1.　陶慕侃一句一句地念出了李白的詩句。
Tao Mukan recited Li Bai's poem line by line.

2.　他把請假的理由一一寫出。
他把請假的理由一條一條地寫出。
He wrote out one by one his reasons for requesting leave.

變換

1. 歷史家把那些人的事情都記下來給後人看。

2. 天氣暖和起來了，他把冷天的衣服都收起來放進箱子裏。

VI. 越發： all the more; even more

Adverb used in comparative constructions

cf. 更加: *EX 6.I*

PATTERN: [S 本來 SV,] . . . 〔現在〕S 越發（地）SV

　　　　S 越 SV1, 越發（地）SV2

例

35.5　〔剛打完球，陶嵐出汗了。〕陶嵐口渴地喝着熱茶，她臉上的汗越發多了。

[Tao Lan was sweating from having just finished playing ball.] Tao Lan thirstily drank the hot tea, [causing] her face to sweat even more.

1.　〔他本來有點兒激動。〕他喝酒之後越發地興奮。
[He already was a little bit excited.] He became even more excited after drinking.

2.　心裏越是有心事，就越發要喝酒。
The more one is preoccupied with something, the more one wants to drink.

22.21　采莲——唤着陶校长、方老师。。。。
One by one Cailian greeted Principal Tao, Teacher Fang. . . .

1.　陶慕侃一句一句地念出了李白的诗句。
Tao Mukan recited Li Bai's poem line by line.

2.　他把请假的理由一一写出。
他把请假的理由一条一条地写出。
He wrote out one by one his reasons for requesting leave.

变换

1. 历史家把那些人的事情都记下来给后人看。

2. 天气暖和起来了，他把冷天的衣服都收起来放进箱子里。

VI. 越发：　all the more; even more

Adverb used in comparative constructions

cf. 更加：*EX 6.I*

PATTERN:〔S 本来 SV,〕. . .〔现在〕S 越发（地）SV

　　　　　S 越 SV1, 越发（地）SV2

例

35.5　〔刚打完球，陶岚出汗了。〕陶岚口渴地喝着热茶，她脸上的汗越发多了。
[Tao Lan was sweating from having just finished playing ball.] Tao Lan thirstily drank the hot tea, [causing] her face to sweat even more.

1.　〔他本来有点儿激动。〕他喝酒之后越发地兴奋。
[He already was a little bit excited.] He became even more excited after drinking.

2.　心里越是有心事，就越发要喝酒。
The more one is preoccupied with something, the more one wants to drink.

完成

1. 剛才就已經起了一點兒風。現在快要下雨了，。。。

2. 你。。。他就越發關心。

VII. 聚精會神： lit., to concentrate the spirit: to do sth. with great concentration; absorbed

Set phrase with VOVO construction: stands alone as a predicate or functions as a modifier

例

35.21 兩人聚精會神地看着，討論着。

The two read and discussed with great concentration.

1. 　工作的時候要聚精會神地工作。遊戲的時候也要聚精會神地遊戲。

When working, one should work with great concentration. When playing, one should also play with great concentration.

2. 　他專心得很，無論作甚麼總是聚精會神的。

He is so single-minded; no matter what he is doing, he is always so absorbed.

回答

1. 他為甚麼那麼聚精會神呢？

2. 你怎麼知道他在聚精會神地學習呢？

三。生詞練習

填空一

冷漠；安排；激動；振奮；否認；囑咐；光明正大；再三；更加；一本一本地；
　　　　何以；盡興；起伏；隨口；激烈；蒼白

1. 錢正興並不（　　）他的辭職與蕭澗秋有關係。

完成

1. 刚才就已经起了一点儿风。现在快要下雨了，。。。

2. 你。。。他就越发关心。

VII. 聚精会神： lit., to concentrate the spirit: to do sth. with great concentration; absorbed

Set phrase with VOVO construction: stands alone as a predicate or functions as a modifier

例

35.21 两人聚精会神地看着，讨论着。
The two read and discussed with great concentration.

1.   工作的时候要聚精会神地工作。游戏的时候也要聚精会神地游戏。
When working, one should work with great concentration. When playing, one should also play with great concentration.

2.   他专心得很，无论作什么总是聚精会神的。
He is so single-minded; no matter what he is doing, he is always so absorbed.

回答

1. 他为什么那么聚精会神呢？

2. 你怎么知道他在聚精会神地学习呢？

三。生词练习

填空一

冷漠；安排；激动；振奋；否认；嘱咐；光明正大；再三；更加；一本一本地；
何以；尽兴；起伏；随口；激烈；苍白

1. 钱正兴并不（   ）他的辞职与萧涧秋有关系。

2. 別的孩子都在嬉笑遊戲，只有那小女孩子臉色（　　），皺着眉頭，一個人坐在那裏很不舒服的樣子。

3. 他學了客氣話《哪裏》以後，覺得這句話很好用。有一天，朋友說他寫字寫得非常難看，他也（　　）說道：「哪裏，哪裏。」

4. 他把他所擔心的事說了又說，（　　）告訴我要小心。說了好幾次，恐怕我不注意。

5. 他為甚麼要寫那樣的信？又（　　）不敢寫上自己的名字？

6. 你太容易（　　）了。怎麼一聽了悲哀的故事就想哭？

7. 晚會開始的時候那位先生對大家說：「今天的節目是這樣為您（　　）的。」

8. 他覺得自己是（　　）的。對別人的閑話並不介意。

9. 他把書房裏的書（　　）都翻完了，還是找不到好題目來作文。

10. 他知道自己並不受歡迎，對於人們（　　）的眼色已經習慣了。

11. 奶奶（　　）孫子說：「到了學校要聽老師的話，好好學習。」

12. 陶嵐對錢正興很不滿意；其實蕭澗秋（　　）對錢正興不滿意。

13. 昨晚那場籃球比賽打得非常（　　）。雙方你不讓我，我不讓你，打到最後半分鐘還不知道誰勝利了。

14. 記得我念中學的時候，每天下午非打三小時的籃球不可，不然不能（　　），總覺得玩得不夠痛快。

15. 欸，別整天喝酒麻醉自己吧！你應該（　　）起來。有很多有意義的事等着你去做呢。

16. 他認為他老家的風景最美。那裏四周有青山（　　），又有綠水悠悠的流過。

2. 别的孩子都在嬉笑游戏，只有那小女孩子脸色（　　），皱着眉头，一个人坐在那里很不舒服的样子。

3. 他学了客气话《哪里》以后，觉得这句话很好用。有一天，朋友说他写字写得非常难看，他也（　　）说道：「哪里，哪里。」

4. 他把他所担心的事说了又说，（　　）告诉我要小心。说了好几次，恐怕我不注意。

5. 他为什么要写那样的信？又（　　）不敢写上自己的名字？

6. 你太容易（　　）了。怎么一听了悲哀的故事就想哭？

7. 晚会开始的时候那位先生对大家说：「今天的节目是这样为您（　　）的。」

8. 他觉得自己是（　　）的。对别人的闲话并不介意。

9. 他把书房里的书（　　）都翻完了，还是找不到好题目来作文。

10. 他知道自己并不受欢迎，对于人们（　　）的眼色已经习惯了。

11. 奶奶（　　）孙子说：「到了学校要听老师的话，好好学习。」

12. 陶岚对钱正兴很不满意；其实萧涧秋（　　）对钱正兴不满意。

13. 昨晚那场篮球比赛打得非常（　　）。双方你不让我，我不让你，打到最后半分钟还不知道谁胜利了。

14. 记得我念中学的时候，每天下午非打三小时的篮球不可，不然不能（　　），总觉得玩得不够痛快。

15. 欸，别整天喝酒麻醉自己吧！你应该（　　）起来。有很多有意义的事等着你去做呢。

16. 他认为他老家的风景最美。那里四周有青山（　　），又有绿水悠悠的流过。

填空二

悔不該；一瞬不瞬；要挾；氣憤；擔心；表現；越發；聚精會神；陰沈；隱瞞；
驅逐；煩惱；昂首闊步；禁不住；殘忍；卑鄙

1. 啊，你現在寫的字比從前更好了。你看，一筆一劃都（　　）有力了。

2. 烏雲滿天，快要下雨了。天氣（　　）。

3. 最近小李好像很（　　），常常跟先生大哭大鬧。

4. 張小姐很久沒有接到母親的來信了。不知道家中的情形怎麼樣，是不是人人都很平安。她非常（　　）。

5. 學生們都全神貫注、（　　）地聽講。

6. 他眼睛（　　）地盯着那個陌生人，很懷疑他的來意。

7. 激戰勝利後，他在橋上一會兒（　　）地走來走去，眺望遠方。一會兒又低下頭來看橋下的流水。

8. 他常說（　　）當初不去當律師而要學藝術。

9. 他是個誠實的孩子。這事情不會（　　）着不告訴父母的。

10. 他只敢在人背後指指戳戳、竊竊私語，而不敢站出來面對面地說。真（　　）。

11. 蕭潤秋猛力的彈着鋼琴，是不是勇敢的（　　）？

12. 鄉鎮裏的人都不歡迎這個陌生人，所以想要把他（　　）出去。

13. 他連小孩哭都不能忍受，你怎麼能說他（　　）？

14. 他寫了十封信（　　）十個有錢的人道：「如果你三天之內不拿出十萬塊錢來，你的事就會暴露出來！」

15. 他很（　　）地說：「他開我的汽車，出了事，竟然還要怪我。你說氣不氣人？」

16. 聽說今年的考試比較難，學生們都（　　）更加緊張起來。

填空二

悔不该；一瞬不瞬；要挟；气愤；担心；表现；越发；聚精会神；阴沉；隐瞒；
驱逐；烦恼；昂首阔步；禁不住；残忍；卑鄙

1. 啊，你现在写的字比从前更好了。你看，一笔一划都（　　）有力了。

2. 乌云满天，快要下雨了。天气（　　）。

3. 最近小李好像很（　　），常常跟先生大哭大闹。

4. 张小姐很久没有接到母亲的来信了。不知道家中的情形怎么样，是不是人
人都很平安。她非常（　　）。

5. 学生们都全神贯注、（　　）地听讲。

6. 他眼睛（　　）地盯着那个陌生人，很怀疑他的来意。

7. 激战胜利后，他在桥上一会儿（　　）地走来走去，眺望远方。一会儿又低下
头来看桥下的流水。

8. 他常说（　　）当初不去当律师而要学艺术。

9. 他是个诚实的孩子。这事情不会（　　）着不告诉父母的。

10. 他只敢在人背后指指戳戳、窃窃私语，而不敢站出来面对面地说。真
（　　）。

11. 萧涧秋猛力的弹着钢琴，是不是勇敢的（　　）？

12. 乡镇里的人都不欢迎这个陌生人，所以想要把他（　　）出去。

13. 他连小孩哭都不能忍受，你怎么能说他（　　）？

14. 他写了十封信（　　）十个有钱的人道：「如果你三天之内不拿出十万块钱
来，你的事就会暴露出来！」

15. 他很（　　）地说：「他开我的汽车，出了事，竟然还要怪我。你说气不气
人？」

16. 听说今年的考试比较难，学生们都（　　）更加紧张起来。

四。説話練習

用你的瞭解來說：

1. 蕭澗秋所接到的那一首詩表示甚麼？
2. 從陶慕侃喝酒時所說的詩句講他對人生的看法。

討論：

1.一個人想要喝酒的理由是甚麼？
2.「文明」在這段故事裏指的是甚麼？

五。作文

　蕭澗秋是不是一個很勇敢的人？

四。说话练习

　　　　用你的了解来说：

1. 萧涧秋所接到的那一首诗表示什么？

2. 从陶慕侃喝酒时所说的诗句讲他对人生的看法。

　　　　讨论：

1.一个人想要喝酒的理由是什么？

2.「文明」在这段故事里指的是什么？

五。作文

　　萧涧秋是不是一个很勇敢的人？

練習七：第三十九景至第四十四景

一。閱讀測驗

三十九至四十一景

1. 說說茶館中的情形。

2. 方謀說錢正興辭職後同仁們感覺怎麼樣？

3. 錢正興回學校教書的條件是甚麼？

4. 方謀將野鴨比作誰？

5. 阿寶怎麼不舒服？阿寶的體溫有多高？

6. 中醫為甚麼看見蕭澗秋和陶嵐在看體溫表就不高興？中醫怎麼為孩子看病？

7. 關於阿寶的病，中醫對文嫂說甚麼？中醫認為非開藥方不可嗎？

8. 文嫂信中醫的話嗎？為甚麼？

9. 中醫對蕭澗秋的態度怎麼樣？

10. 陶嵐回家時，陶媽媽跟她談了些甚麼？

四十二至四十四景

1. 蕭澗秋怎麼教采蓮認字？

2. 蕭澗秋怎麼看護阿寶？

3. 文嫂感激蕭澗秋，她對蕭澗秋說甚麼？

练习七：第三十九景至第四十四景

一。阅读测验

三十九至四十一景

1. 说说茶馆中的情形。

2. 方谋说钱正兴辞职后同仁们感觉怎么样？

3. 钱正兴回学校教书的条件是什么？

4. 方谋将野鸭比作谁？

5. 阿宝怎么不舒服？阿宝的体温有多高？

6. 中医为什么看见萧涧秋和陶岚在看体温表就不高兴？中医怎么为孩子看病？

7. 关于阿宝的病，中医对文嫂说什么？中医认为非开药方不可吗？

8. 文嫂信中医的话吗？为什么？

9. 中医对萧涧秋的态度怎么样？

10. 陶岚回家时，陶妈妈跟她谈了些什么？

四十二至四十四景

1. 萧涧秋怎么教采莲认字？

2. 萧涧秋怎么看护阿宝？

3. 文嫂感激萧涧秋，她对萧涧秋说什么？

4. 蕭澗秋要離開采蓮家時，采蓮說的話為甚麼使他很窘？

5. 阿榮來找蕭澗秋，是誰叫他來的？

6. 陶校長的同仁對甚麼事情看不慣？

7. 陶慕侃認為《人言可畏》指的是甚麼？

8. 陶嵐為甚麼向她哥哥發脾氣？

9. 陶慕侃請蕭澗秋來談話的原意是甚麼？

10. 蕭澗秋認為他現在離開芙蓉鎮有甚麼結果？

二。語法練習

I. 故作 SV（的樣子）： to act intentionally as if SV-ing; to feign SV; to pretend to be SV

Verb-object construction

例

40.22　醫生故作輕鬆地說：「沒甚麼病。」
　　　　The doctor said in an intentionally relaxed manner, "He doesn't have anything serious."

1.　　　他故作專心看書的樣子，叫人不會疑心他。
　　　　He acts as if he's studying with such single-minded concentration, so that no one will suspect [otherwise].

2.　　　其實他一點也不感動，只是故作感動而已。
　　　　Actually, he is not the least bit moved; he's only pretending to be moved, that's all.

回答

1. 一個人為甚麼要故作驚喜呢？

2. 一個人為甚麼要故作擔憂呢？

4. 萧涧秋要离开采莲家时，采莲说的话为什么使他很窘？

5. 阿荣来找萧涧秋，是谁叫他来的？

6. 陶校长的同仁对什么事情看不惯？

7. 陶慕侃认为《人言可畏》指的是什么？

8. 陶岚为什么向她哥哥发脾气？

9. 陶慕侃请萧涧秋来谈话的原意是什么？

10. 萧涧秋认为他现在离开芙蓉镇有什么结果？

二。语法练习

I. 故作 SV（的样子）： to act intentionally as if SV-ing; to feign SV; to pretend to be SV

Verb-object construction

例
40.22 医生故作轻松地说：「没什么病。」
The doctor said in an intentionally relaxed manner, "He doesn't have anything serious."

1. 他故作专心看书的样子，叫人不会疑心他。
He acts as if he's studying with such single-minded concentration, so that no one will suspect [otherwise].

2. 其实他一点也不感动，只是故作感动而已。
Actually, he is not the least bit moved; he's only pretending to be moved, that's all.

回答

1. 一个人为什么要故作惊喜呢？

2. 一个人为什么要故作担忧呢？

II. 如 N1, N2, . . . 之類： like N1, N2, . . . ; for example, N1, N2, . . .

例

42.2   〔小方紙塊〕上面有畫有字，如麥冬、半夏、桂枝之類。
[On the little squares of paper] there were drawings and words, like Maidong, Banxia, and Guizhi.

1.   書架上的書大多是小說，如作家史坦貝克 *[Shǐtǎnbèikè]* 的《人鼠之間》、迪耿斯 *[Dígěngsī]* 的《雙城記》之類。
Most of the books on the bookshelf are novels, like Steinbeck's *Of Mice and Men* and Dickens's *A Tale of Two Cities*.

2.   他正在學説客氣話。常常説着如「對不起、」「不敢當」之類的詞。
He is just in the process of learning how to use polite language; he often says things like "Sorry!" and "You flatter me!"

完成

1. 。。。如孔雀野鴨之類。

2.「哪種人喜歡去茶館呢？」「。。。」

III.   藉此： to take this [opportunity]; thus; in this way
為此： because of this; thus; in this way
以此： by means of this; thus; in this way

PATTERN: CV 此 VE

例

17.17   我現在點名，藉此和你們認識一下。
I will begin roll call now, and thus take this opportunity to get to know you a little bit.

22.20   蕭澗秋帶着采蓮進來，屋內的僵局為此打破。
Xiao Jianqiu brought Cailian in. The tension in the room was thus broken.

42.2   〔小方紙塊〕上面有畫兒有字。。。。蕭澗秋以此來教采蓮認字。
[On the little squares of paper] there were drawings and words. . . . By this means Xiao Jianqiu taught Cailian to read characters.

1.   陶嵐編織着毛綫，以此消磨無聊的時光。
Tao Lan knits and knits [sweaters]. In this way, she fritters away her times of boredom.

II. 如 N1, N2, . . . 之类： like N1, N2, . . . ; for example, N1, N2, . . .

例

42.2　〔小方纸块〕上面有画有字，如麦冬、半夏、桂枝之类。

[On the little squares of paper] there were drawings and words, like Maidong, Banxia, and Guizhi.

1.　书架上的书大多是小说，如作家史坦贝克 *[Shǐtǎnbèikè]* 的《人鼠之间》、迪耿斯 *[Dígěngsī]* 的《双城记》之类。

Most of the books on the bookshelf are novels, like Steinbeck's *Of Mice and Men* and Dickens's *A Tale of Two Cities*.

2.　他正在学说客气话。常常说着如「对不起、」「不敢当」之类的词。

He is just in the process of learning how to use polite language; he often says things like "Sorry!" and "You flatter me!"

完成

1. 。。。如孔雀野鸭之类。

2. 「哪种人喜欢去茶馆呢？」「。。。」

III. 借此： to take this [opportunity]; thus; in this way

　　为此： because of this; thus; in this way

　　以此： by means of this; thus; in this way

PATTERN: CV 此 VE

例

17.17　我现在点名，借此和你们认识一下。

I will begin roll call now, and thus take this opportunity to get to know you a little bit.

22.20　萧涧秋带着采莲进来，屋内的僵局为此打破。

Xiao Jianqiu brought Cailian in. The tension in the room was thus broken.

42.2　〔小方纸块〕上面有画儿有字。。。。萧涧秋以此来教采莲认字。

[On the little squares of paper] there were drawings and words. . . . By this means Xiao Jianqiu taught Cailian to read characters.

1.　陶岚编织着毛线，以此消磨无聊的时光。

Tao Lan knits and knits [sweaters]. In this way, she fritters away her times of boredom.

2.   他每天接、送孩子上、下學，藉此可以運動運動。
Everyday he takes the children to school and picks them up. In this way he can get some exercise.

3.   老張很厭惡他那種紈綺子弟，為此總不願跟他談話。
Lao Zhang detests the kind of profligate son of the rich that he is. Because of this [Lao Zhang] is never willing to talk to him.

完成

1. 。。。，為此他擔任芙蓉鎮中學的校長。

2. 。。。，以此引起老太太的注意。

3. 。。。，藉此可以多了解一些外面的世界。

IV. 繼而： continuing; then

轉而： to turn; changing to (contrastive)

Conjunction

cf. 而：*EX 2.VI, 3.I, 3.V, 5.IV, 9.V*

例
42.5   文嫂欣喜地叫了幾聲阿寶，繼而對。。。蕭澗秋説。。。
Wen Sao delightedly called out Abao's name several times, then . . . said to Xiao Jianqiu . . .

17.55   蕭澗秋的口氣稍微急迫了一些。王福生的眼淚快要流出來了。。。。蕭澗秋又轉而溫和地説：「好了。。。。」
Xiao Jianqiu's tone became a little bit more pressing. Wang Fusheng's tears were just about to start flowing. . . . But then Xiao Jianqiu turned gentle as he said: "It's OK. . . ."

1.   他知道了以後，先是緊鎖眉頭，繼而嘆起氣來。
After he found out, he first frowned, then began to sigh.

2.   他本來是要哭的，看見了大皮球以後，轉而高興地跑過去。
He was going to cry, but when he saw the big rubber ball, he ran over, [his tears] turning to happiness.

2. 他每天接、送孩子上、下学，借此可以运动运动。
   Everyday he takes the children to school and picks them up. In this way he can get some exercise.

3. 老张很厌恶他那种纨袴子弟，为此总不愿跟他谈话。
   Lao Zhang detests the kind of profligate son of the rich that he is. Because of this [Lao Zhang] is never willing to talk to him.

完成

1. 。。。，为此他担任芙蓉镇中学的校长。

2. 。。。，以此引起老太太的注意。

3. 。。。，借此可以多了解一些外面的世界。

IV. 继而： continuing; then

转而： to turn; changing to (contrastive)

Conjunction

cf. 而： EX 2.VI, 3.I, 3.V, 5.IV, 9.V

例

42.5 文嫂欣喜地叫了几声阿宝，继而对。。。萧涧秋说。。。。
Wen Sao delightedly called out Abao's name several times, then . . . said to Xiao Jianqiu . . .

17.55 萧涧秋的口气稍微急迫了一些。王福生的眼泪快要流出来了。。。。萧涧秋又转而温和地说：「好了。。。。」
Xiao Jianqiu's tone became a little bit more pressing. Wang Fusheng's tears were just about to start flowing. . . . But then Xiao Jianqiu turned gentle as he said: "It's OK. . . ."

1. 他知道了以后，先是紧锁眉头，继而叹起气来。
   After he found out, he first frowned, then began to sigh.

2. 他本来是要哭的，看见了大皮球以后，转而高兴地跑过去。
   He was going to cry, but when he saw the big rubber ball, he ran over, [his tears] turning to happiness.

完成

1. 她先用眼色勸蕭澗秋不要喝酒，後來轉而。。。。

2. 她先用眼色勸蕭澗秋不要喝酒，繼而。。。。

V. 何況：let alone; much less; not to mention; never mind

Conjunction

例

43.6　人言可畏，何況已經傳到鎮長的耳朵裏去了。
What people say is worthy of deference; not to mention that the mayor has already heard about it.

1.　小孩子不舒服就得看醫生，何況燒得那麼厲害。
When a child doesn't feel well, he should go to see a doctor, let alone when he has such a severe fever.

2.　他本來已經不耐煩講這件事了，何況你還去問長問短。他當然會發脾氣。
He already had no patience in discussing this, never mind [having to answer] all your many questions. Of course he was going to lose his temper.

完成

1. 這件事情連三歲小孩都知道，。。。。

2. 。。。。，何況一個寡婦。

VI. 難以 VE: to find it hard to VE; to have difficulty VE-ing

(where VE commonly consists of two characters)

Verb construction

cf. EX 2.I, 2.II, 7.VI

完成

1. 她先用眼色劝萧涧秋不要喝酒，后来转而。。。。

2. 她先用眼色劝萧涧秋不要喝酒，继而。。。。

V. 何况： let alone; much less; not to mention; never mind

Conjunction

例

43.6　人言可畏，何况已经传到镇长的耳朵里去了。

What people say is worthy of deference; not to mention that the mayor has already heard about it.

1.　　小孩子不舒服就得看医生，何况烧得那么厉害。

When a child doesn't feel well, he should go to see a doctor, let alone when he has such a severe fever.

2.　　他本来已经不耐烦讲这件事了，何况你还去问长问短。他当然会发脾气。

He already had no patience in discussing this, never mind [having to answer] all your many questions. Of course he was going to lose his temper.

完成

1. 这件事情连三岁小孩都知道，。。。。

2. 。。。。，何况一个寡妇。

VI. 难以 VE: to find it hard to VE; to have difficulty VE-ing

(where VE commonly consists of two characters)

Verb construction

cf. EX 2.I, 2.II, 7.VI

例

40.29 文嫂。。。問：「蕭先生，看樣子，會沒病嗎？」蕭澗秋難以回答。
Wen Sao . . . asked: "Mr. Xiao, from the looks of it, he doesn't really have anything serious, does he?" Xiao Jianqiu found it hard to reply.

42.12 蕭澗秋強笑着，似有些難以為情。
Smiling in a forced way, Xiao Jianqiu seemed as if he were having some difficulty responding.

1. 他聽了這個消息，實在難以隱藏他的心酸，不禁眼淚盈眶。
When he heard this news, he found it truly difficult to hide his pain. He could not stop the tears from welling in his eyes.

2. 世界上的事千變萬化，難以猜測。
With things always changing in the world, it is hard to guess [how things will go next].

變換

1. 阿寶燒得厲害，雖然文嫂用濕毛巾為他敷在頭上，仍是沒法子降低溫度。

2. 文嫂認為要報答蕭澗秋的恩德十分困難。

VII. 惹 N V: to cause N to V (often with negative consequences); to invite or ask for N to V (a form of trouble)

Causative verb construction

例

44.18 這樣不清不白地走了，不更要惹人笑罵嗎？
Wouldn't leaving now in this sullied way just cause people to ridicule me even more?

1. 陶嵐並不介意是否惹人議論，她說她要我行我素。
Tao Lan did not really care whether or not [her actions] provoked discussion; she said she would stick to her ways no matter what anyone else thought.

2. 他的大紅衣服惹人注意。
His scarlet clothing drew [unwanted] attention.

回答

1. 作了甚麼樣的事情會惹人笑罵呢？

2. 作了甚麼樣的事情會惹人喜歡呢？

例

40.29 文嫂。。。问：「萧先生，看样子，会没病吗？」萧涧秋难以回答。

Wen Sao . . . asked: "Mr. Xiao, from the looks of it, he doesn't really have anything serious, does he?" Xiao Jianqiu found it hard to reply.

42.12 萧涧秋强笑着，似有些难以为情。

Smiling in a forced way, Xiao Jianqiu seemed as if he were having some difficulty responding.

1. 他听了这个消息，实在难以隐藏他的心酸，不禁眼泪盈眶。

When he heard this news, he found it truly difficult to hide his pain. He could not stop the tears from welling in his eyes.

2. 世界上的事千变万化，难以猜测。

With things always changing in the world, it is hard to guess [how things will go next].

变换

1. 阿宝烧得厉害，虽然文嫂用湿毛巾为他敷在头上，仍是没法子降低温度。

2. 文嫂认为要报答萧涧秋的恩德十分困难。

VII. 惹 N V: to cause N to V (often with negative consequences); to invite or ask for N to V (a form of trouble)

Causative verb construction

例

44.18 这样不清不白地走了，不更要惹人笑骂吗？

Wouldn't leaving now in this sullied way just cause people to ridicule me even more?

1. 陶岚并不介意是否惹人议论，她说她要我行我素。

Tao Lan did not really care whether or not [her actions] provoked discussion; she said she would stick to her ways no matter what anyone else thought.

2. 他的大红衣服惹人注意。

His scarlet clothing drew [unwanted] attention.

回答

1. 作了什么样的事情会惹人笑骂呢？

2. 作了什么样的事情会惹人喜欢呢？

三。生詞練習

填空一

恰巧；果決；昏迷；狀態；難以；執拗；緩和；惹；何況；以此；繼而；之類；光；故作；理會；依

1. 這件事很不簡單，將來的發展實在（　）猜測。

2. 因為方謀説同仁們都希望錢正興早些回校，錢正興首先感到自己是勝利者，（　）大聲説非趕走姓蕭的不可。

3. 四月一號那天，他（　）緊張地看着窗外説：「快整理你的房間，校長就要來看你來了。」

4.《（　）説不練》的意思是只是説而不練習。

5. 在那困難的時刻，他（　）地作了決定，救活了好多人。

6. （　）他看來，這兒的天氣比他從前住的地方暖和多了。

7. 他們雙方的關係太緊張了，想法子幫他們（　）一下吧！

8. 因為剛到一個新地方，他每天帶着字典出門，（　）幫助自己認識當地的街名，地名和飯館兒的名字。

9. 我正想找他談話呢，（　）在學校碰見了他。

10. 書桌上放着如鋼筆，紙張，小刀（　）的一些東西。

11. 這地方連夏天晚上都很涼，（　）現在已經是秋天了，當然晚上得多穿點衣服。

12. 孩子不聽爸爸的話，（　）爸爸生氣了。

13. 他不能瞭解中醫為甚麼按脈就能知道病人的身體（　）。

14. 他脾氣像牛似的，（　）得很，別人的意見他很難聽得進。

15. 現在雖然有人提倡保護環境，可是多數人並不（　）。

16. 小孩兒發燒得太高，就容易（　）。

三。生词练习

填空一

恰巧；果决；昏迷；状态；难以；执拗；缓和；惹；何况；以此；继而；之类；
光；故作；理会；依

1. 这件事很不简单，将来的发展实在（　　）猜测。

2. 因为方谋说同仁们都希望钱正兴早些回校，钱正兴首先感到自己是胜利者，（　　）大声说非赶走姓萧的不可。

3. 四月一号那天，他（　　）紧张地看着窗外说：「快整理你的房间，校长就要来看你来了。」

4. 《（　　）说不练》的意思是只是说而不练习。

5. 在那困难的时刻，他（　　）地作了决定，救活了好多人。

6. （　　）他看来，这儿的天气比他从前住的地方暖和多了。

7. 他们双方的关系太紧张了，想法子帮他们（　　）一下吧！

8. 因为刚到一个新地方，他每天带着字典出门，（　　）帮助自己认识当地的街名，地名和饭馆儿的名字。

9. 我正想找他谈话呢，（　　）在学校碰见了他。

10. 书桌上放着如钢笔，纸张，小刀（　　）的一些东西。

11. 这地方连夏天晚上都很凉，（　　）现在已经是秋天了，当然晚上得多穿点衣服。

12. 孩子不听爸爸的话，（　　）爸爸生气了。

13. 他不能了解中医为什么按脉就能知道病人的身体（　　）。

14. 他脾气像牛似的，（　　）得很，别人的意见他很难听得进。

15. 现在虽然有人提倡保护环境，可是多数人并不（　　）。

16. 小孩儿发烧得太高，就容易（　　）。

填空二

人言可畏；自鳴得意；緊鎖眉頭；擔憂；難以為情；比喻；藉此；靈；為此；
我行我素；盼望；無辜；沈吟；報答；匆匆忙忙地；詫異

1. 我最喜歡聽新聞廣播了，不但可以瞭解天下大事，而且又能（　）學到最新的有用的生辭。

2. 中文常用含苞待放來（　）年輕美麗的女孩子。

3. 他寫了一首詩，自己認為自己是很了不起的詩人，就（　）地大聲念給別人聽。不知道別人都覺得討厭。

4. 一位名女人自殺了。她留下一封信說：「外界的輿論弄得我不清不白，我不能不用自殺來說明我的清白。」這就是那句老話所說的（　）啊！

5. 母親（　）兒子快快回家。

6. 你為甚麼（　），連笑也不肯笑一下呢？有甚麼不開心的事情？

7. 你對我這麼好，我怎麼（　）你的恩德呢？

8. 陶校長認為陶嵐的思想太文明了，文明得使他（　），在同事們面前感到不好意思。

9. 十幾歲的孩子第一次自己開着車到遠地去旅行，母親非常（　）。

10. 因為昨天晚上睡得晚了一點兒，今天早上（　）起來去上課，沒時間吃早飯。

11. 這藥很（　），吃了兩片，就退燒了。

12. 陶校長聽到采蓮變成了蕭澗秋的乾女兒，覺得十分奇怪，使他很（　）。

13. 他對社會輿論一點兒都不介意。他說：「怕甚麼？我就是（　）。我怎麼能為輿論所打倒？」

14. 小孩子是天真（　）的，不會有甚麼壞心，也不會做甚麼壞事，當然沒有罪。

15. 他想了半天，最後才（　）道：「好吧，只好這麼辦了，目前也沒有更好的辦法。」

填空二

人言可畏；自鸣得意；紧锁眉头；担忧；难以为情；比喻；借此；灵；为此；
我行我素；盼望；无辜；沉吟；报答；匆匆忙忙地；诧异

1. 我最喜欢听新闻广播了，不但可以了解天下大事，而且又能（　）学到最新的有用的生辞。

2. 中文常用含苞待放来（　）年轻美丽的女孩子。

3. 他写了一首诗，自己认为自己是很了不起的诗人，就（　）地大声念给别人听。不知道别人都觉得讨厌。

4. 一位名女人自杀了。她留下一封信说：「外界的舆论弄得我不清不白，我不能不用自杀来说明我的清白。」这就是那句老话所说的（　）啊！

5. 母亲（　）儿子快快回家。

6. 你为什么（　），连笑也不肯笑一下呢？有什么不开心的事情？

7. 你对我这么好，我怎么（　）你的恩德呢？

8. 陶校长认为陶岚的思想太文明了，文明得使他（　），在同事们面前感到不好意思。

9. 十几岁的孩子第一次自己开着车到远地去旅行，母亲非常（　）。

10. 因为昨天晚上睡得晚了一点儿，今天早上（　）起来去上课，没时间吃早饭。

11. 这药很（　），吃了两片，就退烧了。

12. 陶校长听到采莲变成了萧涧秋的干女儿，觉得十分奇怪，使他很（　）。

13. 他对社会舆论一点儿都不介意。他说：「怕什么？我就是（　）。我怎么能为舆论所打倒？」

14. 小孩子是天真（　）的，不会有什么坏心，也不会做什么坏事，当然没有罪。

15. 他想了半天，最后才（　）道：「好吧，只好这么办了，目前也没有更好的办法。」

16. 最近中國有個學校請他去教英文，他高興極了，（　　）特別開了兩瓶酒請
　　朋友喝。

四。説話練習

　　　　　用括號中的詞來說：

1. 你認字片的經驗。（字片；漢字；圖畫）
2. 中醫看病時的過程。（按脈；體溫；藥方）

　　　　　討論：

陶慕侃為了甚麼事為難？

五。作文

　　論《人言可畏》。

16. 最近中国有个学校请他去教英文，他高兴极了，（　　）特别开了两瓶酒请朋友喝。

四。说话练习

　　　　用括号中的词来说：

1. 你认字片的经验。（字片；汉字；图画）
2. 中医看病时的过程。（按脉；体温；药方）

　　　　讨论：

陶慕侃为了什么事为难？

五。作文

　　论《人言可畏》。

練習八：第四十五景至第五十三景

一。閱讀測驗

四十五至四十九景

1. 那天蕭澗秋去上課，發現了甚麼異常情況？蕭澗秋的反應如何？

2. 關於學生們不來上課，陶家兄妹兩人所得到的消息怎麼不一樣？

3. 陶嵐為甚麼跟她的哥哥特別親密起來？

4. 陶嵐說阿寶死時的情形怎麼樣？

5. 阿寶死了，文嫂有甚麼反應？

6. 阿寶死了，蕭澗秋對文嫂說些甚麼安慰的話？

7. 文嫂本來要怎麼報答蕭澗秋？

8. 關於采蓮以後的生活，文嫂想蕭澗秋可以怎麼幫忙？

9. 蕭澗秋以為文嫂可以怎麼解決生活問題？

10. 蕭澗秋為甚麼提出改嫁的辦法後又覺得說錯了話呢？

五十至五十三景

1. 蕭澗秋又徘徊起來，他想要解決甚麼問題？

2. 蕭澗秋正要寫信給陶嵐，陶嵐知道了以後怎麼想？

3. 蕭澗秋為甚麼認為陶嵐會同意他的決定？

4. 蕭澗秋的想法是甚麼？

练习八：第四十五景至第五十三景

一。阅读测验

四十五至四十九景

1. 那天萧涧秋去上课，发现了什么异常情况？萧涧秋的反应如何？

2. 关于学生们不来上课，陶家兄妹两人所得到的消息怎么不一样？

3. 陶岚为什么跟她的哥哥特别亲密起来？

4. 陶岚说阿宝死时的情形怎么样？

5. 阿宝死了，文嫂有什么反应？

6. 阿宝死了，萧涧秋对文嫂说些什么安慰的话？

7. 文嫂本来要怎么报答萧涧秋？

8. 关于采莲以后的生活，文嫂想萧涧秋可以怎么帮忙？

9. 萧涧秋以为文嫂可以怎么解决生活问题？

10. 萧涧秋为什么提出改嫁的办法后又觉得说错了话呢？

五十至五十三景

1. 萧涧秋又徘徊起来，他想要解决什么问题？

2. 萧涧秋正要写信给陶岚，陶岚知道了以后怎么想？

3. 萧涧秋为什么认为陶岚会同意他的决定？

4. 萧涧秋的想法是什么？

5. 錢正興說他來找蕭澗秋做甚麼？那是真的嗎？

6. 錢正興說芙蓉鎮的人對蕭澗秋的態度怎麼樣？

7. 錢正興對蕭澗秋說，聽說蕭澗秋要和誰組織家庭？

8. 錢正興向蕭澗秋要求甚麼？

9. 錢正興要給蕭澗秋一千元，蕭澗秋為甚麼不要？

二。語法練習

I. N1 SV 於 N2: N1 is more SV than N2
Preposition: comparative construction
cf. EX 2.III, 4.III, 9.II

例
45.13 苛政猛於虎。
Tyranny is more savage than a tiger.

1. 陶校長的閱歷多於其他在座的人。
Principal Tao has more experience than everybody else here.

2. 三加二大於三。
Three plus two is greater than three.

變換

1. 重男輕女。

2. 反對的聲音不如贊成的聲音大。

5. 钱正兴说他来找萧涧秋做什么？那是真的吗？

6. 钱正兴说芙蓉镇的人对萧涧秋的态度怎么样？

7. 钱正兴对萧涧秋说，听说萧涧秋要和谁组织家庭？

8. 钱正兴向萧涧秋要求什么？

9. 钱正兴要给萧涧秋一千元，萧涧秋为什么不要？

二。语法练习

I. N1 SV 于 N2: N1 is more SV than N2

Preposition: comparative construction

cf. EX 2.III, 4.III, 9.II

例

45.13　苛政猛于虎。

Tyranny is more savage than a tiger.

1.　　陶校长的阅历多于其他在座的人。

Principal Tao has more experience than everybody else here.

2.　　三加二大于三。

Three plus two is greater than three.

变换

1. 重男轻女。

2. 反对的声音不如赞成的声音大。

II. 毫： the least bit; in the slightest; lit., the finest hair

Adverb used for emphasis in negative constructions

PATTERN: 毫無 N   to not have any N at all   *Verb-object construction*

毫未 VE（過）   to not have VE-ed at all;   *Adverbial construction*
              to have never VE before in the slightest

毫不 SV   to not be SV at all   *Adverbial construction*

例

46.11 〔交涉得〕毫無結果。
    [Our negotiations] did not have any results at all.

31.12 陶慕侃毫未介意。
    Tao Mukan had yet to take offense in any way.   =
    Tao Mukan did not take the least bit offense.

20.2 一家人已經對他毫不陌生了。
    [By this time] already, the family did not treat him in the least bit like a stranger [anymore].

1.   他走時毫無再跟她見面的意思。
    When he left, he didn't have the least intention of ever seeing her again.

2.   他走時毫未想過再跟她見面。
    When he left, he had yet to think of seeing her ever again   =
    When he left, it had not occurred to him in the least that he would ever see her again.   *or*
    When he left, he didn't want to ever see her again.

3.   他走時毫不想再跟她見面。
    When he left, he did not in the slightest ever want to see her again.

變換

1. 我告訴他抽煙對身體不好，他一點兒也沒有醒悟。還是一樣地抽。

2. 我告訴他抽煙對身體不好，他一點兒要改變的決心也沒有。還是一樣地抽。

3. 我告訴他抽煙對身體不好，他一點兒也不改變。還是一樣地抽。

II. 毫：　the least bit; in the slightest; lit., the finest hair

Adverb used for emphasis in negative constructions

PATTERN: 毫无 N　　　　　to not have any N at all　　　　　*Verb-object construction*

毫未 VE（过）　to not have VE-ed at all;　　　　*Adverbial construction*
　　　　　　　　to have never VE before in the slightest

毫不 SV　　　to not be SV at all　　　　　*Adverbial construction*

例

46.11　〔交涉得〕毫无结果。
　　　　[Our negotiations] did not have any results at all.

31.12　陶慕侃毫未介意。
　　　　Tao Mukan had yet to take offense in any way.　　=
　　　　Tao Mukan did not take the least bit offense.

20.2　一家人已经对他毫不陌生了。
　　　　[By this time] already, the family did not treat him in the least bit like a stranger [anymore].

1.　　他走时毫无再跟她见面的意思。
　　　When he left, he didn't have the least intention of ever seeing her again.

2.　　他走时毫未想过再跟她见面。
　　　When he left, he had yet to think of seeing her ever again　　　　　=
　　　When he left, it had not occurred to him in the least that he would ever see her again.　　*or*
　　　When he left, he didn't want to ever see her again.

3.　　他走时毫不想再跟她见面。
　　　When he left, he did not in the slightest ever want to see her again.

变换

1. 我告诉他抽烟对身体不好，他一点儿也没有醒悟。还是一样地抽。

2. 我告诉他抽烟对身体不好，他一点儿要改变的决心也没有。还是一样地抽。

3. 我告诉他抽烟对身体不好，他一点儿也不改变。还是一样地抽。

III. 有所 VE: lit., to have something to VE: to VE to a certain extent; to somewhat VE

　　無所 VE: to have nothing to VE

（V=顧惜；振奮；關心；表現；羞愧；

醒悟；討論；考慮；補充；了解）

Verb-object construction

例

46.16　陶校長有所醒悟。

Principal Tao had something of a realization.

37.22　我們是無所顧惜。

We don't anything to worry about.

1.　　如果家長們有所抗議，校長也會有所考慮。

If parents protest some; the principal will also think it over some.

2.　　對於他的意見，校長無所補充。

The principal had nothing to add to his suggestions.

3.　　你別問我；我對這件事無所了解。

Don't ask me; I don't know anything about this affair.

變換

1.他們都諷刺鎮長。

2.他認為自己作得很對，不必羞愧。

IV. 止不住： cannot stop

Resultative verb

PATTERN: N 止不住（地）V　　　N cannot stop from V-ing　　　*Adverbial construction*

　　　　　N1 止不住 N2　　　　　N1 cannot stop N2　　　　　*Pre-pivotal verb construction*

例

49.18　文嫂聽了止不住（地）湧出淚來。

When Wen Sao heard [this], she could not stop the tears from gushing forth.

III. 有所 VE: lit., to have something to VE: to VE to a certain extent; to somewhat VE

无所 VE: to have nothing to VE

(V=顾惜；振奋；关心；表现；羞愧；
醒悟；讨论；考虑；补充；了解）

Verb-object construction

例

46.16　陶校长有所醒悟。

Principal Tao had something of a realization.

37.22　我们是无所顾惜。

We don't anything to worry about.

1.　如果家长们有所抗议，校长也会有所考虑。

If parents protest some; the principal will also think it over some.

2.　对于他的意见，校长无所补充。

The principal had nothing to add to his suggestions.

3.　你别问我；我对这件事无所了解。

Don't ask me; I don't know anything about this affair.

变换

1. 他们都讽刺镇长。

2. 他认为自己作得很对，不必羞愧。

IV. 止不住： cannot stop

Resultative verb

PATTERN: N 止不住（地）V　　N cannot stop from V-ing　　*Adverbial construction*

N1 止不住 N2　　N1 cannot stop N2　　*Pre-pivotal verb construction*

例

49.18　文嫂听了止不住（地）涌出泪来。

When Wen Sao heard [this], she could not stop the tears from gushing forth.

1.　他看見教室裏沒有學生，止不住(地)詫異起來。
When he saw that there were no students in the classroom, he could not stem his astonishment.

2.　校長止不住家長的抗議，最後辭職了。
The principal could not stop the parents' protests; so in the end, he resigned.

校長止不住家長抗議，最後辭職了。
The principal could not stop the parents from protesting; so in the end, he resigned.

變換

1. 聽了人家的笑罵，她不禁哭出聲兒來。

2. 看見哥哥得勝地跑來，陶嵐不由得拉着哥哥跳了起來。

3. 水總是從高處往低處流，不能叫它不往下流。

V. 具有：　to have; to possess

Verb

PATTERN: S 具有 modified 2-character abstract N

(N= 思想；看法；認識；友誼；精神)

例

52.17　你和我具有同樣的思想。
You and I have the same kind of thinking.

1.　他們兩人之間具有深厚的友誼。
The two of them have a deep friendship.

2.　人必須具有和命運苦鬥的精神。
People have to possess the spirit to engage in bitter struggle against fate.

變換

1. 他的意志很堅強。

2. 那地方的菜風味與別地不同。

1. 他看见教室里没有学生，止不住（地）诧异起来。

When he saw that there were no students in the classroom, he could not stem his astonishment.

2. 校长止不住家长的抗议，最后辞职了。

The principal could not stop the parents' protests; so in the end, he resigned.

校长止不住家长抗议，最后辞职了。

The principal could not stop the parents from protesting; so in the end, he resigned.

变换

1. 听了人家的笑骂，她不禁哭出声儿来。

2. 看见哥哥得胜地跑来，陶岚不由得拉着哥哥跳了起来。

3. 水总是从高处往低处流，不能叫它不往下流。

V. 具有： to have; to possess

Verb

PATTERN: S 具有 modified 2-character abstract N

　　　（N= 思想；看法；认识；友谊；精神）

例

52.17 你和我具有同样的思想。

You and I have the same kind of thinking.

1. 他们两人之间具有深厚的友谊。

The two of them have a deep friendship.

2. 人必须具有和命运苦斗的精神。

People have to possess the spirit to engage in bitter struggle against fate.

变换

1. 他的意志很坚强。

2. 那地方的菜风味与别地不同。

VI. 遭到 2-character V/N: to suffer V/N; to meet with V/N

(where V/N has negative connotations; e.g. 懷疑；天災人禍；驚駭）

Verb-object construction

例

52.21　陶嵐遭到霹靂似地周身發抖。

Tao Lan's whole body shook as if she had been struck by lightning.

1.　飛機出事了，他遭到了不幸。

The airplane had an accident, and he met with misfortune.

2.　革命黨革命了十次，其中九次遭到失敗。

The revolutionary party led ten revolutions, of which nine met with defeat.

變換

1. 開會時大多數的人都反對他的意見。

2. 他是真心想幫助朋友，誰知輿論卻誹謗他。

VII. 節外生枝： to hit a snag; to have complications crop up unexpectedly

Verb-object phrase: stands alone as a predicate or functions as a modifier

例

52.29　真是節外生枝，枝外又生節地永遠弄不清楚。

With complications on top of more complications, [no one] will ever be able to really get it straight.

1.　當工作已經完成一半的時候，他忽然辭職不幹了。節外生枝地找麻煩。

Suddenly, he quit [even though] he had already finished more than half the job. This unexpectedly complicated things, making for [more] trouble.

2.　本來我們大家都同意了，誰知道王先生又節外生枝，改變了原來的安排。

We had all agreed; who knew that Mr. Wang would unexpectedly introduce complications and change our original plans.

VI. 遭到 2-character V/N: to suffer V/N; to meet with V/N
(where V/N has negative connotations; e.g. 怀疑；天灾人祸；惊骇）

Verb-object construction

例
52.21　陶岚遭到霹雳似地周身发抖。
Tao Lan's whole body shook as if she had been struck by lightning.

1.　飞机出事了，他遭到了不幸。
The airplane had an accident, and he met with misfortune.

2.　革命党革命了十次，其中九次遭到失败。
The revolutionary party led ten revolutions, of which nine met with defeat.

变换

1. 开会时大多数的人都反对他的意见。

2. 他是真心想帮助朋友，谁知舆论却诽谤他。

VII. 节外生枝： to hit a snag; to have complications crop up unexpectedly
Verb-object phrase: stands alone as a predicate or functions as a modifier

例
52.29　真是节外生枝，枝外又生节地永远弄不清楚。
With complications on top of more complications, [no one] will ever be able to really get it straight.

1.　当工作已经完成一半的时候，他忽然辞职不干了。节外生枝地找麻烦。
Suddenly, he quit [even though] he had already finished more than half the job. This unexpectedly complicated things, making for [more] trouble.

2.　本来我们大家都同意了，谁知道王先生又节外生枝，改变了原来的安排。
We had all agreed; who knew that Mr. Wang would unexpectedly introduce complications and change our original plans.

完成

1. 。。。這真是節外生枝。

2. 。。。他們節外生枝地。。。

三。生辭練習

填空一

滋潤；眼看着；遭到；笑容可掬；具有；猶豫；抑制；毫不；有所；反應；於；
稀疏；下意識；意想不到；毫無；相當；憤怒；枯乾

1. 南方革命軍的兵力大（　　）北方政府的兵力。

2. 他（　　）救人救世界的革命精神，同情所有受苦受難的人。

3. 啊！真靈！用濕手巾敷頭竟有（　　）的結果。

4. 時間過得好快。老師（　　）學生畢業了，結婚了，長大成人了。

5. 希望校長對學生們的抗議（　　）諒解，讓他們都能畢業。

6. 晚飯後，也不知是怎麼回事，他發現自己又（　　）地來到了橋邊。

7. 大風暴來了。住在海邊的人都（　　）風災、水災。

8. 人們不僅誤會了他的想法，而且不斷地用流言蜚語傷害他。這使他
（　　），也使他變得勇敢。

9. 陶嵐要幫助蕭澗秋反對惡人是（　　）疑問的。

10. 他離開學校後，總找不到一個（　　）的工作，很不得志。

11. 你自己說教育是神聖的事業。現在有人要和你訂約，請你去教書。我不知
你為甚麼還（　　）不定。

12. 風雨過去了，雨水（　　）了土地，地上的草都綠得發亮了。

13. 月光明亮的晚上，星星顯得少了。只有（　　）的幾顆在天上隱閃。

完成

1. 。。。这真是节外生枝。

2. 。。。他们节外生枝地。。。。

三。生辞练习

填空一

滋润；眼看着；遭到；笑容可掬；具有；犹豫；抑制；毫不；有所；反应；于；
稀疏；下意识；意想不到；毫无；相当；愤怒；枯干

1. 南方革命军的兵力大（　　）北方政府的兵力。

2. 他（　　）救人救世界的革命精神，同情所有受苦受难的人。

3. 啊！真灵！用湿手巾敷头竟有（　　）的结果。

4. 时间过得好快。老师（　　）学生毕业了，结婚了，长大成人了。

5. 希望校长对学生们的抗议（　　）谅解，让他们都能毕业。

6. 晚饭后，也不知是怎么回事，他发现自己又（　　）地来到了桥边。

7. 大风暴来了。住在海边的人都（　　）风灾、水灾。

8. 人们不仅误会了他的想法，而且不断地用流言蜚语伤害他。这使他
（　　），也使他变得勇敢。

9. 陶岚要帮助萧涧秋反对恶人是（　　）疑问的。

10. 他离开学校后，总找不到一个（　　）的工作，很不得志。

11. 你自己说教育是神圣的事业。现在有人要和你订约，请你去教书。我不知
你为什么还（　　）不定。

12. 风雨过去了，雨水（　　）了土地，地上的草都绿得发亮了。

13. 月光明亮的晚上，星星显得少了。只有（　　）的几颗在天上隐闪。

14. 他參加了電視上的遊戲節目，因為（　　）很快，問題都答得出來，終於得勝。

15. 文嫂竭力地（　　）自己的悲哀，不願意哭出聲來。

16. 今年夏天雨水太少了，小河都（　　）得露出石頭來了。

17. 公司裏的服務員永遠用一張（　　）的臉問：「您有甚麼事要我幫忙嗎？」

18. 陶慕侃說他妹妹的脾氣不好，陶嵐聽了（　　）生氣。她說她只不過不懂人情世故罷了。她不管別人說甚麼。

填空二

節外生枝；救濟；無所；醒悟；交涉；抗議；挽留；侮辱；沈重；緩緩；鎮定；沒好氣；退讓；諒解；作對；毫未；附和

1. 考試的時候必須十分（　　），不能慌亂，不然一定考不好。

2. 他的汽車跟對面來的汽車碰上了，得去跟保險公司辦（　　）。

3. 向文嫂提出改嫁的意見，就是（　　）她嗎？

4. 本來這件事我們發出了通知就沒有問題了。誰想他竟沒有收到。因此（　　）地惹出麻煩來了。簡單的事變得很不簡單了。

5. 他（　　）了。知道以前所做的是不對的，以後一定要改變。

6. 雖然社會上關於他的閑話很多，他卻說他（　　）受到暗箭的傷害。

7. 學生們在辦公大樓前開會、演講、遊行，認為學校不應該提高學費。他們向學校（　　）。

8. 校長問大家同意不同意時，大多數人都同聲（　　），只有極少數的人反對。

9. 他要辭職離開，校長竭力地（　　），他才同意繼續擔任教務。

10. 聽說，一個人早上起來下床下錯了邊，一整天都會（　　），見了誰都生氣，覺得甚麼都不對。

14. 他参加了电视上的游戏节目，因为（　　）很快，问题都答得出来，终于得胜。

15. 文嫂竭力地（　　）自己的悲哀，不愿意哭出声来。

16. 今年夏天雨水太少了，小河都（　　）得露出石头来了。

17. 公司里的服务员永远用一张（　　）的脸问：「您有什么事要我帮忙吗？」

18. 陶慕侃说他妹妹的脾气不好，陶岚听了（　　）生气。她说她只不过不懂人情世故罢了。她不管别人说什么。

填空二

节外生枝；救济；无所；醒悟；交涉；抗议；挽留；侮辱；沉重；缓缓；镇定；没好气；退让；谅解；作对；毫未；附和

1. 考试的时候必须十分（　　），不能慌乱，不然一定考不好。

2. 他的汽车跟对面来的汽车碰上了，得去跟保险公司办（　　）。

3. 向文嫂提出改嫁的意见，就是（　　）她吗？

4. 本来这件事我们发出了通知就没有问题了。谁想他竟没有收到。因此（　　）地惹出麻烦来了。简单的事变得很不简单了。

5. 他（　　）了。知道以前所做的是不对的，以后一定要改变。

6. 虽然社会上关于他的闲话很多，他却说他（　　）受到暗箭的伤害。

7. 学生们在办公大楼前开会、演讲、游行，认为学校不应该提高学费。他们向学校（　　）。

8. 校长问大家同意不同意时，大多数人都同声（　　），只有极少数的人反对。

9. 他要辞职离开，校长竭力地（　　），他才同意继续担任教务。

10. 听说，一个人早上起来下床下错了边，一整天都会（　　），见了谁都生气，觉得什么都不对。

11. 人們在爭錢、爭地位時，誰也不願意（　　）。

12. 我們怎麼向鎮長解釋，他都不（　　），認為鎮上的人太對不起他了。

13. 鎮長拿出一些錢（　　）受災的人，幫助他們暫時生活下去。

14. 他老是跟我（　　）。我所同意的，他都反對。他想出各種辦法來為難我。

15. 他這兩天心情特別（　　），腳步怎麼輕鬆得起來？

16. 一個老人（　　）從那邊走了過來。他走得那麼慢，彷彿走了一年。

17. 他說世界上的東西他是（　　）不吃的。凡是天上飛的，地下跑的他都歡迎。

四。說話練習

　　　　用你的瞭解來說：

1. 陶校長辦交涉。

2. 蕭澗秋在胡思亂想。

　　　　討論：

1. 蕭澗秋已經決定要娶文嫂來幫助她解決生活問題，為甚麼不能接受錢正興的一千塊錢呢？

2. 蕭澗秋應當跟誰結婚呢？

五。作文

　　完成蕭澗秋給陶嵐的信。

11. 人们在争钱、争地位时，谁也不愿意（　　）。

12. 我们怎么向镇长解释，他都不（　　），认为镇上的人太对不起他了。

13. 镇长府拿出一些钱（　　）受灾的人，帮助他们暂时生活下去。

14. 他老是跟我（　　）。我所同意的，他都反对。他想出各种办法来为难我。

15. 他这两天心情特别（　　），脚步怎么轻松得起来？

16. 一个老人（　　）从那边走了过来。他走得那么慢，仿佛走了一年。

17. 他说世界上的东西他是（　　）不吃的。凡是天上飞的，地下跑的他都欢迎。

四。说话练习

　　用你的了解来说：

1. 陶校长办交涉。
2. 萧涧秋在胡思乱想。

　　讨论：

1. 萧涧秋已经决定要娶文嫂来帮助她解决生活问题，为什么不能接受钱正兴的一千块钱呢？
2. 萧涧秋应当跟谁结婚呢？

五。作文

　　完成萧涧秋给陶岚的信。

練習九：第五十四景至第六十二景

一。閱讀測驗

五十四至五十六景

1. 那天早上是誰送采蓮來上學的？

2. 蕭澗秋見到采蓮，采蓮說甚麼？

3. 蕭澗秋送采蓮去上課以後，走向教務處時，那些教師正在高談闊論着甚麼問題？

4. 教師們對軍閥孫傳芳的看法怎麼樣？

5. 「一滴油不能融於水」比喻甚麼？

6. 陶校長被什麼事弄得莫名其妙？

7. 解釋一下蕭澗秋回答陶校長的話。

8. 老奶奶來找采蓮有甚麼重要的事？

9. 蕭澗秋要采蓮去哭她媽媽幾聲嗎？為甚麼呢？

10. 采蓮要媽媽，蕭澗秋告訴采蓮她媽媽怎麼了？

五十七至六十二景

1. 陶慕侃怎麼勸蕭澗秋喝酒？

2. 陶嵐怎麼勸蕭澗秋喝酒？

3. 蕭澗秋說「我哪是你們的對手？」說明甚麼問題？

练习九：第五十四景至第六十二景

一。阅读测验

五十四至五十六景

1. 那天早上是谁送采莲来上学的？

2. 萧涧秋见到采莲，采莲说什么？

3. 萧涧秋送采莲去上课以后，走向教务处时，那些教师正在高谈阔论着什么问题？

4. 教师们对军阀孙传芳的看法怎么样？

5. 「一滴油不能融于水」比喻什么？

6. 陶校长被什么事弄得莫名其妙？

7. 解释一下萧涧秋回答陶校长的话。

8. 老奶奶来找采莲有什么重要的事？

9. 萧涧秋要采莲去哭她妈妈几声吗？为什么呢？

10. 采莲要妈妈，萧涧秋告诉采莲她妈妈怎么了？

五十七至六十二景

1. 陶慕侃怎么劝萧涧秋喝酒？

2. 陶岚怎么劝萧涧秋喝酒？

3. 萧涧秋说「我哪是你们的对手？」说明什么问题？

4. 人們對西村的事情都怎麼議論？

5. 方謀認為阿寶的死，是甚麼好機會？文嫂吊死說明甚麼？

6. 蕭澗秋說他憤怒的是甚麼？

7. 蕭澗秋為甚麼說他自己對不起陶嵐？

8. 蕭澗秋認為王福生為甚麼不能上學？他可以怎麼幫助他？

9. 陶嵐見了蕭澗秋為甚麼又驚又喜？蕭澗秋委託她作甚麼事情？

10. 文嫂的自殺和王福生的退學對蕭澗秋說明了甚麼？

二。語法練習

I. 不堪：to not be able to withstand

PATTERN: 不堪 N   cannot stand N   *Verb-object construction*

      SV 不堪   SV to an unbearable extreme   *Intensifying complement*

例

55.3 孫傳芳的兵是不堪一擊的。
Sun Chuanfang's army cannot withstand a single attack.

1. 不堪入耳的話不要聽；不堪入目的事不要看。
Don't listen to talk that you cannot bear to have in your ears; don't look at things that you cannot bear to have in [front of] your eyes.

2. 他的衣服破舊不堪。
His clothes are unbearably old and shabby.

變換

1. 他因受不了侮辱而自殺。

2. 孫傳芳的政府腐敗極了，人民都受不了。

4. 人们对西村的事情都怎么议论？

5. 方谋认为阿宝的死，是什么好机会？文嫂吊死说明什么？

6. 萧涧秋说他愤怒的是什么？

7. 萧涧秋为什么说他自己对不起陶岚？

8. 萧涧秋认为王福生为什么不能上学？他可以怎么帮助他？

9. 陶岚见了萧涧秋为什么又惊又喜？萧涧秋委托她作什么事情？

10. 文嫂的自杀和王福生的退学对萧涧秋说明了什么？

二。语法练习

I. 不堪： to not be able to withstand

| PATTERN: 不堪 N | cannot stand N | *Verb-object construction* |
| SV 不堪 | SV to an unbearable extreme | *Intensifying complement* |

例

55.3　孙传芳的兵是不堪一击的。
Sun Chuanfang's army cannot withstand a single attack.

1.　　不堪入耳的话不要听；不堪入目的事不要看。
Don't listen to talk that you cannot bear to have in your ears; don't look at things that you cannot bear to have in [front of] your eyes.

2.　　他的衣服破旧不堪。
His clothes are unbearably old and shabby.

变换

1. 他因受不了侮辱而自杀。

2. 孙传芳的政府腐败极了，人民都受不了。

II. 於：in, of, at, on

Particle: prepositional usage

cf. EX 2.III, 4.III, 8.I

例
55.11　他彷彿一滴油不能融於水一般。

It was as if he were a drop of oil that could not mix with water.

1.　飄蕩於天空的雲千變萬化。

The clouds drifting in the sky are ever changing.

2.　蕭澗秋要幫助文嫂一家完全是出於同情革命黨。

Xiao Jianqiu wanted to help Wen Sao's family, purely out of his sympathies for the Revolutionary Party.

3.　同學們都聚集於教室之內。

The students all gathered in the classroom.

變換

1. 魚在水中游。

2. 朋友們在茶館品茗。

III. 惟恐。。。：afraid of nothing but . . . ; for fear that . . .

Verb introducing a clause

例
56.3　他惟恐驚動她們似地。。。在門邊的一張凳子上坐下。

Appearing to be afraid of nothing but startling them . . . he sat down on a stool by the door.

1.　「他怎麼那麼用功？」「他惟恐落後於人，所以更加努力。」

"Why is he so hardworking?" "He's afraid of nothing but falling behind, so he's trying even harder."

2.　我幾次提醒他，惟恐他忘了。

I have reminded him several times, for fear that he would forget.

II. 于：in, of, at, on

Particle: prepositional usage

cf. EX 2.III, 4.III, 8.I

例

55.11　他仿佛一滴油不能融于水一般。

It was as if he were a drop of oil that could not mix with water.

1.　飘荡于天空的云千变万化。

The clouds drifting in the sky are ever changing.

2.　萧涧秋要帮助文嫂一家完全是出于同情革命党。

Xiao Jianqiu wanted to help Wen Sao's family, purely out of his sympathies for the Revolutionary Party.

3.　同学们都聚集于教室之内。

The students all gathered in the classroom.

变换

1. 鱼在水中游。

2. 朋友们在茶馆品茗。

III. 惟恐。。。：afraid of nothing but . . . ; for fear that . . .

Verb introducing a clause

例

56.3　他惟恐惊动她们似地。。。在门边的一张凳子上坐下。

Appearing to be afraid of nothing but startling them . . . he sat down on a stool by the door.

1.　「他怎么那么用功？」「他惟恐落后于人，所以更加努力。」

"Why is he so hardworking?" "He's afraid of nothing but falling behind, so he's trying even harder."

2.　我几次提醒他，惟恐他忘了。

I have reminded him several times, for fear that he would forget.

完成

1. 陶嵐一直哄着采蓮，給她說故事，彈鋼琴給她聽，唯恐。。。

2. 王福生急忙向教室跑去，唯恐。。。

IV. N1 作 N2 論： to consider N1 as N2; to speak of N1 as N2

應該把 N1 看作 N2; N1 應該被看作 N2

Coverb construction

例

57.23　誰都說文嫂應當作節婦輪。

Everyone says that Wen Sao should be considered a woman who has died in defense of her honor.

1.　歷史是不是科學？研究歷史應當作研究科學論嗎？

Is history a science? Should research in history be considered scientific research?

2.　我們豈能將革命家作軍閥論？

How could we consider a revolutionary to be a warlord?

變換

1. 夫妻分手了就是離婚了嗎？

2. 他政治上失敗了，人們就認為他是土匪。

V. 反而： but instead; but on the contrary

Conjunction: introduces a statement counter to expectations

cf. 而：*EX 2.VI, 3.I, 3.V, 5.IV, 7.IV*

PATTERN: 不但。。。，反而

　　　　　不僅。。。，反而

　　　　　並不。。。，反而

完成

1. 陶岚一直哄着采莲，给她说故事，弹钢琴给她听，唯恐。。。。

2. 王福生急忙向教室跑去，唯恐。。。。

IV. N1 作 N2 论： to consider N1 as N2; to speak of N1 as N2

应该把 N1 看作 N2; N1 应该被看作 N2

Coverb construction

例

57.23　谁都说文嫂应当作节妇轮。

Everyone says that Wen Sao should be considered a woman who has died in defense of her honor.

1.　历史是不是科学？研究历史应当作研究科学论吗？

Is history a science? Should research in history be considered scientific research?

2.　我们岂能将革命家作军阀论？

How could we consider a revolutionary to be a warlord?

变换

1. 夫妻分手了就是离婚了吗？

2. 他政治上失败了，人们就认为他是土匪。

V. 反而： but instead; but on the contrary

Conjunction: introduces a statement counter to expectations

cf. 而： *EX 2.VI, 3.I, 3.V, 5.IV, 7.IV*

PATTERN: 不但。。。。，反而
　　　　　不仅。。。。，反而
　　　　　并不。。。。，反而

例

57.43 〔我想要救活她們，不但〕我沒有救活他們，反而害死了她們。

[I wanted to save them, but not only] did I not save them, but on the contrary, [ended up] killing them!

1. 他的左臉被人打了，他不僅不生氣，反而轉過臉去讓人打另一邊。

When he got slapped on his left cheek, not only did he not get angry but on the contrary, he turned the other cheek for it to be slapped.

2. 聽到那些人的讚美，他並不感到高興，反而以為是不祥之兆。

When he heard those people praising him, he wasn't really very happy about it. On the contrary, he thought it was an inauspicious omen.

完成

1. 。。。反而幫助他。

2. 我本來並沒有請他來，只請他太太來的。誰知道。。。

VI. 居然： unexpectedly; to one's (pleasant) surprise

Movable adverb, typically used for unexpected positive events

例

57.43 有人背後冷言冷語，現在卻居然為我舉杯喝彩了。

People were making sarcastic remarks behind my back, but now, to my surprise, they've come to honor me raising their cups in a toast. *[sarcastic usage]*

1. 他本來告訴他母親吃不下飯的，後來居然(他)吃了兩大碗。

He originally told his mother he couldn't eat anything, but later, to her pleasant surprise, he ate two big bowlfuls.

2. 小時候他不愛念書，非常調皮，現在(他)居然當博士了。

He didn't like to study when he was young; he was very mischievous. But now surprisingly, he is a Ph.D.

完成

1. 三年以前他們倆因意見不同而分手，昨天。。。

2. 。。。居然勝利了。

例

57.43　〔我想要救活她们，不但〕我没有救活他们，反而害死了她们。

[I wanted to save them, but not only] did I not save them, but on the contrary, [ended up] killing them!

1.　他的左脸被人打了，他不仅不生气，反而转过脸去让人打另一边。

When he got slapped on his left cheek, not only did he not get angry but on the contrary, he turned the other cheek for it to be slapped.

2.　听到那些人的赞美，他并不感到高兴，反而以为是不祥之兆。

When he heard those people praising him, he wasn't really very happy about it. On the contrary, he thought it was an inauspicious omen.

完成

1.。。。反而帮助他。

2.我本来并没有请他来，只请他太太来的。谁知道。。。

VI. 居然：　unexpectedly; to one's (pleasant) surprise

Movable adverb, typically used for unexpected positive events

例

57.43　有人背后冷言冷语，现在却居然为我举杯喝彩了。

People were making sarcastic remarks behind my back, but now, to my surprise, they've come to honor me raising their cups in a toast. [sarcastic usage]

1.　他本来告诉他母亲吃不下饭的，后来居然（他）吃了两大碗。

He originally told his mother he couldn't eat anything, but later, to her pleasant surprise, he ate two big bowlfuls.

2.　小时候他不爱念书，非常调皮，现在（他）居然当博士了。

He didn't like to study when he was young; he was very mischievous. But now surprisingly, he is a Ph.D.

完成

1.三年以前他们俩因意见不同而分手，昨天。。。

2.。。。居然胜利了。

VII. 煞費苦心：   painstaking; to take great pains

Verb-object construction: functions as stative verb

煞費苦心地 V: to take great pains to V

Adverbial construction

例

57.40 像你這樣煞費苦心地去救濟他們，實在是令人佩服。

[People] like you who take such great pains to help them in their time of distress, truly give us cause for admiration.

1.   錢正興煞費苦心地跟蕭澗秋較量。

Qian Zhengxing took great pains to compete with Xiao Jianqiu.

2.   陶校長一方面要弄到足夠的錢聘請好教師，一方面要滿足家長們的要求，還要顧及鎮長的面子，能把學校辦出這樣的成績，真是煞費苦心了。

On the one hand, Principal Tao has to get enough money to hire good teachers. On the other, he has to satisfy parents' demands, and also attend to the mayor's reputation. He has really gone to great lengths to be able to get these kinds of results in his administration of the school.

回答

1. 甚麼事值得你煞費苦心？

2. 小王給他父親過生日（招待朋友吃飯）。他是怎麼煞費苦心地安排的？

VII. 煞费苦心：　　　　painstaking; to take great pains

Verb-object construction: functions as stative verb

煞费苦心地 V:　to take great pains to V

Adverbial construction

例

57.40　像你这样煞费苦心地去救济他们，实在是令人佩服。

[People] like you who take such great pains to help them in their time of distress, truly give us cause for admiration.

1.　钱正兴煞费苦心地跟萧涧秋较量。

Qian Zhengxing took great pains to compete with Xiao Jianqiu.

2.　陶校长一方面要弄到足够的钱聘请好教师，一方面要满足家长们的要求，还要顾及镇长的面子，能把学校办出这样的成绩，真是煞费苦心了。

On the one hand, Principal Tao has to get enough money to hire good teachers. On the other, he has to satisfy parents' demands, and also attend to the mayor's reputation. He has really gone to great lengths to be able to get these kinds of results in his administration of the school.

回答

1. 什么事值得你煞费苦心？

2. 小王给他父亲过生日（招待朋友吃饭）。他是怎么煞费苦心地安排的？

三。生詞練習

填空一

會意；較量；何必；作；反而；惟恐；不堪；終止；不出；欲；由此可見；豈；
自我譏諷；按期；惆悵

1. 畢業的一天來到了。同學們一方面因走向社會而興奮，同時又不免因大家就要分手而（　　）。

2. 每個月雜誌都（　　）寄來，準時收到。

3. 本地的兩所大學今天要比賽籃球，（　　）誰強誰弱。

4. 他雖然沒有大學畢業，但大家都知道他的學問好。我們既然要聘請他來教書，當然應該將他（　　）教授論。

5. 在那次比賽中，他（　　）對手沈重的一擊，倒了下去。

6. 對於那些人的誹謗，他不但沒有介意，（　　）大笑起來。

7. 既然一切都已成為過去，人們都諒解了。你（　　）非要離開不可？

8. 他提出的問題總是令人深思。（　　），他是很有頭腦的。

9. 你說這麼做沒有壞影響嗎？我看很難說，（　　）十年問題就會暴露出來。

10. 朋友對他皺眉頭、擠鼻子，示意他不要再說那個問題，他都不能（　　），繼續一直不停地講下去。

11. 他紅着臉緊緊地以手蓋杯，並連聲說：「我不能再喝了，我不能再喝了。」他（　　）主人再給他斟酒，喝得太多。

12. 蕭澗秋（　　）地說：「我得發了。錢先生今天要送我一千塊錢，讓我娶文嫂呢。」

13. 他喝了十大杯酒，（　　）能不醉？

14. 方謀仍（　　）繼續發表高論，稱贊文嫂，卻沒有人理會。

15. 被侮辱的寡婦自殺了，流言也隨即（　　）了。

三。生词练习

填空一

会意；较量；何必；作；反而；惟恐；不堪；终止；不出；欲；由此可见；岂；
自我嘲讽；按期；惆怅

1. 毕业的一天来到了。同学们一方面因走向社会而兴奋，同时又不免因大家
   就要分手而（　　）。

2. 每个月杂志都（　　）寄来，准时收到。

3. 本地的两所大学今天要比赛篮球，（　　）谁强谁弱。

4. 他虽然没有大学毕业，但大家都知道他的学问好。我们既然要聘请他来教
   书，当然应该将他（　　）教授论。

5. 在那次比赛中，他（　　）对手沉重的一击，倒了下去。

6. 对于那些人的诽谤，他不但没有介意，（　　）大笑起来。

7. 既然一切都已成为过去，人们都谅解了。你（　　）非要离开不可？

8. 他提出的问题总是令人深思。（　　），他是很有头脑的。

9. 你说这么做没有坏影响吗？我看很难说，（　　）十年问题就会暴露出来。

10. 朋友对他皱眉头、挤鼻子，示意他不要再说那个问题，他都不能（　　），继
    续一直不停地讲下去。

11. 他红着脸紧紧地以手盖杯，并连声说：「我不能再喝了，我不能再喝了。」
    他（　　）主人再给他斟酒，喝得太多。

12. 萧涧秋（　　）地说：「我得发了。钱先生今天要送我一千块钱，让我娶文嫂
    呢。」

13. 他喝了十大杯酒，（　　）能不醉？

14. 方谋仍（　　）继续发表高论，称赞文嫂，却没有人理会。

15. 被侮辱的寡妇自杀了，流言也随即（　　）了。

填空二

居然；腐敗；委託；舒暢；輕便；喝彩；得人心；蒙在鼓裏；煞費苦心；堅持；
謙讓；招呼；清醒；首當其衝；是非；意味

1. 他花了很多工夫，又請教了很多人，（　　）地把家中佈置好，歡迎客人。

2. 病人的生命已經很危險了，但他本人還（　　），醫生不應該告訴他嗎？

3. 政府的這一政策，對一般的人並無幫助。這政策是很不（　　）的。

4. 臺上的人唱得好極了。臺下的人為他的歌聲所感染，一曲唱完，大家靜寂了一刻，才發出鼓掌（　　）聲。

5. 那些政府大官們都很（　　）。不送禮是辦不了事的。

6. 要打官司，應該（　　）哪個律師好呢？

7. 現代人穿鞋不但要漂亮好看，而且要（　　）舒服。

8. 昨天他還被罵為卑鄙小人，今天（　　）有人說他稱得起品學並茂了，真想不到。

9. 早晨起來，空氣清新，不再像昨天那麼氣悶。使人感覺心胸（　　）。

10. 我們都知道你是有能力的，別（　　）了。既然大家都要你幫忙，你就為我們大家辦這件事吧！

11. 那公司要辭去一部分工作人員，（　　）地受到影響的大概是工作經驗較少的人吧。

12. 你太糊塗了。怎麼能（　　）不分呢？誰給你錢你就聽誰的話嗎？

13. 他決定辭職不幹了。他不知道每天在家與公司之間來來去去（　　）着甚麼。他覺得這種生活異常無聊。

14. 我最喜歡早晨早早起來念書，那時頭腦最（　　），是用功的好時候。

15. 他結婚請客的時候，老朋友都去飯館兒幫他（　　）客人。

16. 當兩個力量相當的人較量時，誰能（　　）到最後誰就是勝利者。

填空二

居然；腐败；委托；舒畅；轻便；喝彩；得人心；蒙在鼓里；煞费苦心；坚持；
谦让；招呼；清醒；首当其冲；是非；意味

1. 他花了很多工夫，又请教了很多人，（　）地把家中布置好，欢迎客人。

2. 病人的生命已经很危险了，但他本人还（　），医生不应该告诉他吗？

3. 政府的这一政策，对一般的人并无帮助。这政策是很不（　）的。

4. 台上的人唱得好极了。台下的人为他的歌声所感染，一曲唱完，大家静寂了一刻，才发出鼓掌（　）声。

5. 那些政府大官们都很（　）。不送礼是办不了事的。

6. 要打官司，应该（　）哪个律师好呢？

7. 现代人穿鞋不但要漂亮好看，而且要（　）舒服。

8. 昨天他还被骂为卑鄙小人，今天（　）有人说他称得起品学并茂了，真想不到。

9. 早晨起来，空气清新，不再像昨天那么气闷。使人感觉心胸（　）。

10. 我们都知道你是有能力的，别（　）了。既然大家都要你帮忙，你就为我们大家办这件事吧！

11. 那公司要辞去一部分工作人员，（　）地受到影响的大概是工作经验较少的人吧。

12. 你太糊涂了。怎么能（　）不分呢？谁给你钱你就听谁的话吗？

13. 他决定辞职不干了。他不知道每天在家与公司之间来来去去（　）着什么。他觉得这种生活异常无聊。

14. 我最喜欢早晨早早起来念书，那时头脑最（　），是用功的好时候。

15. 他结婚请客的时候，老朋友都去饭馆儿帮他（　）客人。

16. 当两个力量相当的人较量时，谁能（　）到最后谁就是胜利者。

四。說話練習

用你的瞭解來說：

1. 蕭澗秋對方謀十分生氣。
2. 比較文嫂生前與死後的社會地位。

討論：

1. 采蓮和阿寶在文嫂生命中的地位。
2. 甚麼叫作「投身到時代的洪流中」？

五。作文

評論《早春二月》。

四。说话练习

用你的了解来说：

1. 萧涧秋对方谋十分生气。
2. 比较文嫂生前与死后的社会地位。

讨论：

1. 采莲和阿宝在文嫂生命中的地位。
2. 什么叫作「投身到时代的洪流中」？

五。作文

评论《早春二月》。

填空解答
Fill-in-the-Blank Answer Key

一。一至五景

填空一

1. 至		8. 向		15. 其中	
2. 為	为	9. 將	将	16. 破舊	破旧
3. 使		10. 似		17. 異常	异常
4. 隨即	随即	11. 要	几乎	18. 寬敞	宽敞
5. 引起		12. 顯得	显得	19. 珍惜	
6. 卻	却	13. 似乎			
7. 唯有		14. 幾乎	几乎		

填空二

1. 足足		8. 輕鬆	轻松	15. 無可奈何	无可奈何
2. 世外桃源		9. 消磨		16. 約	约
3. 呆呆地		10. 扭捏		17. 興隆	兴隆
4. 微微		11. 勉強	勉强	18. 不自在	
5. 悲哀		12. 心不在焉		19. 探索	
6. 無聊	无聊	13. 不時地	不时地	20. 模樣	模样
7. 氣悶	气闷	14. 厭倦	厌倦		

二。六至十景

填空一

1. 以
2. 待
3. 抱歉
4. 非
5. 敝
6. 白
7. 凡
8. 閱歷　　　　阅历
9. 冷落
10. 難道　　　　难道
11. 呈現　　　　呈现
12. 一般
13. 其實　　　　其实
14. 就是了
15. 至於　　　　至于
16. 嘛
17. 東奔西跑　　东奔西跑
18. 領　　　　　领
19. 變化　　　　变化
20. 負擔　　　　负担

填空二

1. 興致勃勃　　兴致勃勃
2. 人情世故
3. 旁若無人　　旁若无人
4. 按
5. 原諒　　　　原谅
6. 沈寂　　　　沉寂
7. 吃不來　　　吃不来
8. 光臨　　　　光临
9. 程度
10. 感觸　　　　感触
11. 各色各樣　　各色各样
12. 熱氣騰騰　　热气腾腾
13. 順水推舟　　顺水推舟
14. 一飲而盡　　一饮而尽
15. 不祥之兆
16. 高談闊論　　高谈阔论
17. 生疏
18. 示意
19. 而已
20. 竭力

三。十一至十五景

填空一

1. 感情衝動　　感情冲动
2. 而且
3. 多餘　　　　多余
4. 偏
5. 不料
6. 不成其為　　不成其为
7. 寒冷
8. 立即
9. 終究　　　　终究
10. 説不上　　　说不上
11. 僅是　　　　仅是
12. 好不容易
13. 徬徨　　　　彷徨
14. 感染
15. 緩一緩　　　缓一缓
16. 簡短　　　　简短
17. 補充　　　　补充
18. 介意

填空二

1. 見外　　　　见外
2. 胡亂　　　　胡乱
3. 誤會　　　　误会
4. 監視　　　　监视
5. 躊躇　　　　踌躇
6. 冒昧
7. 認真　　　　认真
8. 見笑　　　　见笑
9. 暴露　　　　暴露
10. 受委曲
11. 天無絕人之路
　　　　　　　　天无绝人之路
12. 慌亂　　　　慌乱
13. 感激
14. 顫抖　　　　颤抖
15. 手足無措　　手足无措
16. 不禁
17. 來得及　　　来得及
18. 感興趣　　　感兴趣

四。十六至二十二景

填空一

1. 之間	之间	7. 除此以外		13. 擔任	担任
2. 一一		8. 考慮	考虑	14. 殷勤	
3. 不盡然	不尽然	9. 稱得起	称得起	15. 溫柔	温柔
4. 甚至		10. 既然		16. 幸福	
5. 推卻	推却	11. 尷尬	尴尬	17. 支持	
6. 氣息	气息	12. 孝敬		18. 不敢當	不敢当

填空二

1. 心神不寧	心神不宁	7. 羨慕		13. 稱贊	称赞
2. 廢寢忘食	废寝忘食	8. 精緻	精致	14. 孤單	孤单
3. 品學並茂	品学并茂	9. 休養	休养	15. 愛護	爱护
4. 連跑帶跳	连跑带跳	10. 拿		16. 張望	张望
5. 心切		11. 問長問短	问长问短	17. 稍微	
6. 含苞待放		12. 活躍	活跃	18. 截住	

五。二十三至二十九景

填空一

1. 究竟		7. 為難	为难	13. 當真	当真
2. 決不		8. 曾經	曾经	14. 隱約	隐约
3. 認	认	9. 招呼		15. 任性	
4. 果然		10. 懷疑	怀疑	16. 受累	
5. 修改		11. 焦慮	焦虑	17. 叫	
6. 不便		12. 當初	当初		

填空二

1. 指指戳戳		7. 掩飾	掩饰	13. 兒戲	儿戏
2. 結結巴巴	结结巴巴	8. 突破		14. 眺望	
3. 莫名其妙		9. 竊竊私議	窃窃私议	15. 懇求	恳求
4. 終身大事	终身大事	10. 精明		16. 不安	
5. 責備	责备	11. 拖延		17. 竟	
6. 照顧	照顾	12. 打擾	打扰		

六。三十至三十八景

填空一

1. 否認	否认	7. 安排		13. 激烈	激烈
2. 蒼白	苍白	8. 光明正大		14. 盡興	尽兴
3. 隨口	随口	9. 一本一本地		15. 振奮	振奋
4. 再三		10. 冷漠		16. 起伏	
5. 何以		11. 囑咐	嘱咐		
6. 激動	激动	12. 更加			

填空二

1. 越發	越发	7. 昂首闊步	昂首阔步	13. 殘忍	残忍
2. 陰沈	阴沉	8. 悔不該	悔不该	14. 要挾	要挟
3. 煩惱	烦恼	9. 隱瞞	隐瞒	15. 氣憤	气愤
4. 擔心	担心	10. 卑鄙		16. 禁不住	
5. 聚精會神	聚精会神	11. 表現	表現		
6. 一瞬不瞬		12. 驅逐	驱逐		

七。三十九至四十四景

填空一

1. 難以	难以	7. 緩和	缓和	13. 狀態	状态
2. 繼而	继而	8. 以此		14. 執拗	执拗
3. 故作		9. 恰巧		15. 理會	理会
4. 光		10. 之類	之类	16. 昏迷	
5. 果決		11. 何況			
6. 依		12. 惹			

填空二

1. 藉此	借此	7. 報答	报答	13. 我行我素	
2. 比喻		8. 難以為情	难以为情	14. 無辜	无辜
3. 自鳴得意	自鸣得意	9. 擔憂	担忧	15. 沈吟	沉吟
4. 人言可畏		10. 匆匆忙忙地		16. 為此	为此
5. 盼望		11. 靈	灵		
6. 緊鎖眉頭	紧锁眉头	12. 詫異	诧异		

八。四十五至五十三景

填空一

1. 於	于	7. 遭到		13. 稀疏	
2. 具有		8. 憤怒	愤怒	14. 反應	反应
3. 意想不到		9. 毫無	毫无	15. 抑制	
4. 眼看着		10. 相當	相当	16. 枯乾	枯干
5. 有所		11. 猶豫	犹豫	17. 笑容可掬	
6. 下意識	下意识	12. 滋潤	滋润	18. 毫不	

填空二

1. 鎮定	镇定	7. 抗議	抗议	13. 救濟	救济
2. 交涉		8. 附和		14. 作對	作对
3. 侮辱		9. 挽留		15. 沈重	沉重
4. 節外生枝	节外生枝	10. 没好氣	没好气	16. 緩緩	缓缓
5. 醒悟		11. 退讓	退让	17. 無所	无所
6. 毫未		12. 諒解	谅解		

九。五十四至六十二景

填空一

1. 惆悵	惆怅	7. 何必		13. 豈	岂
2. 按期		8. 由此可見	由此可见	14. 欲	
3. 較量	较量	9. 不出		15. 終止	终止
4. 作		10. 會意	会意		
5. 不堪		11. 惟恐			
6. 反而		12. 自我嘲諷	自我嘲讽		

填空二

1. 煞費苦心	煞费苦心	7. 輕便	轻便	13. 意味	
2. 蒙在鼓裏	蒙在鼓里	8. 居然		14. 清醒	
3. 得人心		9. 舒暢	舒畅	15. 招呼	
4. 喝彩		10. 謙讓	谦让	16. 堅持	坚持
5. 腐敗	腐败	11. 首當其衝	首当其冲		
6. 委託	委托	12. 是非			

索引

suǒyǐn

Index

索引

遭到		zāo dào	52.21; *EX 8.VI*
早		zǎo	12.50, 17.35
早點	早点	zǎo diǎn	17.35
灶台		zào tái	8.2
責	责	zé	11.49, 14.12, 24.6, 40.26
責備	责备	zé bèi	24.6
責怪	责怪	zé guài	14.12
責任	责任	zé rèn	11.49
責問	责问	zé wèn	40.26
增		zēng	9.59, 37.13
增加		zēng jiā	9.59
增添		zēng tiān	37.13
乍一		zhà yī	19.15
炸裂		zhà liè	30.26
展	发展	zhǎn	9.12, 57.36
展覽	展览	zhǎn lǎn	57.36
盞	盏	zhǎn	20.1
戰	战	zhàn	7.14, 35.2
戰爭	战争	zhàn zhēng	7.14
佔領	占领	zhàn lǐng	7.33
顫	颤	zhàn; chàn	11.14, 55.41
顫抖	颤抖	zhàn dǒu; chàn dǒu	11.14
張	张	zhāng	17.3, 17.36
張望	张望	zhāng wàng	17.3
長	长	zhǎng	4.5, 17.5, 41.4, 46.11 另见 *cháng*
掌		zhǎng	17.15
丈夫		zhàng fu	46.4
帳	帐	zhàng	55.50
招		zhāo	7.23, 17.41, 22.21, 57.14
招待		zhāo dài	7.23
招呼		zhāo hu	22.21, 57.14
招手		zhāo shǒu	17.41
找		zhǎo	7.25
兆		zhào	7.10
照顧	照顾	zhào gù; zhào gu	28.7
罩		zhào	51.1

哲學	哲学	zhé xué	7.42
者		zhě	35.2
浙		Zhè	55.2
着		zhe	14.3 另見 *zhuó*
珍		zhēn	2.7, 8.8
珍惜		zhēn xī; zhēn xí	2.7
真		zhēn	7.42, 12.39, 15.19, 24.4, 44.8
真誠	真诚	zhēn chéng	44.8
真正		zhēn zhèng	7.42
貞節	贞节	zhēn jié	49.30
斟		zhēn	57.2
診療費	诊疗费	zhěn liáo fèi	40.32
鎮	镇	zhèn	1.2, 19.15, 25.7, 41.4, 45.3
鎮定	镇定	zhèn dìng	45.3
鎮靜	镇静	zhèn jìng	25.7
鎮長	镇长	zhèn zhǎng	41.4
震		zhèn	7.14, 37.11
震動	震动	zhèn dòng	37.11
陣亡	阵亡	zhèn wáng	9.51
振奮	振奋	zhèn fèn	31.17
睜	睁	zhēng	4.12
爭	争	zhēng	7.14, 9.12, 21.3
整		zhěng	21.7
正		zhèng	4.7, 7.42, 9.31, 37.16, 55.7, 57.24
正常		zhèng cháng	9.31
正好		zhèng hǎo	55.7
正派		zhèng pài	57.24
政		zhèng	45.13, 55.10; *EX 8.I*
政府		zhèng fǔ	55.10
織	织	zhī	4.6, 53.18
之		zhī	7.10, 11.39, 22.28, 42.2; *EX 7.II*
之間	之间	zhī jiān	22.28
之類	之类	zhī lèi	42.2; *EX 7.II*
知		zhī	7.43, 7.52, 30.21, 46.13
知識	知识	zhī shì; zhī shi	7.43
支持		zhī chí	22.6
枝		zhī	42.2, 52.29; *EX 8.VII*

CORNELL EAST ASIA SERIES

Order online: www.einaudi.cornell.edu/eastasia/CEASbooks, or contact Cornell East Asia Series Distribution Center, 369 Pine Tree Rd., Ithaca, NY 14853-2820, USA; toll-free: 1-877-865-2432, fax 607-255-7534, ceas@cornell.edu

IBT/12-03/.4M pb